For Cami and Jimmy

University of Hertfordshire

College Lane, Hatfield, Herts. AL10 9AB
Information Hertfordshire
Services and Solutions for the University

For renewal of Standard and One Week Loans,
please visit the web site http://www.voyager.herts.ac.uk

This item must be returned or the loan renewed by the due date.
A fine will be charged for the late return of items.

Experimental Latin American Cinema

EXPERIMENTAL LATIN AMERICAN CINEMA
HISTORY AND AESTHETICS

by Cynthia Tompkins

University of Texas Press 〜 Austin

Requests for permission to reproduce material from this work
should be sent to:
    Permissions
    University of Texas Press
    P.O. Box 7819
    Austin, TX 78713-7819
    http://utpress.utexas.edu/about/book-permissions

♾ The paper used in this book meets the minimum
requirements of ANSI/NISO Z39.48-1992 (R1997)
(Permanence of Paper).

Library of Congress Cataloging-in-Publication Data

Tompkins, Cynthia, 1958–
    Experimental Latin American cinema : history and aesthetics /
by Cynthia Margarita Tompkins. — 1st ed.
    p.   cm.
    Includes bibliographical references and index.
    ISBN 978-0-292-74415-8 (cloth : alk. paper)
    1. Experimental films—Latin America—History and criticism. I. Title.
    PN1993.5.L3T75 2013
    791.43098—dc23   2012024686

doi:10.7560/744158

CONTENTS

ACKNOWLEDGMENTS

I thank Arizona State University for providing research funds to present preliminary versions of the material included in this book at local, national, and international venues. I am grateful to audiences in Arizona (Council for Latin American Studies and Association of Spanish Professors—ADEUU, 2010), Utah (International Association of Feminine Literature and Culture Conference—AILCFH, 2006), San Diego (American Association of Teachers of Spanish and Portuguese—AATSP, 2007), and San Francisco (National Popular Culture Association and American Culture Association, 2007). Feedback and comments at international venues was crucial in re-thinking the theoretical approach. My appreciation extends to colleagues in London and Cambridge, England (Visual Synergies conference, 2006); Seville, Spain; Córdoba (Facultad de Lenguas, 2007) and Buenos Aires, (Argentine Association of Film and Media Studies, ASECA Argentina, 2009); Rio de Janeiro (Latin American Studies Association, 2009); and Morelia, Mexico (Permanent Seminar on Film Analysis, SEPANCINE con-ference, 2009). I am especially appreciative for the interaction and feed-back provided by students and faculty at the eight-hour workshop offered at the first regional conference of the Brazilian Society of Cinema and Audiovisual Studies—SOCINE, Universidade Federal de São Carlos, Bra-zil, May 2011. I am extremely grateful to Inés de Oliveira Cézar, Fernando

Pérez, Carlos Reygadas, and Carlos Sorín for sharing frames of their films and to the Learning Support System at the School of International Letters and Cultures at ASU, and especially to Zach Mills and Andrew Ross, for the invaluable technical support throughout this process.

Preliminary versions of chapters appeared in the following refereed articles: "Fabián Bielinsky's *El aura* [*The Aura*]: Neo-Noir Inscription and Subversion of the Action Image," *Confluencia* 24.1 (Fall 2008): 17–27; "A Deleuzian Approach to Carlos Reygadas' *Japón* and *Battle of Heaven*," *Hispanic Journal* 29.1 (Spring 2008): 155–169; "Paradoxical Inscription and Subversion of the Gendered Construction of Time, Space, and Roles in María Victoria Menis' *El cielito* (2004) and Inés de Oliveira Cézar's *Como pasan las horas* (2005) and *Extranjera* (2007)," *Chasqui* 38.1 (May 2009): 38–56; "Walter Salles's *Central do Brasil*: The Paradoxical Effect of the Conventions of the Documentary," *Studies in Twentieth and Twenty-First Century Literature* 33.1 (Winter 2009): 9–27; "A Deleuzian Approach to Jorge Furtado's *O Homem que Copiava* (2003) and Heitor Dhalia's *O Cheiro do Ralo* (2006)," *Dissidences* 6–7 (May 2010): 1–31; "A Deleuzian Approach to Carlos Reygadas's *Stellet Licht* [*Silent Light*] (2008)," University of New Mexico Latin American and Iberian Institute Research Paper Series, no. 51 (November 15, 2010); and "Montage in Fernando Pérez's *Suite Habana* (2003)," *Confluencia* 26.2 (Spring 2011): 31–45.

My debt of gratitude to Elizabeth Rosa Horan, editor extraordinaire, David William Foster, and Isis Costa McElroy at Arizona State University for their generous and sustained intellectual support throughout this project. I extend my appreciation for the keen observations of the anonymous readers and especially to Jim Burr at University of Texas Press for believing in this project. I am also grateful to Lynne Chapman at UT Press for her keen sense of structure and to Tana Silva for a superb copyediting job. Finally, all shortcomings are only my own.

INTRODUCTION

Mise-en-Scène, a Seemingly International Staging

In this book I analyze experimental films from Argentina, Brazil, Cuba, Mexico, Paraguay, and Peru of the past twenty years. The focal films in the chapters were made in 1998–2010. These films are experimental in that they have been influenced by the first (late 1920s–early 1930s) and second (1960s–1970s) avant-gardes as evidenced by the paratactical use of montage, the similarities with Italian neorealism, and an antihegemonic stance regarding the industrial, Hollywood model. While many Latin American films of this period share the conventions of the documentary and neorealism, that is, shooting real subjects on location and focusing on actual events, only a few feature an experimental deployment of montage that results in breaks in causality. These breaks are related to the "interval," which Gilles Deleuze defines as a delay between an action and a reaction. More importantly, the break suggests the unforeseeable nature of the reaction (Rodowick, 60; Deleuze, *Cinema 1*, 81). In the corpus of this text, the interval is represented by montage defined in a broad manner. Indeed, rather than a style of cutting, montage becomes a logic of composition and to that extent a concept or an overriding idea that regulates the system (Rodowick, 51).

The selection of films is always already arbitrary; in this book I offer a range of genres and conclude with a few suggestions. No other book on the market presents a comparative analysis across the contemporary cinematic production of some of the most important national traditions, underscoring shared thematic and formal preoccupations. I take a philosophical approach to emphasize the filmmakers' preoccupation with time as possibility as well as the portrayal of characters who witness events rather than react to them, resulting in an affective reading and thus broadening the Latin American imaginary in terms of counterhegemonic readings.

The Deleuzian approach underscores the difference between the features associated with the structure of classic Hollywood films—in other words, linear narratives propelled by strict causality, as epitomized by Hitchcock's films (Deleuze, *Cinema 1*)—and the impact of Italian neorealism and the French New Wave, explicitly regarding neorealism's signature concern with the protagonist as witness, thus stressing the voyage, the dispersive situation, the intentionally weak links, the deliberate condemnation of plot, and the consciousness of clichés (Deleuze, *Cinema 2*).

Most of the filmmakers in this text contest the classic Hollywood mode of a linear narrative (based on a single diegesis) that appears to be anchored in (the illusion of) realism as well as in spatial and temporal verisimilitude and psychologically motivated characters. Ideological and economic factors caused neorealist features to pervade the New Argentine Cinema, the Brazilian Cinema da Retomada, and the work of a variety of relatively young filmmakers in countries with rich cinematic traditions, among them Brazil, Mexico, Argentina, and Cuba. Countries with less-sustained national cinematic traditions, such as Paraguay and Peru, have contributed to understanding the impact of neorealism, for this diverse gamut of directors who, like Deleuze, translate the time-image into an emphasis on sight in films that represent time as possibility.

In these films, experimentation increases as their directors distance themselves from the industrial, Hollywood model. The term "experimental" follows Umberto Eco's definition, which proposes a contrast between the typically revolutionary and antagonistic features of the avant-garde versus the desire for acceptance of experimentalism, where innovation and critique occur from within an established tradition, with the intent of becoming the norm (Eco, 102–103). Insofar as the avant-garde montage techniques of the 1920s and 1930s have become canonical, the deployment of montage in the films in this book is experimental, while representing a broad range of themes and a variety of genres. These films do not necessarily constitute a coherent whole but are rather in dialogue with one another in terms of shared aesthetic features.

The rest of the introduction offers a historical contextualization of the cinematic tradition in Argentina, Brazil, Cuba, Mexico, Paraguay, and Peru. The chronological approach is complemented by a discussion of montage as typical of the first avant-garde, in Europe, the United States, and Latin America, and the inception of the documentary as a genre, in Britain and Latin America. By focusing on the aesthetics of neorealism, I underscore its traditional fusion with the conventions of the documentary in Latin American cinematic production. While the different manifestations of the New Latin American Cinema of the late 1960s and the 1970s tie in experimentation with montage, a documentary approach, and neorealist aesthetics, the recent boom in film production in Argentina, Brazil, and Mexico includes a strong industrial production but also suggests a development and continuation of the aesthetics of the New Latin American Cinema. The section on the most relevant philosophical concepts that Gilles Deleuze applied to cinema contextualizes discussion in the following chapters as briefly presented at the end of the introduction.

THE DEVELOPMENT OF NATIONAL CINEMATIC TRADITIONS

Silent movies arrived in Latin American capitals fast on the heels of their Parisian premières. The first film screenings took place in Buenos Aires on July 6, 1896, and in Rio de Janeiro two days later. By the following month, August 1896, Lumière's cameramen were in Mexico shooting Porfirio Díaz and his entourage. In Peru the first film screenings took place on January 2, 1897, and later that month in Cuba, still a Spanish colony, on January 24.

From 1900 to 1912, the annual production of more than one hundred Brazilian films dominated that country's domestic market. In 1913 Enrique Díaz Quesada (1882–1923) initiated the Cuban national cinematic tradition with a series of nine films focused on events related to country's new independence. From 1917 through 1921, Mexico produced an average of ten movies per year. That success was short-lived, since Hollywood took over the market by 1923. In Peru, realism and social commentary soon emerged as the dominant mode, as evidenced by Enrique Cornejo Villanueva's *Luis Pardo* (1927), the first Peruvian feature film, which focused on a famous bandit. Although Hipólito Carrón's ten-minute film *Alma paraguaya* (*Paraguayan Soul*) dates to 1925, Paraguay still lacks a significant cinematic tradition, so each new production is hailed as "the first Paraguayan film" (Etcheverry, 156).

The following sections explore the topics of montage, documentary, and realism, beginning with their respective historization and ending with their application in the most contemporary Latin American cinema.

Montage

Latin American experimental cinema begins, ironically, *comme il faut*, in Paris with the urban symphony *Rien que les heures* (1926) by Brazilian filmmaker Alberto Cavalcânti (1897–1982). Though it could be argued that Cavalcânti was merely applying the avant-garde montage concepts with which he had become familiar, the Brazilian director was to prove an instrumental figure in the history of cinema.[1] Cavalcânti's *Rien que les heures* is an intertextual pastiche that inscribes and subverts generic conventions. A shot of a group of elegant women that then becomes a photo is subsequently shredded into minute pieces. Texts dissolve, first into a self-reflexive image of an eye, then into an alternation of paintings, sketches, and pictures that reference varied styles—impressionism, cubism, and expressionism—before leading into abstract images. Names of well-known artists retrospectively anchor the references. The flags of different countries that fly in unison unexpectedly give way to sets of masklike eyes fluttering like fish. Snippets of stories of the underclass, such as a prostitute looking for a one-night stand, are set against series of flowers. As dissolves lead into other series, this riotously associative montage pushes still further into sets of brimming baskets that signal the beginning of another busy day. We are reminded of cosmopolitan Cavalcânti's admonitory proviso, "Toutes les villes seraient pareilles si leurs monuments ne les distinguaient pas" (All cities would be alike if not for their monuments). So did his Paris prefigure Berlin, as in collaboration with Walter Ruttmann (1887–1941) Cavalcânti produced *Berlin: Die symphonie der Großstadt* (1927).

This urban-symphony genre crossed the Atlantic, as Brazilian filmmakers Adalberto Kemeny (1901–1961) and Rodolfo Lustig (1901–1970) produced *São Paulo: Sinfonia de uma metrópole* (1929), a film designed to reveal the "grandeza desta soberbia metrópole, graças à energia construtiva do seu povo" (greatness of this proud metropolis, resulting from the constructive energy of its people). Adhering to the nationalist ideology, the movie presents the feverish activity of a day in São Paulo, emphasizing the city's continued progress (Stam, "On the Margins," 307). Experimental flourishes include alternating documentary shots with a montage of images structured by association that give way to a kaleidoscopic, simultaneous projection in three or five sections of the screen. Using film, he stresses the modernity of the city and thus of the nation.

Cavalcânti's contribution to and connection with the avant-garde occur within roughly the same context as those of a close contemporary, Russian filmmaker Sergei Eisenstein (1898–1948), who had produced *Strike* (1924) and *Battleship Potemkin* (1924). At that point, Eisenstein's influence on Latin American cinema was even more direct than Calvacânti's, as the Russian traveled to Mexico in 1930 just as the Brazilian filmmaker Mário Peixoto (1910–1992) was directing *Limite* (1931). Peixoto, who was only nineteen at the time, became conversant with the European avant-garde during his trips to England and France (Stam, "On the Margins," 307), reinforcing the motif of the international nature of cinematic cross-fertilization. Peixoto's *Limite* intertwines three stories through highly metaphoric visual language. Though there is nothing particularly Brazilian in these stories, Peixoto's film continues to enjoy its status as a cult movie in Brazil, perhaps due to the suggestive and ambiguous effect of the young director's use of montage.[2]

Limite opens with shots of vultures flying into a nest, followed by a shocking image of a woman's face over cuffed hands. After a dissolve the handcuffed fists become the focal point. Then they fuse into the woman's eyes, which subsequently dissolve into the reflection of the sun on the sea. As the process continues, the audience realizes that these eyes and hands belong to two women and a man whose intertwined stories converge, as they are stranded together on a boat in high sea. Two years after the inception of *Limite*, Brazilian director Humberto Mauro (1897–1983) fused German expressionism and Russian montage in *Ganga bruta* (Rough Scum, 1933). More importantly, Mauro's record of daily life in *Favela dos meus amores* (*Favela of My Loves*, 1934) precedes neorealism.

The foundation of national film traditions gained momentum with the arrival of sound. European wars of 1936–1945 prompted embargos on film stock. Argentina, in the years 1937–1940, produced 168 films, Mexico 161, Brazil 34, and Peru 22 (Schumann, 270). In the 1930s, sound track brought a new genre to Brazil as the *chanchada* (from Paraguayan Spanish slang meaning "trash," "mess," or "trick") implied the easy accessibility of these films to a culturally deprived public that was somewhat familiar with U.S.

musicals as epitomized by Carmen Miranda. The chanchada generated hundreds of movies from the late '30s well into the '50s (Johnson and Stam, 27). Meanwhile, from the 1940s on, Mexico became a main film producer in Spanish, as perceived competition from Argentine tango films was assuaged by the United States; cuts to the provision of film stock had a fatal impact on the nascent industry. The golden age of Mexican cinema was consolidated by the emergence of several important directors, a star system, and a proven formula (King, *Magical Reels*, 47). Subsidized by the state, Mexican films reinforced old-fashioned notions about national character in melodramas, *rancheras*—musical comedies focused on the ups and downs of rural people—and *rumberas* or *cabareteras* based on the stereotype of the fallen woman with a heart of gold (Hershfield and Maciel, 34). Legends of this era include El Indio Fernández (Emilio Fernández Romo), Dolores del Río, María Félix, Cantinflas (Mario Moreno), and Tin Tan (Germán Valdés).

Like Mexico and Brazil, Argentina pursued a policy of official support for the nascent national film industry, yet the period had few memorable projects. The Perón administration (1945–1955) saw the completion of Hugo del Carril's marvelous but ideologically flawed *Las aguas bajan turbias* (*Dark River*, 1952), whose focus on the overriding force of nature, including unbridled passions, precluded dwelling on the working conditions of the exploited peons. The 1955 coup d'état prompted improvements in the Argentine film industry: Leopoldo Torre Nilsson's hermetic movies *La casa del ángel* (*The House of the Angel*, 1957) and *La caída* (*The Fall*, 1959) inaugurated a national auteur cinema with an international aesthetics (Beceyro, 42–43). Brazilian producers similarly tried to emulate an international aesthetics. Backed by an industrial production and distribution system, Vera Cruz Studios, founded in São Paulo in 1949, imported top-quality equipment and experienced European technicians. Actors, decor, costumes, and music were to evoke a European ambience. Vera Cruz produced eighteen feature films; the most famous, Lima Barreto's *O cangaceiro* (1953), won two prizes at Cannes and was a worldwide success. Vera Cruz improved the technical quality of Brazilian films, increased investment, and incorporated an international cinematic language. Cavalcânti stayed until 1951, and Vera Cruz's production system went bankrupt in 1954, largely because its industrial films failed to connect with local audiences and lacked appropriate distribution to reach the international market. As Cavalcânti ignored his experimental beginnings he came to be seen as an agent of imperialism as well as a catalyst for Cinema Novo (Johnson, *Cinema Novo × 5*, 5–7).

—

As well known for his directorial work as for his theoretical musings on the nature of montage, Sergei Eisenstein is remembered for his dialectical method, which posited that a new concept would arise from the juxtaposition of two film pieces of any kind (*Film Sense*, 4). Eisenstein understood that the visual counterpoint within the shot could be defined in terms of graphic or spatial conflict, conflict between planes or volumes, or conflict in lighting or tempo ("Dramaturgy of Film Form," *Selected Works*, 166–172). By 1929 Eisenstein added other types of montage, namely metric, rhythmic, tonal, overtonal, and intellectual ("Fourth Dimension", ibid., 186–194). Like Eisenstein, Dziga Vertov (1896–1954), a practicing filmmaker, was interested in the theoretical nature of montage. Indeed, Vertov's *Man with a Camera* (1929) presented machines, landscapes, buildings, or men as part of a material system in perpetual interaction. Vertov is essentially recognized for freeing the camera from human intervention.

The importance of montage in the first European (Eisenstein, Vertov, Ruttmann) and Latin American (Cavalcânti, Peixoto) avant-garde appears throughout the films discussed in this book. These films share the deployment of montage as a paratactical structuring device in the act of literally placing scenes side by side. Just as in language we expect clauses or phrases to follow one after another without coordinating or subordinating connectives, paratactical structures in film result from noticeably omitting editing transitions. Montage is a factor in Fernando Pérez Valdés's *Suite Habana*, which incorporates Eisenstein's dialectic, rhythmic, tonal, and associative montage, while Fabián Bielinsky's *El aura* naturalizes the experimental use of montage as repetition in terms of conventional representations of psychic processes. Those processes involve the protagonist's epileptic seizures, his stream of consciousness (scenes of the initial heist at the cash register in the museum), recollections, and mental preparation to face a traumatic event (such as the killing of a deer and of his enemies at the end).

Montage, as a rapid succession of shots, appears in industrial roadies such as Walter Salles's *Central do Brasil* to suggest the female protagonist's fainting as a result from hunger and overexertion. Salles resorts to montage in both interview sections, purportedly as a thematic editing device but also as a way to safeguard the interviewees' privacy, at least in the first series. Similarly, during the initial thirty minutes of *El camino de San Diego* Carlos Sorín relies on montage to buttress characterization by juxtaposing recollections focused on different aspects of the protagonist's idolization of soccer player Diego Armando Maradona. In *El cielito*, María Victoria Menis portrays the protagonist's dreams by way of the experimental use of montage.

As a paratactical structuring device, montage is deployed to edit frames and shots or to alternate plot lines. In Carlos Reygadas's films, the abrupt juxtaposition of scenes reinforces the importance of the interval, which results in a *verfremdungs-effekt*, as the need to fill in the blanks becomes obvious. Oliveira Cézar deploys montage as a structuring device that allows for intertextual relations between similar narratives across temporal and spatial disjunctions. Montage appears with more latitude in Heitor Dhalia's *O cheiro do ralo* by naturalizing the protagonist's path to self-destruction through a series of seemingly interchangeable scenes that offer multiple permutations of a pattern of exchange.

Montage takes a different route in *Días de Santiago*, in which Josué Méndez's experimental aesthetics may be defined as the alternation between shots in color, designed to suggest contemporary reality, with others in black and white, to allude to the protagonist's past. By contrast, Paz Encina suggests montage by varying the distance of the shots from a fixed camera in *Hamaca paraguaya*, whose paratactical articulation is apparent at the end of the film, since the trauma experienced by the characters allows the audience to consider the possible arbitrariness of the order of the scenes, insofar as the protagonists obsessively recall their son's farewell. As a structuring device in Pérez Valdés's *Madrigal* (2006), montage underscores the juxtaposition of alternate reversible plots, such as the play, the personal lives of the actors, and their transformation in the short story.

The Documentary

According to John Grierson (1898–1972), founder of the British documentary movement, documentary depicts the story of a living scene as well as its original or native actors. Generic conventions include respect for the content of the image, the interpretive potential of editing, and the representation of social relationships (Aitken, 41, 83). These factors enter into our tendency to associate documentaries with commentary by voice-over narrators or exchanges between reporters and interviewees. Even if we become aware of the multiple perspectives on an issue, the commentator's words usually acquire an aura of truthfulness. Thus, documentaries present events as history reclaimed (Nichols, 21).[3]

Classical cinema deploys voice to buttress the impression of reality, yet it subordinates sound to sight and noise to speech. Synchronization is fundamental to identifying the source of sound, and to emphasizing speech, which serves to suture the spectator into the story, quite in the same way as the shot/reverse shot formation (Silverman, *Acoustic Mirror*, 43–45). While contemporary critics challenge the objectivity of the documentary by citing the socially constructed nature of reality, the documentary has thrived, spawning many subgenres such as the ethnographic film, *cinema vérité*, autobiographical documentary, documentary drama, indigenous documentary productions, and television documentary journalism (Beattie, 2).[4] The current revival may be traced to the influx of new media, that is, the widespread availability of video recorders, and a renewed emphasis on realism.[5]

In her foundational book on the social documentary in Latin America, Juliane Burton identifies four modes of the documentary—expository, observational, interactive, and reflexive—noting that the admixture of modes constitutes a fifth category. Since the observational mode recurs in the films examined in this corpus, we shall proceed to define its main characteristics.[6] Thematically, observational documentaries tend to focus on the behavior of subjects within social formations (families, institutions, communities) at moments of historical or personal crisis. Technically, the observational mode is noted for presenting the voice of the observed in indirect verbal address. There is a general predominance of synchronous sound and long takes. While the interaction between observer and observed is kept to a minimum, the mode provides a sense of impartiality that results from the intimate detail and texture of the lived experience (Burton, 4).

Writing at about the same time as Burton, Bill Nichols notes that the observational mode appears to provide direct access to the events taking place in front of the camera (38). The audience seems to be watching social actors, that is, individuals whose performance consists of representing themselves to others by playing out their daily lives. In terms of generic conventions, the observational mode is noticeable for its indirect address: speech is overheard as social actors engage with one another rather than speak to the camera. Synchronous sound and relatively long takes anchor speech to images that locate dialogue (and sound) in a specific moment and historical place. The observational documentary adheres to the conventions of classic narrative fiction: it displays a three-dimensional full-ness and unity in which the observer's location is readily determined and the space appears to have been carved from the historical world. In sum, observational documentaries share such narrative conventions of fiction as plot, character, and situation. To the extent that they build tension and offer closure, they both inscribe and subvert the purported objectivity of documentary (Nichols, 39, 107).

—

Peruvian directors Manuel Chambi and Luis Figueroa, who founded the Cuzco Film Club in 1955, produced ethnographic documentaries primarily based on the cultures of indigenous peoples. The Cuzco School (as per Georges Sadoul's coinage) earned prestigious international prizes. During the 1960s Luis Figueroa, Eulogio Nishiyama, and César Villanueva shared directorial responsibilities as they shot *Kukuli* (1960), spoken entirely in Quechua, a tragic love story in which the indigenous female protagonist falls prey to an *ukuku*, a mythical kidnapping bear, which kills her after hav-ing pushed her lover from a bell tower. After the bear is hunted down, the spirits of the lovers live on, transmuted into a pair of affectionate llamas.

European influences preceded much Latin American work with documentary. Nelson Pereira dos Santos spent two months in Paris in 1949. Upon his return he produced *Rio 40 graus* (*Rio 100 Degrees*, 1955), a semidocumentary on the people of Rio, as the camera follows boys who come down from the *favela* (slum) to sell peanuts in Copacabana. Cubans Tomás Gutiérrez Alea and Julio García Espinosa and Argentine Fernando Birri traveled to Rome to study filmmaking at the Centro Sperimentale di Cinematografia in the early 1950s. Returning to Argentina in the mid-1950s, Birri founded the Escuela Documental de Santa Fe. In so doing he drew from Grierson's definition of the documentary as a genre that offered a creative elaboration of reality based on actual events, nonprofessional actors, and issues emerging from the specific locations (Birri, 36). Birri involved his students in a sociological study that focused on the prole-tarians who lived by the railway tracks—especially those children who regularly risked their lives as they ran along the bridge while begging for a dime. This project began with a photographic exhibition and culminated in the film *Tire dié* (*Toss Me a Dime*, 1956–1958).

There were other collaborative ventures, too. *La hora de los hornos* (*Hour of the Furnaces*, 1968) was co-directed by Argentine filmmakers Fernando E. Solanas, Octavio Getino, and Gerardo Vallejo, who were part of the collective Cine Liberación. While political conditions in Argentina forced Solanas, Getino, and Vallejo to film clandestinely, they posited a guerrilla cinema that proved both influential and forward and whose manifestations varied according to its practitioners. The production of *La hora de los hornos* involved input from the workers as well as an active audience subjected to a constant barrage of images designed to illustrate the ideas of that essay-film. The screening also called for interruptions intended to engage the audience in live discussions, part of an aesthetic of seeking impromptu interactions termed *cine-actos* (film-acts) that aimed to subvert cinematic illusion by transforming the passive experience of watching a movie into an active performance or living theater.

La hora de los hornos appears to have a polyphonic structure resulting from the montage of images of multiple sources such as other films, TV images, advertisements, and interviews with real people. Paradoxically, this polyphony is set against an unambiguous message based on a schematic historicist model (*revisionismo histórico*).[7] Concluding the first of three parts in the film's original version, a five-minute shot of Che Guevara's corpse suggests that the movie articulates a call to join the armed struggle. The second part of the film focuses on Juan Perón's first administration (1945–1955), but here the unified ideological tone of the first part breaks down, creating ambiguity as Solanas and Getino—as well as Vallejo—unwittingly fail to situate Peronism in the context of Latin American populism and reinscribe Peronism's constant swing between democracy and authoritarianism through the manipulative and participatory format of the film (Stam, "Hour of the Furnaces," 263–264).[8] Argentine-Israeli film critic Tzvi Tal, who identifies Peronist verticalism (top-down decision making) in the ideological process of *La hora de los hornos*, attributes this ideology to several factors, ranging from Perón's military background to the typical authoritarianism of Argentine culture (69). Part 3 is equally monological in conveying a call to end imperialism and neocolonization enforced by native elites, ironically by way of multiple interviews of victims of state terrorism in the 1930s, 1950s, and 1960s Perón's return becomes the panacea.

Relative to the much larger nations of Mexico, Brazil, and Argentina, film production was sporadic in Cuba until the revolution prevailed when on March 24, 1959, a group of young Cubans founded the ICAIC (Instituto

Cubano del Arte y la Industria Cinematográfica). The ICAIC was to produce newsreels, documentaries, cartoons, and feature films. The revolution would reach a broad audience throughout the island as the ICAIC
deployed mobile units for projecting open-air movies in the countryside.
Among the Cuban directors to emerge out of the ICAIC, only Gutiérrez
Alea and García Espinosa had prior professional training and experience
as filmmakers; they attended the Centro Sperimentale de Cinematografia
and there became aware of neorealism, whose influences proved both immediate and far-reaching not just in Cuba but throughout Latin America.

Upon returning from Rome, Gutiérrez Alea and García Espinosa
produced *El mégano* (*The Charcoal Worker*, 1955). This film about the
substandard living conditions of brick makers anticipates concerns that
Cuban directors would be expressing a decade after the revolution top-
pled Batista in widely circulated movies such as Gutiérrez Alea's *Memorias
del subdesarrollo* (*Memories of Underdevelopment*, 1968) and Humberto
Solás's *Lucía* (1968), both of which privileged aesthetic experimentation
(Elena and Díaz López, 5). As the ICAIC was founded on the premise that
cinema is art and the Cuban government had many friends and sympathizers internationally, a good many Cuban movies garnered prestigious
awards at film festivals in the 1960s and subsequent decades.

Neorealism

Since Italian neorealism has exerted a continuing, profound effect on Latin
American cinema, attention to that genre's or school's origins reveals
the aesthetic concerns that recur into the present. Though Neapolitan
silent-era films foreshadowed neorealist aesthetics, neorealism is to some
degree a moral statement, for it emerges out of the postwar Italian repudiation of fascism, whose proponents were deeply involved in film as a way
of promoting an imperialist agenda. Although filmmakers did not adhere
to the same prescribed techniques, neorealism can be defined as a group
of Italian films produced from 1945 to 1952 that loosely shared certain
aesthetic conventions but never formed a self-conscious movement (Ruberto and Wilson, 6). As neorealists left the studios for the countryside or
the city, their cameras focused on physical and social realities (Shiel, 10).
Production was usually low-budget and artisanal.

Neorealism's representation of the poor working or peasant classes
often explores the point of view of children, who remained largely absent
from previous cinematic treatments of social problems. Though neoreal-

ism was primarily aimed at audience reflection, it also strove for emotional engagement (Hess, 106–107). By offering attractive narrative techniques and focusing on social issues, neorealism redefined national identity, which made it very popular (Ruberto and Wilson, 3). After the Italian period, roughly 1945–1955, neorealism became a politics and an aesthetics that influenced the New Latin American Cinema and Cinema Novo in the 1960s and 1970s, then cinema in Europe (Anglo-Saxon, German rubble films, Czechoslovak New Wave), the United States, Africa, and India, and prevalent in contemporary Latin American cinema.

—

When Gutiérrez Alea and García Espinosa returned to Cuba from their sojourn in Rome, they made films deeply influenced by neorealism, which shares some characteristics with the documentary, such as the use of nonprofessional actors and shooting on location (Hess, 105). While neorealism initially had a documentary flair in that it focused on the factors that affected the daily existence and conditions of the Italian people, by the 1950s, storytelling infused the documentary spirit of neorealism (Kolker, 65). So did a number of foundational Cuban films such as Gutiérrez Alea's *Memorias del subdesarrollo*, Solás's *Lucía*, and Sara Gómez's *De cierta manera* (*One Way or Another*, 1974) fuse the generic conventions of drama with those of the documentary (López, 135–156). After his sojourn in Paris, dos Santos also adapted neorealist techniques in *Vidas secas* (*Barren Lives*, 1963); attracted by their humanistic appeal, he was convinced that Cinema Novo was the Brazilian application of this method.

AESTHETICS AND POLITICS

The devastation resulting from World War II influenced the aesthetics of neorealism. When Cinecittá, founded in 1935 as the "most modern and best equipped studio in Europe (Brunetta, 72, 108), had become a refugee camp by 1945, directors were forced to film on location or to build sets. Whether directors were inspired by true stories or made them up, there was a sense that the camera recorded life in real time (Brunetta, 110), with the harshness of documentaries (Shiel, 10). The lack of resources likewise exerted a powerful impact on the neorealist aesthetics of the New Latin American Cinema and Cinema Novo and would recur in the 1990s to influence the aesthetics of the New Argentine Cinema, the Cinema da

Retomada in Brazil, and the contemporary production of certain directors in other Latin American countries.

The main difference between neorealism and the New Latin American Cinema, including Cinema Novo, was the avowed distance from Hollywood, that is, classical cinema. In other words, neorealism did not go far enough in using film for social commentary. According to some Latin American directors, neorealist filmmakers failed to deploy their techniques to address the revolutionary movements of the 1960s. They certainly neglected to challenge issues of underdevelopment. Although neorealist directors struggled against the imperialist designs of fascism, theirs was a brief interlude in comparison with the impact of colonialism and imperialism in Latin America, especially in view of the struggle to achieve national cinematic traditions.[9]

Moreover, by playing down the role of the people and the state in the fascist past and by positing the unfeasibility of utopia through strategies of containment that allowed for the preservation of the status quo, both in terms of social class and of patriarchal capitalism, neorealism ultimately articulated conservative discourses. As we shall see, the same failure also has been attributed to contemporary Latin American films, which display neorealist features. Despite the apparent break with fascism, neorealism was not as politically revolutionary as to exert widespread social change. Rather, its ideological flaw may be traced to the continuity in personnel, since those who had been fascists were absolved of their ideological sins as long as they were useful in the filmmaking process. In the 1950s, Italian cinema's re-entry into the market was facilitated by a number of measures that encouraged directors to move away from neorealist themes.[10]

In the 1960s and 1970s, Latin American filmmakers were adamant about distancing themselves from Hollywood economic and aesthetic considerations. Argentine and Brazilian directors of the period privileged theoretical and cinematic resources associated with social change. Those resources included 1920s Soviet montage as epitomized by Eisenstein; 1930s French poetic realism, which arose with the ephemeral Popular Front prior to World War II; Italian postwar neorealism; the British documentary tradition, which contributed to the articulation of a national identity as it privileged social responsibility; and Bertolt Brecht's aesthetic and political views (Tal, 77). With the sole exception of French poetic realism, these resources inform *La hora de los hornos*, and they are ubiquitous in contemporary Latin American cinema.

The social critique of the Argentine cinema of the late 1960s was mirrored throughout the continent. Cinema Novo, the Brazilian manifestation of the New Latin American Cinema, was far from unified as a movement. Randal Johnson identifies three different periods of about four years each. The first spans 1960–1964, when filmmakers contributed to the debate on the national question with films about the country's proletariat, often depicted in rural settings. During this first period, Cinema Novo filmmakers hoped to raise consciousness regarding the process of social transformation. This stage would be epitomized by dos Santos's *Vidas secas* and Glauber Rocha's *Deus e o diabo na terra do sol* (*Black God, White Devil*, 1964). Aesthetically, Cinema Novo directors relied on overexposure, the hand-held camera, and nervous framing to present a fragmented narrative suggestive of the cruelty of the sertão and to posit an ethics based on images of pain and revolt (Bentes, 124).

Their hopes were frustrated over the course of the second period, 1964–1968, as the country experienced an extremely repressive military rule. Thus, films such as Rocha's *Terra em transe* (*Land in Anguish*, 1967) and dos Santos's *Fome de amor* (*Hunger for Love*, 1968) turned their focus toward the urban middle class in an attempt to understand the failure of the Left. The last phase, 1968–1972, saw the tightening of censorship and the institution of torture, so Cinema Novo filmmakers opted for allegorical films such as Joaquín Pedro de Andrade's *Macunaíma* (1969) and dos Santos's *Azyllo muito loco* (*The Alienist*, 1970) (Johnson, *Cinema Novo × 5*, 2–3). This last phase encompassed two vastly different manifestations. The cannibal-tropicalist practice alluded to the government's genocidal measures by emphasizing kitsch and the grotesque (tropicalism) but also by suggesting that Brazil should figuratively devour foreign enemies and thus appropriate their force (cannibalism). *Udigrudi* (underground), the second practice, was aimed at marginality and intended to shock the audience by identifying with rebellious lumpen characters as well as by radicalizing Rocha's aesthetics of hunger (Johnson and Stam, 37–39).

Like other national cinematic traditions, Cinema Novo mapped national experience in order to arrive at a general diagnosis of the country's malaise. Social criticism coupled with aesthetic rupture alienated audiences who expected naturalism and a didactic cinema. The formal innovations of young filmmakers linked them to the modernist tradition. While some filmmakers resorted to allegories, Cinema Novo introduced intertextual references that conveyed political engagement opaquely. Into the late 1960s, Brazilian filmmakers thus moved away from a utopian impulse and a social teleology of redemption. By the 1970s Brazilian filmmakers accepted underdevelopment as a state of being, in plots that turned on family dramas and frustrated characters both poor and rich whose lives ended calamitously (Xavier, 41).

As this brief survey of aesthetics, directorial schools, collaborative ventures, and national trends would suggest, the New Latin American Cinema was political, above all. After the 1964 coup d'état, Rocha established a connection between Brazil and the rest of Latin America based on the region's shared dependency. Rocha's interpretation of social reality was resonant for Solanas, Getino, and Vallejo, who used dependency theory to explain the undernourishment of the Argentine rural population. It was in this context that Rocha's "aesthetics of hunger" was presented in Genoa, Italy, in 1965 to promote awareness of the exploitation of the colonized and to incite action to attain change, as Rocha concluded that the industrial and economic integration of Cinema Novo was contingent on Latin America's liberation (*Revolução*, 66–67). Rocha took this rhetoric still further when he argued that Cinema Novo would arise wherever a filmmaker struggled against censorship, commercialism, exploitation, pornography, and to move past mere displays of technical virtuosity (67). Around 1969 García Espinosa called for what he termed an "imperfect cinema" predicated on the need to focus on the problem as process, not just because personal analysis is always already marred by a priori value judgments but because it precludes input from the interlocutor (14–15). In their 1973 book *Cine, cultura, y descolonización*, Solanas and Getino posited a "third cinema," a "militant cinema" that would tackle particular historical conditions over the course of contributing to the process of continental liberation (89).

Among the leading film directors who shared the views expounded by Rocha, Solanas, and Getino were Bolivian film director Jorge Sanjinés and Cuban filmmaker Julio García Espinosa. Each emphasized the need for collective analysis of the underlying causes of the people's struggle. For his part, in 1979 Sanjinés argued against providing a priori judgments: he pointed to how predetermined conditions that structure subjectivity influence the individual's apprehension of reality. Instead, Sanjinés suggested analyzing the dialectic relation between the people's struggle and popular art, so that art could thereby become an instrument of liberation. As collective and revolutionary, popular art would therefore represent a particular culture's *weltanschauung* (Sanjinés and Grupo Ukamau, 79–80).

Likewise, reflecting on the Cuban experience in 1982, Gutiérrez Alea's "viewer's dialectic" argued for transforming the passive and complacent audience into one ready to engage in meaningful action. This would be achieved, he proposed, by presenting a socially productive spectacle that negated the false values crystallized in everyday reality: moved by pleasure, the audience would be attracted to the possible reality offered by the spectacle (26–27). In other words, despite the generalized usage of the label "New Latin American Cinema," each practice and theoretical position stemmed from a specific sociohistorical reality. For instance, despite the initial collective production, the ethnographic approach of the Cuzco School could not have differed more from the cinematic production (and self-reflexive theorization) through which Jorge Sanjinés and the Ukamau Collective attempted to record indigenous reality. Although García Espinosa's imperfect cinema also differed from Gutiérrez Alea's viewer's dialectic, all of these directors' theoretical positions shared certain traits, such as the urge to deploy film as a tool for social change and an attitude of commitment that would further undermine Hollywood's hegemonic model of production and reception. Therefore, I have chosen the term "New Latin American Cinema" to refer to Spanish American cinematic production of that period and "Cinema Novo" to refer broadly to its Brazilian counterpart.[11]

As the effervescence of the 1960s was cut short by a series of coups that installed state terrorism in Brazil (1964–1985), Chile (1973–1990), Argentina (1976–1982), and Uruguay (1973–1985), state censorship— worsened by disappearances and torture—exile, and self-censorship stymied cinematic production. The forceful institutionalization of neoliberal economic policies resulted in a widening economic gap that, coupled with the withdrawal of the welfare state, led to significant decreases in the standard of living, a phenomenon referred to as "the lost decade," during which, for example, Argentine cinematic production was drastically curtailed. The few quality productions include Mario Sábato's *El poder de las tinieblas* (*Power of Darkness*, 1979), a highly metaphorical film about ubiquitous fear.

Piedra libre (*Free for All*, 1976) by the paradigmatic auteur Leopoldo Torre Nilsson was considered subversive and underwent significant cuts prior to being released. Adolfo Aristarain's industrial *Tiempo de revancha* (*Time for Revenge*, 1981), an allegory about the omnipresent power of the military juntas, centers on a worker who succeeds in resisting exploitation. The production of political films resumed with the return of democracy.

Juan José Jusid's *Asesinato en el Senado de la Nación* (*Murder in the
Senate*, 1984) critiques government corruption by alluding to a shady deal
involving the sale of meat to Britain with the connivance of the mafia in
1935. María Luisa Bemberg's melodramatic *Camila* (1984) portrays the
tragic end of Camila O'Gorman during the 1840s dictatorship of Juan
Manuel de Rosas. Luis Puenzo's *La historia oficial* (*The Official Story*, 1985)
tackles the thorny issue of the appropriation of the children of the disappeared and was awarded an Oscar for Best Foreign Film, the first garnered
by a Latin American country (Schumann, 36–45).[12]

The rampant neoliberalism of Carlos Saúl Menem's administration
(1989–1999) had a nefarious impact on Argentine cinema. Most of the
filmic production was unabashedly commercial, but some filmmakers
ensured international distribution by relying on co-productions and the
cachet of foreign actors. The cast of Bemberg's *Yo, la peor de todas*
(*I, the Worst of All*, 1990), an Argentine-French venture on Mexican
nun, author, and protofeminist Sor Juana Inés de la Cruz (1648–1695),
included Assumpta Serna of Spain and Dominique Sanda of France. Lita
Stantic's *Un muro de silencio* (*A Wall of Silence*, 1993), which addresses
the disappearance of the legendary film producer's partner by way of a
complex structure of a play within a play, involves Argentina, Mexico, and
Britain and depends on Vanessa Redgrave's prestige. Martín Rejtman's
El rapado, a co-production involving Argentina and the Netherlands
(1991, released in 1996), sports a minimalist aesthetics in the story of a
youth who feels the need to steal a motorbike after his has been stolen.
This film exerted a powerful influence on a new generation of filmmakers (Maranghello, 221–256). Alejandro Agresti, an auteur with more than
seventeen feature films who has enjoyed success in Argentina and in
the Netherlands, where he lived in the early 1990s, is another influential
precursor of the new Argentine Cinema. Though Agresti has made an
industrial blockbuster film, his contribution lies in the episodic structure
and the improvisational nature of his experimental black and white films.
Like Agresti, Esteban Sapir is another important precursor. Sapir's black
and white *Picado fino* (1986), which follows the protagonist as he shirks
his responsibility in the impregnation of his girlfriend, is groundbreaking in
the use of intellectual montage to supersede dialogue.

Argentina

Despite policies intended to encourage national film (such as legislating
that a percentage of all screen time be devoted to nationally produced

materials), few of the movies associated with the New Argentine Cinema, or the Independent Argentine Cinema, enjoyed official subsidies. Due to economic difficulties, many of the films were made in nonstandard formats such as 16mm, black and white, digital video, Beta, and Super VHS, and most were shot on location with nonprofessional actors (Bernardes, Lerer, and Wolf, 10). The stories tend to be representative of that generation because they are, for the most part, personal. Among the most salient features of the New Argentine Cinema is the slang used throughout the dialogue. Many of the films are set in the city, depicting an urban space that becomes strange due to the inscription of social, cultural, or religious ghettoes or to the uncanny persistence of the past into present-day life. So do characters, locations, and forms of speech blur the limits between fiction and the documentary in the work of these directors (S. Wolf, "Aesthetics," 31, 34–35). In sum, rather than unabashedly identifying with European-influenced culture as their modern antecessors had done, more recent filmmakers portray ethnic minorities and working-class people, projecting a more complex understanding of national identity in Argentina (Falicov, *Cinematic Tango*, 133).

Brazil

The importance of Embrafilme, a state enterprise involved in film production and distribution, was decisive as of 1974. Coupled with legislation regarding screening quotas—movie theaters had to show Brazilian films 133 days per year—this state agency ensured the ongoing development of Brazilian cinema. For the most part, the *pornochanchadas*, vapid erotic comedies of the 1970s that offered a picture of a decadent bourgeoisie, were superseded by an interest in the popular toward mid-decade. Dos Santos was one of the various cultural agents to spearhead the renewed interest in popular culture, envisioned as the cultural expression of the people. Though the controversy over "popular" and "populist" has yet to be settled, Brazilian cinema succeeded in making accessible avant-garde films (Johnson and Stam, 40–50). While the escapism afforded by the pornochanchadas continued unabated in the 1980s, the decade also saw a series of movies focused on political violence and state repression. Most importantly, cinematic production was no longer restricted to metropolitan areas (São Paulo, Rio) but migrated toward Bahia, Pernambuco, Minas Gerais, and other places (Schumann, 116–117).

In Brazil, a new audio-visual law promulgated in 1993 prompted a boom in film production that became known as the "Retomada do Cinema

Brasileiro," the rebirth or boom of Brazilian cinema (Nagib, introduction to *Cinema da Retomada*, 13). The current echoes of emblematic Cinema Novo subjects and spaces such as the sertão reveals certain continuities in the concerns of Cinema da Retomada filmmakers.[13] As contemporary filmmakers are more skeptical than their Cinema Novo predecessors with regard to the national-popular issue, they have resorted to allegorical representations of politics (Xavier, 41). Still other oblique venues have included love stories, generational conflicts, and murder mysteries. Most of the recent films focus on the nation's recurring fault lines: national history, the violence arising from the social class system, and interaction with the other—including foreigners (Oricchio, *Cinemadenovo*, 232).

Cuba

In Cuba the exploration of the first decades after the revolution was, with a few exceptions, superseded by a crisis in representation that led back to traditional formats. *Hasta cierto punto* (*To a Certain Point*, 1983), Gutiérrez Alea's attempted thesis film, establishes a counterpoint with the profound ideological critique of Gómez's *De cierta manera*. The 1980s closed with two formally rewarding self-reflexive films: Juan Carlos Tabío's quirky comedy *¡Plaff! O demasiado miedo a la vida* (*Too Afraid of Life, or Splat*, 1988) parodies the allegories of the nation embodied by female characters, while Orlando Rojas's *Papeles secundarios* (*Supporting Roles*, 1989) employs the performance of shifting identities ranging from sexual orientation to Afro-Cuban magic—all is reflected through the multiple connotations of a theater (Chanan, 436–437, 440–441).

As perestroika destabilized the Cuban economy between 1989 and 1993,[14] there were frequent blackouts and food shortages. Severe gasoline rationing brought about huge cuts in public transport, and bicycles were imported from China. The new constitution of 1992, which modified the concept of property, heralded economic recovery as the dollar was legalized, land ownership was transferred to agricultural cooperatives, and self-employment became an option. While markets for agricultural produce and industrial and artisanal products became available, economic growth was stimulated by foreign investment, especially in tourism. Though the ICAIC kept its annual festival going, the end of state subsidies led to an exodus of personnel, and production ground to a halt. As economic conditions forced the ICAIC to pursue international co-productions, Cuban filmmakers learned that European investors were interested in low-budget films that offered an exotic view of the island presented by poorly remu-nerated but highly qualified labor—technical support and actors (Chanan, 447–448, 479–480). As the quest for co-productions led to more per-sonal narratives, a growing number of films afforded possibilities for social critique (Young, 26).

Mexico

Mexican cinema has been subject to a number of presidential interven-tions designed to revitalize its productivity, in apparent decline since the so-called golden age. The stop-and-go development of the cinematic industry has, from the early 1950s, witnessed the introduction of measures to "save" it with a new model for each *sexenio*, or six-year presidential term. These oscillate between complete liberalism on the one hand and state monopoly on the other. As observed in King, López, and Alvarado (222), one total effect has been to drive the industry, on the whole, into further crisis. The efforts of President Luis Echeverría Álvarez offer a case in point: to offset the loss of confidence resulting from the massacre of Tlatelolco in 1968, Echeverría appointed his brother Rodolfo to the Banco Cinematográfico. Rodolfo, in turn, founded the Cinemateca Nacional de México, the state film archive, and established a film school. Both actions gradually increased the role of the state in key aspects of production and exhibition.

These measures were dismantled in the José López Portillo (1976–1982) administration, while the following regime of Miguel de Lamadrid saw state neglect and rampant commercialism. Lastly, under duress, that is, aware of the privatization of state enterprises as a condition for NAFTA, President Carlos Salinas de Gortari (1988–1994) had Ignacio Durán, the head of Imcine, the Instituto Mexicano de Cinematografía, buttress state funding by seeking private-sector investments (King, "Cinema," 516). Such inconsistency of policies on film production and distribution in Mexico is an all too common feature in other Latin American countries like Brazil and Argentina.

The renaissance of Mexican cinema was heralded by the unexpected, almost blockbuster success of Alfonso Arau's *Como agua para chocolate* (*Like Water for Chocolate*, 1991). Arau's adaptation of Laura Esquivel's homonymous novel (1989) offers the drama of an ill-starred love story, the authenticity of Hispanic customs, local color, a mixture of well-known and nonprofessional actors, and most importantly, a magical realism that

reinscribes Latin America as exotic, fulfilling Euro-American expectations. In line with the plot's conservative ideology, the protagonist's power
remains circumscribed to the kitchen. Moreover, in accordance with the
stereotype of the self-destructive heroine, her suicide restores conventional order. In sum, Arau's mainstream film underscores the qualities of
contemporary Mexican cinematic production, insofar as the movie is light
and the plot revolves around private conflict (Torrents, 225).

Mexican directors debuting in the early 1990s achieved acclaim at
home and abroad because they relied on proven Hollywood genres, such
as action or horror movies, which ensured international cross-over. A
generation of professionally trained filmmakers were graduates of the
Centro de Capacitación Cinematográfica or Centro de Estudios Cinematográficos, institutions that allowed for collaboration with seasoned
directors. These directors were savvy in seeking international funds and
co-productions. For instance, the success of Alfonso Cuarón's *Sólo con
tu pareja* (*Love in the Time of Hysteria*, 1991) and *Y tu mamá también*
(2001) led to his Hollywood productions *Harry Potter and the Prisoner
of Azkaban* (2004) and the futuristic dystopia *Children of Men* (2006).
Likewise, the warm reception of Guillermo del Toro's horror movie *Cronos*
(1993) was the stepping-stone for two other films set in Spain, *El espinazo
del diablo* (*The Devil's Backbone*, 2001) and *El laberinto del Fauno* (*Pan's
Labyrinth*, 2006), the last of which garnered Oscar nominations. The box-
office success of the three interwoven stories in Alejandro González Iñárritu's *Amores perros* (*Love's a Bitch*, 2000) led to Hollywood invitations to
produce *21 Grams* (2003) and to repeat the formula of interwoven stories
in *Babel* (2006). Iñárritu's *Biutiful* (2010), set in Barcelona, also garnered
Oscar nominations.

Paraguay

In Paraguay, Argentine co-productions from the late 1930s to the late '50s
gave way to state propaganda in the '60s, as epitomized by Guillermo
Vera's *Cerro Corá* (1977), which focused on the War of the Triple Alliance
(1867–1970) but was in fact political propaganda aimed at promoting
longtime dictator General Alfredo Stroessner's fascist version of history.
Recent successes include Claudio MacDowell's large-scale co-production
The Call of the Oboe (Paraguay-Brazil, 1998), a fiction film entirely shot
in Paraguay; Etcheverry's *El portón de los sueños* (*The Gate of Dreams*,
1998), documentary-fiction about the most important Paraguayan writer,

Augusto Roa Bastos; and Galia Giménez's *María Escobar* (2001), a film based on a popular Paraguayan song (Etcheverry, 157–159). Thus, given the lack of a strong national cinematic tradition, each production is hailed as the one and only Paraguayan film. In a context of an industrial tradition, Encina's directorial sophistication thrives due to the support garnered at international venues and by adding production incentives to the advantages of transnational co-productions.

Peru

Conversely, in Peru, General Velasco Alvarado's 1968 leftist coup d'état fostered a series of social reforms, including the 1973 law that fomented national film production. But the considerable boom was cut short by the 1975 conservative coup d'état. Francisco Lombardi and Federico García began their prolific careers in the late 1970s. Lombardi, who trained with Fernando Birri in the Santa Fe documentary film school in Argentina in 1968, released his first feature-length movie, *Muerte al amanecer* (*Death at Dawn*), in 1977. While García examined indigenous and historical topics, Lombardi achieved commercial success by exploring social violence (Schumann, 276–277). At present, Lombardi is the most successful director, with more than ten feature films to his name along with an Oscar nomination for *Ojos que no ven* (*What the Eye Doesn't See*, 2003) (Middents, 40–42).

Josué Méndez denies the existence of a Peruvian cinematic tradition. His first feature film, *Días de Santiago* (2004), was an independent venture. Claudia Llosa's *Madeinusa* (2006), completed with funds from the Sundance Festival, heralded the arrival of a new generation of filmmakers who benefit from international programs. Her second feature film, a Catalan co-production, *La teta asustada* (*Milk of Sorrow*, 2010), earned a Golden Bear award at the Berlin festival and was nominated for an Oscar in 2010. Llosa's directorial production evidences the need for engaging in the international circuit of film festivals, seeking production funding or international co-productions. Like Llosa, Méndez has become keenly aware of the pressures involved in submitting well-defined scripts and keeping to the deadlines of the international film-festival circuit. Indeed, while still making a social statement, Méndez's second film, *Dioses* (*Gods*, 2008), is not experimental.[15]

HYPOTHESES OF ORIGINS AND AESTHETIC SIMILARITIES

Despite the inherent flaws of generalizations, this brief summary of cine-matic traditions allows for positing the following hypotheses. Silent movies arrived almost on the heels of the initial French showings. As a veritable cottage industry of producing newsreels, shorts, and feature films, initial cinematic production involved friends and relatives or members of the higher social classes, but Hollywood asserted its hegemonic power early, with devastating effects for the nascent national industries. In the mean-time, relatively isolated from Spanish America, Brazil turned aggressively to the European avant-garde, as the cinematic production of Cavalcânti, Peixoto, and Mauro attests.

The arrival of sound offered new opportunities to the national cin-ematic production: in Mexican rancheras, Argentine tango films, and Brazilian musicals like the chanchadas epitomized by Carmen Miranda. However, with the excuse of implicit support of the Axis, the United States strangled production in Argentina and Peru, cutting at once their imports of virgin film stock and turning to Mexico for its propaganda machine. By importing the international studio model, Mexico arrived at its "golden era."

With Cavalcânti in the vanguard, film directors like Birri turned to documentary in the 1950s. By the mid-1950s, the general mode was in-dustrial, with the few exceptions of auteurs such as the hermetic Leopoldo Torre Nilsson, the ethnographic documentaries of the Cuzco School, and the first films made by Latin American directors who had been influenced by neorealism during their sojourns in Rome. After he returned to Brazil, dos Santos's films initiated Cinema Novo. The political fervor of the 1960s revolutionized cinematic production. Following the Soviet example, the Cuban Revolution turned to film for the reproduction of ideology. Docu-mentaries were favored, but feature films followed, and some mixed the two genres. Both the New Latin American Cinema and Cinema Novo were marked by a variety of aesthetic and political manifestos: while each reflects the sociohistoric conditions of its inception, the mid-1970s was a bleak period. The violent repression of dissent manifested in such atroci-ties as the massacre of Tlatelolco and the disappearance of thousands of dissenters as well as innocent victims in the Southern Cone and Brazil, which were in the grip of state terrorism. Filmmakers went into exile. Few continued to produce films at the same rate. Rampant commercialism ensued. Some filmmakers became more elliptical.

The 1980s marked the arrival of democracy and the end of state censorship, but neoliberalism had been instituted across Latin America. Policies geared to foster domestic cinematic production were systematically ignored. Cuba experienced the Special Period, starved by the unintended consequences of perestroika. Thus, for slightly different reasons and with widely divergent results, Latin American filmmakers were forced to seek international funding in the way of co-productions. Paradoxically, the 1990s saw a veritable boom in the creation of film schools across the continent. The directors who graduated from these schools were soon made aware of the need for international investment, so they heavily relied on the international cycle of film festivals. While their production differs widely, the New Argentine Cinema and Cinema da Retomada share certain aesthetic and thematic features. Despite the examples in this text and a penchant for certain neorealist qualities, current filmmakers seem to favor the industrial Hollywood model in an investment that has led to a number of Oscar nominations and two actual awards, the last being Argentine Juan José Campanella's *El secreto de sus ojos* (*The Secret in Their Eyes*) in 2010.

Neorealist practices made a comeback in the 1990s New Argentine Cinema and Cinema da Retomada. All of the directors featured in the following chapters make a point of shooting on location. Most of them work with casts made up at least partly of nonprofessional actors. While these practices manifest the influence of documentaries on the New Latin American Cinema, especially under the aegis of the Cuban Revolution, they have been labeled "fictual faction" and *realismo sucio* (dirty realism).[16] Thus, a considerable number of directors—Reygadas, Sorín, Pérez Valdés, and Menis among them—work with nonprofessional actors who play roles similar to those of their actual lives. This is particularly evident in the neorealist focus on the child—defined with a certain latitude. Thus, Vinícius de Oliveira, a shoe-shine boy, plays Josué in Salles's *Central do Brasil*. Agustín Alcoba plays Santi in Oliveira Cézar's *Como pasan las horas*, and Agustín Ponce plays Orestes in *Extranjera*.

In this text I discuss films as well whose directors rely on professional actors to play the roles of actors, as in Pérez Valdés's *Madrigal*. While the overwhelming presence of professional actors is also evident in Paz Encina's *Hamaca paraguaya*, Oliveira Cézar's *Extranjera* and *El recuento de los daños* maintain a balanced mix of professional actors and extras. The inclusion of nonprofessional actors may be ironic. Such is the case of

Lourenço Mutarelli, the author of the novel *O cheiro do ralo*, in the role of
the security agent and the extras who anchor the film's structure of repetition with variation by attempting to pawn their belongings in Dhalia's homonymous film. In the more industrial neonoir movies only a few extras are
nonprofessional actors, as in the scenes of the museum, the brothel, and
the casino in Fabián Bielinsky's *El aura* or the street and nightclub scenes
in Jorge Furtado's *O homem que copiava* and Méndez's *Días de Santiago*.
Occasionally the distinction between professional and nonprofessional
actors is hard to make because of the range of national cinematic traditions I have included here.

In addition, these films share a focus on contemporary life, as
epitomized in Oliveira Cézar's work, wherein the enactment of certain
customs (rituals in *Como pasan las horas*), lifestyles (in *Extranjera*), and
rash actions (*El recuento de los daños*) alludes to the pattern of recurrent
lifestyles across time periods and geographical distance. To an extent,
all of the movies address current social issues—the failure of the state,
for example—with the caveat that in Latin America the topic may not be
considered current but rather the status quo. Nonetheless, the context
for *El aura* as well as Bielinsky's previous film, *Nueve reinas* (*Nine Queens*,
2000), is impunity, given the widespread corruption illustrated by the
phrase "Todos roban" (Everyone steals). Sorín and Menis focus on the
lack of opportunities for rural workers, worsened by the withdrawal of the
welfare state. Salles explores the dire predicament of homeless children.

Furtado's protagonists experience a lack of opportunities, but like
Bielinsky's, they are ready to take calculated risks to beat the system.
Rather than defining his identity by way of consumerism, Dhalia's protagonist takes advantage of the lack of opportunities, yet his interactions are
tainted by commodification, while Oliveira Cézar's *Como pasan las horas*
suggests that financial constrictions would only allow for crammed living
conditions if the characters lived in the city. The failure of the state becomes that of the community in *Extranjera*, for co-optation in the sacrifice
purportedly planned to alleviate a long-lasting drought is a thin disguise
to distract group members from becoming aware of their leader's failing
powers. The failure of the state is fully evident in *El recuento de los daños*,
which harks back to the disappearance of dissenters and the appropriation of babies born in captivity during the period of Argentine state terrorism (1976–1982).

While Reygadas points to rural poverty and underdevelopment in

Japón and *Batalla en el cielo* illustrates the gaping abyss between social classes in urban Mexico, *Stellet licht* focuses on the harsh living conditions and the lack of reliable medical attention in isolated rural Mennonite communities. The desperate living conditions of contemporary Cubans, given the ultimate failure of the state, that is, of the revolution, is at the center of Pérez Valdés's films. *Días de Santiago* addresses the failure of the state to reincorporate its veterans. Among other factors, ubiquitous post-traumatic syndrome has a domino effect that influences the predicament of the soldier as well as of his relatives. Insofar as war results from the failure of the state to arrive at a diplomatic solution, the resulting trauma engulfs the nation, symbolized by the peasant couple in *Hamaca paraguaya* (2008).

GILLES DELEUZE AND CINEMA

As is evident in the English versions of Deleuze's *Cinema 1* and *Cinema 2*, his approach to film is based on the fundamental categories of time, movement, and the interval. Actually, Deleuze was inspired by the similarity that Henri Bergson drew between movement and cinematographic illusion. In establishing differences between space and movement, Bergson posits that movement is present and space covered is past and infinitely divisible. Movement, by contrast, cannot be divided without changing qualitatively as it is being divided. Developing these Bergsonian premises, Deleuze argues that two instants can be brought together to infinity, but movement always occurs in the interval between them. Despite the subdivision of time, movement always occurs in a concrete qualitative duration. Cinematic technique has changed significantly since Bergson's time. Initially, the sections, or images, were made to pass consecutively through the apparatus on the basis of a uniform, invisible movement. As montage and the mobile camera emancipated movement from the viewpoint of projection, the shot would no longer be a spatial but a temporal category. The section would no longer be immobile but mobile (*Cinema 1*, 1, 3).

Deleuze's notion of the movement-image develops from Bergson's third thesis on movement and change, which is based in turn on the rationale that movement is a translation in space that involves a qualitative change in the whole. Yet the whole is open because its nature is to change constantly, which is reflected in duration. While sets defined as discernible objects are subject to movement, which modifies both their respective positions and the duration or the whole, the whole in turn is a spiritual real-

ity that constantly changes according to its own relations. Therefore, one
aspect of movement is what happens between objects or parts; another is
that which expresses the duration or the whole. By changing qualitatively,
duration is divided into objects. By gaining depth, objects are united in
duration. Therefore, movement relates the objects between which it
is established to the changing whole that it expresses, and vice versa.
Though the objects are immobile, movement relates them to the duration
of a whole that changes. Unlike instantaneous images—immobile sections
of movement—movement-images are mobile sections of duration, while
time-images include duration-images and change-images (8–11).

As a system that includes sets, characters, and props, the frame is
conceived as a dynamic construction, closely linked to the scene in D. W.
Griffith's iris method, which isolates a face prior to opening up to show the
surroundings. The out-of-field introduces the transpatial and the spiritual
into the system through duration. For instance, Carl Theodor Dreyer's
method closes the image spatially. By reducing it to two dimensions, Dreyer allows for the introduction of the fourth dimension, time, and even of the
fifth, spirit. Conversely, Alfred Hitchcock's frames include the maximum
number of components in the image. Yet, as the components are open to
a play of relations, the mental image becomes pure thought (11–13, 17–18).

While cutting (*decoupage*) determines the shot, the shot determines
the movement established between the parts of the set within the closed
system, expressing in turn a change of the whole. Insofar as the shot relates movement to a whole that changes, the shot is the movement-image.
Originally, the fixed camera defined the frame by a frontal point of view,
that of the spectator. To this extent, the shot indicates "a slice of space"
that varies from close-up to long shot. In the case of these immobile sections, movement remains attached to the elements that serve as its vehicle. Therefore, the whole is identical to the set, in that the movement goes
through as it passes from one spatial shot/plane (plan) to another (22, 24).
Encina's experimental aesthetics greatly depends on the initial use of the
fixed camera, which is why Deleuze's thoughts are so appropriate.

Deleuzian Montage

When Deleuze defines "montage" as the determination of the whole, he
stresses the composition of movement-images that constitute an indirect
image of time, within the organic montage of the American school, Soviet
dialectic montage, the quantitative style of the prewar French school, and

the intensive trend of German expressionism. While Bielinsky and Oliveira Cézar hint at German expressionism in their montage, the other three schools have proven to be the most influential in the films discussed in this book. D. W. Griffith conceived the composition of movement-images as a great organic unity that included differentiated parts set as binary relationships that allowed for parallel alternate montage. The close-up endows the objective set with subjectivity by showing how the characters live their scenes. Finally, a conflict must arise, only to be overcome. In Griffith's time, montage required the alternation of differentiated parts, of relative dimensions, or of convergent actions. Usually, the confrontation and restoration of peace would take the form of a duel or of the convergence of actions.

Eisenstein's dialectical method modifies Griffith's organic montage in that it replaces opposition with the notion of an internal motive as a force that divides the unity, leading to a new unity on another level. However, this unity may arise from the pathetic passage of the opposite into its contrary. In the case of a pathetic jump, such as from sadness to anger, from doubt to certainty, or from resignation to revolt, the power of the first stage is transferred to the second. The transition generates an upsurge of a new quality. Yet, the pathetic jump involves a change in form. Eisenstein suggested a change of dimension, a transition from nature to man and a quality born from the transition by resorting to series of enlarging close-ups. In the French sublime school, montage is based on the interval, a variable and successive numerical unit that enters into metrical relationships with other factors. Where the interval defines the greatest relative quantity of movement, the whole becomes so immense that it confronts the imagination with its own limit (*Cinema 1*, 29–48).

In sum, by putting the cinematographic image into a relationship with the whole, montage gives an indirect image of time. As an individual movement-image it is the variable present. In the whole of the film, montage stands for the immensity of future and past, as the variable present could become interval, a qualitative leap, while the whole could become organic whole, dialectical totalization, measureless totality (55).

Deleuzian Movement-Image and Its Variations

Also important to the Latin American directors who inscribe and subvert the classic Hollywood model, as epitomized by the noir penchant of depicting the protagonist's reasoning and evident in Bielinsky's *El aura*,

Furtado's *O homem que copiava*, and Dhalia's *O cheiro do ralo*, is the notion of the movement-image. Deleuze introduces the movement-image
by reminding us that Bergson posits a state of things in constant change,
with no center of reference, wherein image equals movement. Though the
set is defined as image, everything is indistinguishable from its actions and
reactions, including human beings, viewed in terms of constantly renewed
molecules and atoms. In this infinite set, *movement-image* and *flowing-
matter* are one and the same. Furthermore, as a block of space-time, this
plane of immanence includes the movement established between the
parts of each system as well as between one system and another, which
prevents them from being closed. Despite the interrelation of movement, it
is possible to speak of images because perception and language allow us
to distinguish bodies (nouns), qualities (adjectives), and actions (verbs). In
order to arrive at these distinctions, movement is replaced with an idea of
a place toward which it is directed, a persisting state, or a vehicle to carry
it out, respectively. This process leads to the formation of action-images,
affection-images, and perception-images (*Cinema 1*, 57–58, 60).

—

The notion of the interval acquires especial significance in the work of
experimental Latin American auteurs such as Reygadas, whose films
call for active participation on the part of the audience in deciphering
motivation and eliciting an affective reaction. As everything impinges on
everything else in this acentered universe, an interval—a gap between the
action and the reaction—may appear at any point whatever. The interval
is possible insofar as the plane of matter encompasses time. According
to Bergson (in Deleuze, *Cinema 1*, 61), the interval defines a specific type
of image, which receives actions in certain parts and executes reactions
in others. This specialization, defined as "receptive" or "sensorial," exerts
an effect on the influencing images. If living beings consider external influences indifferent, they let them through (62); however, the isolated ones
become perceptions. After certain actions are isolated, they come to be
anticipated. Yet, the interval allows for delayed reactions, which rather
than simply prolonging the excitation become actions, that is, something
unpredictable or new.

Images provide the black screen in the luminous aspect of the plane
of matter. Yet, when the image runs up against an obstacle that reflects it,
the image becomes a perception; therefore, the living image complements

the center of indetermination or black screen. In other words, there is *a double system of images*. First, individual variations are complemented by the multifaceted interaction of all images. In the second system all images vary for a single one, which receives the actions of the other images on one of its facets and reacts to them on another facet. According to Bergson (62), this double system explains the working of the brain, since it is only on this plane that a single interval of movements can be produced. In other words, the brain is an interval, a gap between an action and a reaction.

Through a process of elimination, the total, objective perception, which is indistinguishable from the thing, becomes a subjective perception. Moreover, when the movement-image is related to a center of indetermination, it becomes perception-image. The process is the following: when the universe of movement-images is related to one of these special images that forms a center in it, the universe is organized to surround it. Thus, perception leads to action in that action is the delayed reaction of the center of indetermination (64). The passage from movement-image to action-image is the second material aspect of subjectivity. Thus, as perception relates movement to "bodies" (nouns), action relates movement to "acts" (verbs) (65).

In addition to a perceptive and active facet, the interval has an in-between, occupied by affection. The affection-image arises in the subject as center of indetermination, between a perception that is somewhat troubling and a hesitant action. The affection-image may be a coincidence of subject and object or a self-reflexive perception. In sum, it associates movement with a "quality" as lived state (adjective) (66). Through montage, movement-images give way to perception-images, action-images, and affection-images; nonetheless, no film is entirely made up of one type.

Deleuze's concept of the action-image is based on the notion of mental image, or thirdness, posited by Charles Sanders Peirce (1839–1914). Thirdness, which may be understood in terms of signification, law, or relation, originates acts such as exchanging that involve the symbolic effect of a law. Additionally, thirdness results in perceptions, which refer back to meaning, and it involves intellectual feelings of relations. Deleuze's movement-image is epitomized by noir. For instance, Hitchcock's films become the exposition of a rationale (reasoning). Yet, rather than focusing on the whodunit, these movies explore the system of actions in which the action and its author are enmeshed (*Cinema 1*, 197, 200).[17] The action-image may result in an indirect reflexive relationship, which occurs when rather than giving way to a suitable action, a situation produces a fictitious action that prefigures an upcoming action (181).

The Close-Up

Deleuze prioritizes the affective power of the close-up, which he identifies with the face. The effect results from the juxtaposition of a face that is seen and a body that is hidden. A reflecting, immobile unit presents intensive expressive movements that contrast with a closer implied corporeality. Following the painting tradition that focuses either on the face as an outline or on dispersed features functioning metonymically, such as quivering lips, Deleuze contrasts the reflexive face, which reflects a quality such as admiration or wonder, with the intensive face, which expresses power, defined in terms such as desire or the conflict between love and hate. The French philosopher concludes that a series of intensive faces allows for passing from one quality to another and thus carries out a qualitative leap. By contrast, a reflecting face, frozen in a specific thought, remains immutable and thus eternal (*Cinema 1*, 87–91).

Affective films allow for a slippage that mimics the sliding of the signifier, caught in the endless play of difference and deferral of différance. The event itself goes beyond its own causes, referring to other effects, while their causes, in turn, fall aside. Rather than referring to the state of things, the affect refers to the faces that reflect it, as Deleuze argues in referring to Dreyer's *La passion de Jeanne d'Arc* (*The Passion of Joan of Arc*, 1928). This is above all an affective film, as the philosopher contends that despite the historical events, characters, and relationships, there is something that allows for the constant intersection of the two presents, articulated as the endless arrival of the one while the other is already established (106).

In terms of technique, Deleuze emphasizes Dreyer's practice of cutting close-ups, which alternate between cutting an image such as a toothless sneer into a face or having the frame cut a face horizontally, vertically, or obliquely or even cutting movements in their course. By isolating a face in a partly filled close-up, Dreyer introduces a virtual conjunction that precludes real human connection. Affective cutting involves Dreyer's signature flowing close-ups, which may be defined as a continuous movement from the close-up to the medium or full shot. Deleuze argues that by flattening the third dimension, Dreyer connects the second dimension with the affect as well as with the fourth dimension, time, and the fifth dimension, spirit (106–107). Conversely, the out-of-field also subverts everyday notions of space and time by generating the impression of a disturbing presence, situated as disturbingly close but still out of reach (17).

Deleuze, Neorealism, and the Time-Image

Endorsing Bazin, Deleuze argues that neorealism should not be defined by its social content but by the representation of a type of dispersive reality, presented in blocks and linked with deliberately weak connections. Deleuze goes beyond the movement-image by suggesting that the goal of neorealism is to connect them to thought, not to extend perceptions into actions. Thus, neorealism is associated with a build-up of optical and, later, sound situations that are different from those of traditional realism; they are not anchored in a setting that presupposes an action but rather in "any space whatever," that is, in disconnected bits of space. Consequently, the protagonist is entranced with a vision instead of being engaged in an action. As the visual description replaces the motor action, the situation becomes suffused with indeterminacy, and whether it is imaginary or not becomes irrelevant (*Cinema 2*, 1–7).

—

According to Deleuze, a number of social, political, moral, and cultural factors brought about the crisis of the traditional cinematic image after World War II. He points to the crisis of the American Dream, the growing awareness of minorities, the overwhelming explosion of images in the world around us, the impact of cinematic productions, and the decadence of Hollywood and its genres. A new aesthetics, marked by the voyage form and the ensuing condemnation of plot, the dispersive situation, and deliberately weak links as well as the consciousness of clichés, appeared first in Italian neorealism and subsequently in the French New Wave. Rather than focusing on causal relations, the new aesthetics that Deleuze engaged explored the situation itself, emphasizing the dispersive nature of reality (*Cinema 1*, 206, 210). As the ideological construction of the protagonist changed, the character became a kind of flâneur vested in recording reality rather than reacting to it (*Cinema 2*, 3).

This set of circumstances had an impact on all of the films that comprise the corpus of this book, which share conventions dear to the documentary and neorealism such as shooting contemporary, true-to-life subjects on location, capturing language in the vernacular, and focusing on social critique. At the same time, the range of movies highlighted in this text allows for variations of other technical conventions, such as natural lighting, lengthy takes, and unobtrusive editing. While all of these films demand active viewer involvement, certain conventions—respect for the continuity of time and space, a predominance of medium and long shots, for example—are more evident in noir films.[18] Most of the remaining films stress the importance of an uncontrived, open-ended plot, and for this reason they favor the loose structure implied by a journey taken by protagonists depicted as seers rather than agents. As we shall see, these latter films illustrate the possibilities opened by the Deleuzian time-image.

Recollections and Dreams

As an introduction to the different types of time-images, we shall explore the nature of recollections and dreams. Bergson (in Deleuze, *Cinema 2*, 44) distinguishes between two types of recognition, namely, automatic and attentive recognition. In automatic or habitual recognition, perception extends itself into habitual movements. Through association of images we pass from one object to another along the same plane (synchronically). Conversely, attentive recognition focuses on some characteristic features of the object. As we identify different features, the object passes through different planes (diachronically) so that the sensory-motor image seems richer because it is the object itself, while the pure optical (and sound) image seems poorer because it is a description (44).

The postwar image heralded a paradigm shift. To the extent that the sensory-motor image retains the features that interest us and its richness arises from the association with similar objects on the same plane, it is an agent of abstraction. Conversely, since the pure optical image is a description and the character may not be able to react to the situation, the minimal features retained by this image emphasize its particularity and the endless possibility of referring to others, which in turn underscores its richness (45). Furthermore, according to Bergson, the optical (and sound) image of attentive recognition calls up a recollection-image. Although the related terms differ in nature, they refer to each other and ultimately slip into indeterminacy. Thus, a zone of recollections, dreams, or thoughts corresponds to a particular aspect of the thing as each circuit paradoxically obliterates and creates an object at the level of the same mental reality, memory, or spirit (46). In the process, the sensory-motor images and their extensions are superseded by circular links between pure optical and sound images, and images from time and thought, on coexisting planes (47).

To determine the role of the virtual image Deleuze resorts to Bergson's "recollection-images," which are involved in automatic recognition in that they insert themselves between simulation and response, contributing to the adjustment of the motor mechanism by providing psychological causality. In sum, recollection-images allow for a new kind of subjectivity. Subjectivity emerges in the movement-image as soon as there is a gap between a received movement and an executed movement, that is, between a perception-image and an action-image. Affection is a dimension of subjectivity because it belongs to the gap but without filling or fulfilling it. Conversely, the recollection-image fills the gap to the extent that it returns us to perception rather than extending into movement. Thus, subjectivity is no longer motor or material but temporal and spiritual (47).

The relation of the actual image to recollection-images is evident in the flashback, which may act as a closed circuit going from the present to the past, only to return to the present. Or it may react as a multiplicity of circuits, each of which goes through a zone of recollections and returns to an even deeper state of the present situation. Therefore, the flashback can indicate psychological causality that, due to its similarity with sensory-motor determinism, confirms the linear progression of narration (48). More importantly, by suggesting an inexplicable secret, the flashback may fragment linearity by introducing forks that break causality (49). Thus, time's forks provide flashback with a necessity, and recollection-images with an authenticity, a weight of the past without which they would remain conventional (50). Dream sequences are not a common feature of Hollywood movies; au contraire, Soviet cinema, German expressionism, and the French school represented psychic phenomena to break away from the American limitations of the action-image. Dream images tend to be depicted by dissolves, superimpositions, complex camera movements, special effects, or montage (55), to suggest an unhinging that resembles a dream, while the objects remain concrete (58). Yet breaking away from classical cinema, avant-garde directors like Federico Fellini (1920–1993) in 8½ (1963) disallow any transition between the representation of dreams and so-called reality.

Images of Time

Speaking about montage Deleuze notes that as a measure of movement, time includes two aspects: chronosigns and the interval. As a great circle or spiral, chronosigns draw together the set of movements in the universe.

Conversely, the interval indicates the smallest unit of movement or action. Thus, the bird that hovers, increasing its circle, illustrates time as a whole, and the beating of its wing represents a numerical unit of movement, the diminishing interval between two actions (*Cinema 1*, 32).

The images presented by the cinema are surrounded with a world; that is, their circuits unite actual images with recollections, dream images, and world images. As the smallest unit, the crystal-image emerges from the Bergsonian coalescence between the actual and virtual images of an object (*Cinema 2*, 68). This is as if a real object reflected itself in a mirror image as a virtual object that engulfs the real, blending both images into one. This coalescence may be further described as if the image of the mirror came to life, even though the actual image resumed its place in the mirror, paradoxically pursuing the double movement of freedom and capture (68). This indiscernibility between the real and the imaginary and/ or the present and the past is evident in the crystal-image (69). While the actual image is the present, the virtual image, reflected on the mirror, constitutes its simultaneous past. Given the parallel process of perception and recollection, our lives mirror themselves in a virtual existence as they unravel in time (79). The crystal-image emerges from the most fundamental operation of time, for the present splits into two directions: one makes the present pass on, and the other preserves all the past. In sum, time consists of this split, and time is what we see in the crystal (81).

In order to introduce the notion of sheets and peaks of time, Deleuze warns against confusing the past with the mental existence of recollection-images that actualize it. Following Bergson's model of time as an inverted cone, Deleuze notes that the past is preserved in time as the virtual element into which we look for the pure recollection that is actualized in a recollection-image. As we perceive things in the present, in space, we remember where they have passed, in time. In neither case is memory in us; rather, it is we who move in a Being-memory, a world-memory. Thus, the past appears as the most general form of an already there, presupposed by our recollections and made use of by our perceptions. The present exists as an infinitely contracted past that is constituted at the extreme point of the already there (98). While the successive is the present that is passing, the past appears as the coexistence of circles, each of which contains everything at the same time, including the present of which it is the extreme limit. The circles appear to be chronologically arranged, although they coexist from the point of view of the actual present insofar as each time represents their common limit (99).

The present is the presence of something that stops being present when it is substituted by something else. Thus, the event simultaneously includes a present of the future, a present of the present, and a present of the past. While the time involved in the event allows for the interrelation of the peaks of the present, the possibility of treating the world as a single episode, involving affect and time, reinforces the simultaneity of these presents (100). In sum, there are two kinds of chronosigns: the former alludes to features such as regions and layers; the latter suggests accents such as peaks or points of view (101). To conclude, the significance of space to create depth in classical cinema is superseded by time in the postwar image. In the new cinema, the depth of time arises from the inter-action of elements in different planes, which constitute the region of past as the continuum of duration (108).

THE BOOK'S STRUCTURE

Experimental Latin American Cinema: History and Aesthetics is con-structed around genres because they provide a framework that allows for underscoring the inscription and subversion of established conventions. Thus, part 1 focuses on movies that inscribe and subvert the generic conventions of noir films. "Film noir" is a descriptive term coined by French critics in the post–World War II period to define a distinctly darker tone that arose in American cinema. In terms of film history, "film noir" refers to Hollywood films of the 1940s and early 1950s that depicted crime and corruption, among other dangers lurking in the dark streets of the city. Ge-nealogically, the genre harks back to gangster films of the 1930s, French poetic realism, Sternbergian melodrama, and German expressionism (Schrader, 214). A lack of social consensus is evident between the upbeat tone of lowbrow, mainstream culture and the gloomier, highbrow culture of dissent represented by film noir (Chopra-Gant, 5–9). Noir's B status in the United States may be attributed to the genre's dependence on choreogra-phy rather than sociology, coupled with American critics' greater interest in theme than style (Schrader, 225). Nonetheless, in contrast to their rela-tively minor significance in Hollywood, noir films constitute a long-standing and important genre within Latin American cinema.

The existential anxiety resulting from Nazi brutality and nuclear power was compounded by U.S. domestic upheaval voiced in terms of the strug-gle for equal rights mainly involving gender and race, the end of an appar-ently transparent social structure, geographical dispersal into the suburbs, and uncertainty about the ubiquitous power of corporations (Dimendberg, 4; Hirsch, *Dark Side*, 21). While postwar realism influenced noir insofar as shooting on location provided an honest but harsh picture of America, Austrian and German expatriate directors like Fritz Lang, Billy Wilder, and Karl Freund brought expressionistic lighting. Finally, film noir is derivative of or connected with hard-boiled U.S. writers of crime-related fiction such as Hemingway, Dashiell Hammett, and Raymond Chandler, who created a "tough," cynical way of acting and thinking (Schrader, 216–218).

But how Hollywood is noir, really? European auteurs of the 1960s and 1970s—Godard, Fassbinder, Truffaut, Wenders, and others—helped create the idea of film noir. Their work is grounded in allusion and hyper-textuality rather than in straightforward attempts to keep a formula alive. Naremore, a leading historian of the genre, proposes that French and German New Waves as well as the Italian tradition of philosophical noir led to noir's emergence during a renaissance of the European art film. For instance, Antonioni and Polanski made English thrillers aimed, partially at least, at the American market (*More than Night*, 202–203). Conversely, Levy opts for an autochthonous origin. Accordingly, noir survives as neonoir because the latter offers a venue to express the distrust of government and paranoia resulting from such paradigm-shifting events as the Vietnam War and the Watergate scandal (221).[19] Tom Conley attributes the 1970s rebirth of noir to economics, for investments became more lucrative due to the growth of distribution networks, recording apparatuses in everyday life, and the pace of production (203). One way or another, neonoir films have enjoyed a resurgence in the work of contemporary U.S. directors such as David Lynch and the Cohen brothers in the 1980s and Tarantino and his imitators in the 1990s (Levy, 218).

In Bielinsky's *El aura* (*The Aura*, 2005), an epileptic taxidermist dreams about applying his prodigious photographic memory to rob a bank. Unforeseen events allow him to discover the plans for an upcoming heist in which he willingly participates. The film is structured as a series of reenactments that allow for neonoir questioning the veracity of events, only to prove that they occurred despite their improbability. By contrast, Furtado's *O homem que copiava* (*The Man Who Copied*, 2003) rewrites neonoir conventions. Furtado focuses on a charming black teenager whose voice-over leads the audience into accepting the necessity of violent actions. Furtado's forté is the emphasis on intermediality—intertextual references to collage, comics, cartoons, and films—to advance the plot. Since the allure of the voice-over resides in sharing the protagonist's reasoning process, the final reversal is all the more unsettling.

Closing the neonoir section, Dhalia's *O cheiro do ralo* (*Drained*, 2006) reinscribes the genre in a psychoanalytic key. The protagonist's fixations establish an intricate web linking profit and feces, the drain, and hell. As Lourenço plummets into self-destruction, he becomes aware of the nature of desire, barely restrained or held in abeyance by an always already receding satisfaction. Structured as a pattern of repetition with variations, the film depicts Lourenço conducting business as a duel aimed at extracting the greatest advantage from the desperate prospective clients. Ironically, the protagonist's comeuppance arrives when least expected.

Part 2 centers on road movies. As a film genre, road movies focus on a road trip, which favors character development, as a bildungsroman of sorts. However, in addition to the journey and like the picaresque in literature, road movies allow for navigating different cultural and geographical environments and thus offer a means for cultural critique. In terms of generic conventions, the journey allows for cultural critique, since the unknown may offer epiphanies and/or refuge from oppressive social circumstances. Characters are usually frustrated or desperate as they embark on open-ended, rambling plot structures. Cinematically, the frame composition might show windshields or rearview mirrors to suggest the driver's point of view (Laderman, 1–2, 16). Since road movies have been a minor genre in Latin American cinema, the effect of *Central do Brasil* (*Central Station*, 1998) may be gauged by subsequent productions like the socioeconomic and cultural critique implicit in Mexican director María Novaro's *Sin dejar huella* (*Without a Trace*, 2000), which fleshes out a *Thelma and Louise* plot by underscoring ubiquitous machismo, violence, and (police) corruption while allowing for character development and female independence. Brazilian director Vicente Amorím's *O caminho das nuvens* (*The Middle of the World*, 2003) registers the difficulties encountered by a man and his family on their 2,000-mile bicycle ride from the state of Paraíba to Rio de Janeiro in search of work.

The Latin American penchant for cultural critique—undoubtedly a recurrent feature of Latin American roadies—is epitomized in Salles's *Diarios de motocicleta* (*The Motorcycle Diaries*, 1998), which depicts Ernesto (Che) Guevara's growing awareness of the pervasiveness of gross economic inequity that leads him to become a firebrand revolutionary. Argentine director Pablo Trapero's roadie, *La familia rodante* (*Rolling*

Family, 2004) narrows down the typical social critique to a clash of family members' ideologies during a three-day journey to a relative's wedding in the claustrophobic environment of a small recreational vehicle. The road movie also structures Alfonso Cuarón's *Y tu mamá también* (2004), which underscores the huge economic disparity in Mexican society that the characters witness from the comfort of their car; the friction comes from the teenager's competition for the attention of their female companion, their different social classes, and their shared homophobia. Finally, Marcelo Gomes's *Cinema, aspirinas, e urubus* (*Cinema, Aspirins, and Vultures*, 2005) marks the inception of the subgenre of period roadies; it centers around the misadventures of a German selling aspirin in the Brazilian Northeast during World War II.

The road-movie structure in Salles's *Central do Brasil* points to how a melodramatic journey from Rio de Janeiro to the *sertão*, the dry backlands of Northeast Brazil, embodies the fusion between the conventions of the documentary and fiction films. Documentary techniques underscore the luminescent beauty of the close-ups of the *nordestinos*, inhabitants of the Northeast. These exert an affective impact on the audience and frustrate it via the scant development of the nordestinos' stories. Significantly, care about their plight turns into an awareness of the lack of viable opportunities in the sertão, pathetically the very same conditions Cinema Novo practitioners denounced fifty years before. Similarly, the light-hearted humor of the road-movie structure in Sorín's *El camino de San Diego* (*The Road to San Diego*, 2006) is undercut by an ironic denunciation of the overriding effects of the economic crisis following three decades of neoliberal policies in Argentina. The conventions of the *grotesco criollo* portray an alienating social order, yet the apparent happy ending barely conceals the continued cycle of loss. Menis's *El cielito* (*Little Sky*, 2004), which also follows the conventions of the roadie, sets a couple's path to self-destruction against a story of redemption. Like Sorín, Menis suggests the withdrawal of the welfare state by showing the vulnerability of the underclass in a lyrical counterpoint with dream sections that deepens the sense of despair.

Part 3 showcases drama. Oliveira Cézar's *Como pasan las horas* (*The Hours Go By*, 2005) underscores the endless repetition of ritual as it embodies the function of film as sculpting time. Similarly, Méndez's approach to post-traumatic stress disorder (PTSD) sheds light on the repetitious nature of trauma, which tends to engulf and thus cancel out the present.

Méndez's *Días de Santiago* (*Days of Santiago*, 2004) suggests that as long as the social order fails to provide assistance, there is no exit for veterans. This represents a kind of modification of drama significant to Latin American cinema because of the implicit and sustained social critique.

Part 4 highlights the work of experimental director and self-proclaimed auteur Carlos Reygadas, who emerged as the *enfant terrible* of Mexican cinema. His career relates to key aspects in the ideological construction of an auteur in ways not diverse from this term's origins in the 1950s, when Paris was partial to American ways, the city had an avant-garde aura, and its practitioners resorted to popular culture to shock the bourgeoisie. The approach may be traced back to a group of intellectuals, film directors, and critics who shared certain objectives and developed a body of writing to disseminate their polemical opinions, largely through the journal *Cahiers du cinema*. The label arose from the extended metaphor of the *camera-stylo*, which was unraveled with the camera as pen, the screen as paper, and the director as author. The larger picture encompassed the decline of the Hollywood studios and the emergence of the French New Wave, which incorporated certain neorealist elements. Andrew Sarris, who wrote *The American Cinema* (1968), identified the canonical works of classic Hollywood on the basis of autonomous personal expression. Thus, Sarris became the most prominent exponent of auteurism in the United States. Despite being displaced by psychoanalysis, Marxism, poststructuralism, and deconstruction and the current vogue of reception theory, auteurism provides an anchor for interpretation; after all, the author becomes no less real because she or he is socially constructed (Naremore, "Authorship," 10, 22).[20]

Notwithstanding the apparent liberalism and the ultimate vagueness of Sarris's definition, the most politically aware contemporary Latin American directors rejected the notion of auteurism. Indeed, like most of the filmmakers of that era, Solanas and Getino were concerned with the widespread notion of cinema as a lucrative standardized spectacle, both in terms of time and language, produced for distribution in large movie theaters and promoting the reproduction of bourgeois ideology by interpellating the spectator as a passive consumer (65). As Solanas and Getino critiqued the notion that auteur cinema provided anything like a real alternative to mainstream or Hollywood film, the two directors acknowledged that auteur cinema offered different screening and distribution venues. They insisted, however, that auteur cinema was co-opted by the ideological and economic constrictions of the mainstream, remained confined to the category of a token, and allowed the democratic ideology of the Hollywood model only as an exception (67).

While on the one hand Sorín has publicly taken on the role of director of independent movies positioned as a complementary niche and offering alternatives to the high-budget, industrial products of the Hollywood studios, most of the filmmakers in this book—with the possible exception of Salles—could be categorized as producers of independent movies, with tremendous variation in range of production, of cultural, political, and socioeconomic background, in access to state and international funding, and/or as co-productions.[21] Ultimately, in most "national" cinemas and with Brazil as a case in point, the divide between commercial and independent films is a false dichotomy, as cinematic production is not overdetermined by market success but rather by the ability of directors and producers to make subsequent films. Even as independent filmmakers subscribe to an auteur mode of production, they receive state funding; symbolic capital, recognized through critical success, enables some directors to produce subsequent films (Johnson, "TV Globo," 15–16).

Reygadas retraces the original meaning of "auteur" when he articulates his preference for evidence of the director's *personalidad y concepción del mundo* (personality and worldview) (in Romero, 180). Accordingly, sharing a sustained polished, industrial, and international style, Argentine director Leopoldo Torre Nilsson (1924–1978) as well as Mexican filmmaker Arturo Ripstein (1943–) would warrant auteur reputation due to the hermetic nature of the work of the former and the latter's focus on intolerance.[22] While the broad definition that Reygadas posits eschews political affinities and allows for the co-optation mentioned by Getino and Solanas, Rocha's equally apolitical desideratum that an auteur should offer a nonconformist, rebellious, violent, and impudent vision applies to the reception of Reygadas's filmography (*Revisión crítica*, 12).

The postmodern end of metanarratives illuminates the ideological differences between the younger generations of filmmakers and those vested in the different traditions of the New Latin American Cinema. Most of the contemporary directors in the corpus of this text engage in social critique but stop short of offering a salvational metanarrative. Conversely, considering that aesthetics and *mise-en-scène* imply an underlying ethical and political stance, many of the directors whose films are analyzed in this book would fit into Rocha's definition of *auteur*, as their work tends to be antithetical to bourgeois (read: classic Hollywood) cinema.

Yet, given that Hollywood has enjoyed a hegemonic position in Latin America for more than a century, the extent to which the films examined in this book are "experimental" stands in inverse relation to their commercial success. Salles's *Central do Brasil* offers a good example since his work received the Golden Bear in Berlin, the British Academy Film Award, and Oscar nominations: it was a commercial success at home and abroad, where more than one and a half million spectators watched it the year it premiered.[23] Conversely, Oliveira Cézar's *Como pasan las horas* and *Extranjera* (*Foreigner*, 2007) were both viewed at the Berlinale, but neither became commercially viable. Menis's *El cielito* similarly received the FIPRESCI (International Federation of Film Critics) prize at the 2004 Havana Film Festival and four awards at the 2004 San Sebastián International Film Festival, yet it was no blockbuster. Lastly, and to a large part due to economic constraints, these aesthetic choices reappear in the contemporary New Argentine Cinema, in the Cinema da Retomada, and in the work of current directors who take an anti-establishment stance. That stance can occur within rich cinematic traditions, such as Reygadas's in Mexico. Rejection of the establishment also appears in Encina, who emerges from the far less established Paraguayan cinematic tradition.

Reygadas's films evidence a continued fixation with taboo, represented as suicide and intergenerational sex in *Japón* (*Japan*, 2002). In *Batalla en el cielo* (*Battle in Heaven*, 2005), taboo involves prostitution, kidnapping, manslaughter, murder, and intercourse across social class and racial or ethnic barriers. In addition to insisting on iconoclastic topics, Reygadas's technical experimentation is defined by audacious camera work, unusual expectations for nonprofessional actors, and the use of ellipsis to mystify motivation.

Part 5 focuses on experimental auteurs whose films weave a complicated intertextual web of echoes and reverberations, beginning with Reygadas's *Stellet licht* (2008), a remake of Carl Theodor Dreyer's masterpiece *Ordet* (1954), set in the Mennonite colonies of northern Mexico. Reygadas's penchant for taboo is evident in the production of the film, given the Mennonite interdiction on physical representation. Intertextual reverberations displace the protagonist's death, which is caused by sheer desolation due to her husband's continued extramarital affair. Similarly, the contested miracle is wrought by a passionate kiss from her rival, who brings the wife back from her catatonic state.

Reygadas's use of minimalist settings and long takes that freeze movement echo Dreyer. Oliveira Cézar's work likewise continues to stress the function of film as sculpting time by underscoring the endless repetition of ritual by way of foundational myths that are revived and live on as they are rewritten. Thus *Extranjera*, which offers a free rendition of Euripides's *Iphigenia in Aulis*, explores the willingness of a community to sacrifice a young woman and her acceptance of such fate in the hopes that it will contribute to the common good. *El recuento de los daños* (*The Recount of the Damages*, 2010) dives into the unconscious in a powerful contemporary rendition of Sophocles's *Oedipus Rex*.

Pérez Valdés's *Madrigal* (2006) sheds light on the subjective construction of reality by showing the effect of point of view in the determination of meaning in a Pirandellian rendition that successfully weaves three interconnected stories, only to subvert the audience's expectations regarding plot reversal. The apparent certainties offered by anchoring events around the performance of a play and the private lives of the members of a theater troupe are debunked by an alternative plot that reframes those characters and circumstances into a dystopia, which is in turn subverted.

Part 6 opens and closes with a circular movement, centering on two films that inscribe and subvert the conventions of the documentary. Pérez Valdés's urban symphony *Suite Habana* (*Havana Suite*, 2003) examines the lives of a dozen Cuban residents of different ages and walks of life whose heroic acts of resistance respond to the island's severe economic crisis. The virtuosity of Pérez Valdés's montage recalls the inception of cinema, underscoring the primacy of the image and harking back to silent films insofar as the audience of *Suite Habana* cannot hear the exchanges of the protagonists. Contrary to the generic expectations of the documentary, no talking head provides didactic commentary. Nor do the protagonists share their stories with the audience. Background sounds, traffic, a jackhammer, children counting, the fragment of a savant's reading of the tarot, lyrics, and music fill the contextual function of the orchestra in the silent movies and underscore the rhythm of the action.

Encina's opera prima *Hamaca paraguaya* (*Paraguayan Hammock*, 2008) offers a similarly haunting rendition of national trauma. The film portrays the suffering of an elderly couple awaiting their son's return from war. The mechanical repetition of habitual actions allows their minds to wander, haunted by the recollection of their son's farewell. Both husband and wife refrain from addressing the intimations of their son's death, thus paradoxically prolonging the agony of waiting. Their isolated, rural, daily life reinforces the oppressive atmosphere, which Encina inscribes via the documentary device of shooting on location. Deploying a fixed camera, Encina reproduces the effect of montage by altering the distance of the shots. While the haunting effect of national trauma remains, Encina subverts the conventions of the documentary, as the protagonists are well-known professional actors who are acting out a period story, and the distance at which they are shown both disguises and underscores speech that is not anchored in standard lip synchronization. Therefore, the audience perceives that the plausibility of the apparent linear reading of the film is undercut by the traumatic repetition of the couple's memories of their son's farewell.

In sum, the inscription and subversion of generic conventions provides a useful framework for comparing the range of experimentation of the films I discuss in this book.

PART ONE
A NEONOIR SKEW TO THE ACTION-IMAGE

CHAPTER ONE
A SHIMMERING SUTURE

Fabián Bielinsky's Epileptic *El aura*

El aura (2005) is the last film that the late Fabián Bielinsky (1959–2006) completed in his lifetime. Bielinsky achieved international acclaim for *Nueve reinas* (*Nine Queens*, 2000), which chronicles an elaborate scheme to exchange a set of purportedly highly valued postage stamps for a forged replica. The film's plot turns on reversals as the con man falls victim to his own greed and most of the characters are revealed to have conspired to deprive him of the share of an inheritance that he in actuality owed his siblings. As if life imitated art, a tragic reversal grew out of the critical and commercial success of *Nueve reinas*. Instead of distributing the film, Warner Brothers commissioned an American remake titled *Criminal* (2004). Though Bielinsky was in Hollywood, the industry insider Gregory Jacobs worked with him to adapt the screenplay and then directed the remake.

Unlike other directors of his generation in Argentina (and to some extent elsewhere in Latin America) who preferred the European tradition, Bielinsky admired American cinema. In terms of specific directors, Bielinsky acknowledges the influence of Hitchcock and Mamet.[1] Despite working within more classical narrative structures, Bielinsky, in the first generation of directors to graduate from Argentine film schools, is considered an industry auteur because of his personal approach to filmmaking

(Bernardes, Lerer, and Wolf, 119–120).[2] *El aura* is experimental in that it inscribes and subverts Hollywood conventions of noir, which Deleuze associates with the movement-image.

El aura opens with a shot that shows Esteban Espinosa (Ricardo Darín) lying on his back on the floor. The intermittent mechanical and electronic chugging and whirring sounds of an ATM establish the location as Espinosa stands up, takes his cash, and exits. As in *Nueve reinas*, much of the action is tightly choreographed but within a timeline of about one week, as opposed to *Nueve reinas*'s approximately thirty hours. Espinosa, a taxidermist, appears to have marital problems, as may be inferred from the loud music with which he drowns out the words of a woman who is vying for his attention from behind a glass door. On the morning following the opening scene, Espinosa delivers a fox to the museum, where he meets his colleague Sontag (Alejandro Awada). While the two men wait in line to be paid for their work, Espinosa plans a flawless robbery, an idea he shares with his friend. Sontag dismisses the plan and urges Espinosa to join him hunting in Patagonia instead. Espinosa accepts the invitation when he realizes that his wife has left him. Only after Sontag and Espinosa arrive at the Lauquén Hotel in Bariloche do they learn that the hotel rooms have been sold out to a sudden wave of customers, all descending to take advantage of the impending closure of the casino. The hotel owner suggests that the two men try Dietrich's cabins, which are closer to the hunting grounds. When the two men arrive at the cabins an unfriendly young man, Julio (Nahuel Pérez Biscayart), tells them there are no vacancies. However, his sister, Diana (Dolores Fonzi), who is married to Carlos Dietrich (Manuel Rodal), the owner of the cabins, overrides Julio's objections and signs them in. Sontag is forced into an early and abrupt return to Buenos Aires by his wife's botched suicide attempt, and Espinosa remains on the hunting grounds, where he falls into an epileptic seizure.

As Espinosa comes to, he spots a deer but kills a man instead. After Espinosa ascertains that the victim is Dietrich, the owner of the cabins, he tries to find out why (unbeknownst to his wife) Dietrich was holed up in a remote cabin. The resulting discoveries lead Espinosa to become increasingly enmeshed in the plans for an upcoming heist. Inferring from the notes, pictures, and maps at the cabin, Espinosa learns that Urién (Jorge D'Elía), the manager, provided data about the casino's revenues and the number of men assigned to the armored vehicle on its weekly runs. Espinosa also discovers Dietrich's motives: the indebted Dietrich needed to repay an overdue loan. After following Dietrich's notes about an upcoming meeting at a factory named Cerro Verde, Espinosa witnesses a bungled robbery. As he follows a fatally wounded man who escapes by climbing down a wall, Espinosa obtains the key to the armored vehicle's inner safe, a rather contrived coincidence. Following Dietrich's notes, Espinosa calls on two hit men, Sosa and Montero, to carry out the heist. Espinosa, however, forgets that a third man, who will not open the back doors of the armored vehicle, is deployed on long weekends. This sudden distraction seems to trigger another seizure, after which Espinosa arrives just in time to witness Montero being wounded in a shoot-out with the guards and Sosa killing the two guards who rode in the front of the vehicle, all of which Espinosa previously envisioned.

The third guard locks himself up in the back of the armored vehicle, thus cheating the robbers of the money from the casino. So, rather than remain exposed in front of a bordello, Espinosa suggests driving to Dietrich's secluded cabin in search of tools to pry the back doors of the vehicle open. Upon arrival, Sosa props Montero against a tree and follows Espinosa into the cabin to look for the tools. Once they locate them, Sosa walks out and shoots Julio point blank. Sosa attempts to gun down Espinosa, too, but realizes he has run out of ammunition, which forces him to shove Espinosa back into the cabin so he can reload. Espinosa struggles to free himself, grabs the gun hidden behind the stuffed deer's head, and rushes out of the cabin. Even though Sosa and Montero shoot at him, Espinosa finally kills Sosa, and Montero appears to have bled to death. The trail of blood dripping down from the back doors of the armored vehicle implies that the guard suffered the same fate.

El aura has many of the hallmarks of noir stories, psychological tales relying on characterization and verisimilitude, with even the most violent or exciting actions paling in comparison to the effects of faces, expressions,

Figure 1.1
Kaleidoscopic trees: Espinosa comes to after seizure.

and words (Frank, 23). Generic conventions in noir call for three major characters: the criminal, the middle-class victim, and the scapegoat. All three are prone to deception at the hands of dangerous dames prowling through the city and promising easily and ill-gotten money. Ironically, film noir displaces into the sexual realm the strength that women acquired during their wartime experience; therefore, they usually appear as dangerous temptresses. Since the same process of distortion affects men, they are represented as weak and neurotic. Indeed, the victim is usually a middle-class family man, an anti-hero who gets trapped between the cynical private eye and the experienced criminal (Hirsch, *Dark Side*, 12–13, 20).[3] The protagonist is usually aware of and even complicit in the events in which he is caught, but he is unable to do anything about them because he is immersed in a corrupt, immoral world (Stephens, 273). The killer likewise remains a sympathetic character because the victim is often as suspect as the man who kills him (Borde and Chaumeton, 65).

With time, generic conventions were pared down to ensure international success: increased violence and sexuality compensated for the diminished complexity of the narrative (Conley, 203). Neonoir shows a shift in characterization as well. Heroes and villains alike are represented as cynical, disenchanted, insecure, and prone to clinging to the past, given their uncertainty about the future (Levy, 220). The postmodern neonoir protagonist is always chasing after transparent self-consciousness only to learn that it recedes indefinitely (Abrams, 19).

A treacherous femme fatale is important to both noir and neonoir. *El aura* seems to subvert this convention, as Espinosa's wife abandons him. Diana's deceit, if any, is a self-preservation ruse that backfires, as is often the case in neonoir: although she manipulated Dietrich, who is thirty years her senior, into marriage because she hoped to escape from an abusive father, she finds to her dismay that her husband is just as abusive. The bruises on her back lend credence to the story that he tracked her down when she tried to escape. Although Espinosa shows interest in Diana, she takes flight as soon as he reassures her that Dietrich will not return.

Noir's reliance on the detective and mystery means that the pursuit is a major factor in the development of the plot and characters' motives. To that extent, Espinosa is an unlikely noir protagonist. Sontag invites him hunting with the proviso "No tenés que matar nada" (You don't have to kill anything). Instead of plotting to kill the femme fatale's husband, Espinosa shoots Dietrich accidentally. Conversely, Dietrich is a more likely film noir victim because his compulsion to play lures him into a plot that offers the promise of easy money (Hirsch, *Dark Side,* 13). Bielinsky repeatedly inscribes and subverts the noir tradition that, once trapped, the noir protagonist is unable to escape (Stephens, 273). If Dietrich is the noir victim, however, he does not expect to be shot. In fact, his unforeseen death happens before the beginning of the action—and propels it. Taking Dietrich's place, Espinosa becomes ensnared. As Julio warns him, there is no exit. And like the noir protagonist, Espinosa is unafraid. In the best noir tradition, the protagonist allows himself to be severely beaten (Borde and Chaumeton, 65). Espinosa is roughed up repeatedly by Sosa; however, rather than (and in addition to) waiting for the final showdown, Sosa threatens to kill Espinosa in the middle of the action. Despite Sosa's bravado, Espinosa survives him. Detective and villain are fused in neonoir. As per these generic conventions, Espinosa is morally ambiguous.

The noir detective hero is normally crippled either emotionally or physically. This is the case with Hemingway's heroes, who are usually physically maimed in some way, while Chandler's and Hammett's heroes tend to be loners, outsiders, incapable of closeness. By representing Espinosa as an epileptic, Bielinsky inscribes a long-standing noir and neonoir tradition in which the detective often suffers a traumatic accident that causes some type of amnesia or is haunted by hallucinations or multiple personalities. He may have artificial memory implants, high-tech devices that reveal the future, or a number of other alterations in the continuum of self-consciousness (Abrams, 10). Espinosa offers Diana an ambiguous description of his condition:

Unos segundos antes yo sé que voy a tener un ataque. Hay un momento, hay un cambio. Los médicos le dicen aura. De pronto las cosas cambian. Es como si el mundo se detuviera y se abriera una pequeña puerta en la cabeza que dejara pasar cosas . . . ruidos, música, voces, imágenes, olores, a escuela, a cocina, a familia . . . Me dice que el ataque es inminente. No se puede hacer nada para detenerlo, es horrible y perfecto. Y durante unos segundos sos libre. No hay alternativa. Todo se ajusta, se estrecha. Uno se entrega.

[A few seconds before it happens I know I'm going to have an attack. There's a moment, a shift. The doctors call it aura.

```
Things suddenly change. It's as if everything stopped and
a door opened in your head that lets things in . . . sounds,
music, voices, images, smells, [the smell] of school, of
kitchen, of family . . . It tells me that the fit is coming
and there's nothing you can do to stop it. It's horrible and
it's perfect. During those seconds, you're free. There's no
alternative. Everything tightens up, gets narrower. And you
surrender.]
```

Bielinsky refers to the power of the paradigm shift the postwar image elicits. The richness of the sensory-motor image arises from its
associations. As an epileptic, Espinosa is aware of the symptoms signal-
ing an impending seizure. Recollections surface poignantly, apparently
unconsciously, from the sheets of the past. As a neonoir protagonist,
the maimed Espinosa cannot predict the seizures; yet the aura in those
instants prior to the seizure also allows for rejoicing in pleasant memories
pushed back into the unconscious, thus heralding the time-image.

Sosa and Montero are more conventional noir criminals. While Montero's poor physical health and his repeated complaints about being out
of breath make him into something of an anti-hero, the grim, gun-toting
Sosa obeys his commands. Greed prods them to drive 500 miles to meet
Dietrich. Sosa constantly belittles Espinosa, yet his tenderness toward
the wounded Montero evidences a strong homosexual undercurrent. In
contrast to the reticent evocation of homosexuality in noir, neonoir affirms
its essential role in American violence (Rafter, 79–80). Bielinsky follows
neonoir conventions as the depth of Sosa and Montero's relationship
is suggested before the heist. While Montero's reply "Voy a ir con quien
tenga que ir" (I will go with whoever I have to) suggests he is willing to go
with Espinosa, the final remark reinscribes the mutuality of the two men's
commitment, "Con vos como siempre" (With you, as usual).

In terms of setting, neonoir is as likely to take place in the pestilential
city as in vast open spaces such as the (Sonoran) desert in Orson Welles's
Touch of Evil (1958), which displaces the criminal actions from Los Angeles to Mexico. Either way, the maze is as typical of neonoir as the detective,
the crime, or the femme fatale (Hirsch, *Detours*, 8, 14–15). While *El aura*
opens in Buenos Aires, once in Patagonia the urban referent is the casino,
and the woods include their own maze. *El aura* was shot on location,
alternating the arid mesas of the Patagonian landscape with the woods

encircling the scenic tourist town of Bariloche at the foothills of the Andes surrounded by lakes and mountains. Despite the spectacular outdoor settings, most of the scenes, faithful to the stylistics of film noir, take place in rather darkly lit interiors (Espinosa's workroom, the museum, Dietrich's cabins, the casino) or outdoors at night. German expressionism's oblique and vertical lines appear most strikingly in those scenes that are shot in the woods. Since the setting tends to be as important as the characters, both receive equal lighting emphasis. Additionally, Bielinsky institutes a clear chronological order by referring explicitly to each day of the week (Schrader, 219–221).[4] The predominant bluish hues that color the walls in Espinosa's bedroom as well as the brothel, his clothing, and the misty tones of the forest all reinforce the dark/noir tone of the film. Although Bielinsky's is an industrial film that involves well-known performers with the exception of the extras in public spaces, it was shot on location, and their exchanges involve slang, reinforcing the film's neorealist features along with its allusions to the widespread corruption typical of the turn of the twenty-first century and, for wearier audiences, of Argentine ethos.

As mentioned in the introduction, Deleuze conceived of noir as the prime illustration of the movement-image. Rather than focusing on the whodunit, Hitchcock's plots became the exposition of reasoning amid the unraveling of a set of circumstances in which the action and its agent are caught (*Cinema 1*, 200). Following generic conventions, Bielinsky's *El aura* also hinges on the clockwork precision of plot: after the accidental killing of Dietrich, Espinosa could have returned immediately to Buenos Aires, given Sontag's abrupt departure. However, Bielinsky weaves in clues from the beginning of the movie. For instance, the headlines of the newspapers Espinosa keeps at his workshop allude to his penchant for dwelling on the perfect heist. In other words, his background makes him the ideal detective/protagonist.

Espinosa contends that the plan he concocts in the cashier's office is based on his photographic memory. Thus, when Sontag asks Espinosa to verify his claim by repeating the serial number of the bags with the cash, Bielinsky must offer another shot of the bags, this time presumably from Sontag's point of view. With the exception of the preceding change in viewpoint, Bielinsky resorts to repetition of images, using minimalist flashbacks to convey how Espinosa infers the planned heist based on data he committed to memory. As we have seen, the set of relationships becomes more complicated with repetition. Espinosa performs under duress when Urién threatens him and when Sosa and Montero interrogate him. However, the plan becomes clearer as the different characters provide information. Espinosa thus understands the motivation of the plot when Urién calms down and volunteers the amount of Dietrich's debt, $67,000, a figure that the camera shows jotted down in the notebook.

Whether as flashbacks or as flash-forward shots that prefigure events, repetition unquestionably structures the film. Departing from Hume's thesis on the null effect of repetition on the object vis-à-vis its influence on the contemplating mind, Deleuze concludes that the force of habit binds repetition into the form of living present that is constantly renewed. Repetition is particularly apt for Espinosa because it provides reassurance. Repetition results in pleasure when the id subordinates psychic life; more importantly, the satisfaction arising from a specific hallucination endows the ego with a narcissistic image of itself (Deleuze, *Difference and Repetition*, 108). Therefore, while repetition—defined as an imagined enactment that is more precisely a foreshadowing of the exact same events, or a flash-forward—prepares the protagonist for a more satisfactory reaction, the information provided for the audience varies. For instance, the imagined enactment of the heist at the cashier's office is significant not only because it sheds light on Espinosa's thoughts but also because it proves a recurrent device that ultimately casts doubts on whether the heist occurred.

Another imagined enactment takes place when Sosa, Montero, Espinosa, and Julio drive toward the brothel to plan the heist. Although someone is counting the seconds required for each phase as in the first enactment, the audience expects a truthful depiction of the events presented. Another reenactment is suggested but not shown when Espinosa suffers a seizure at the casino after Urién reminds the protagonist about the third man in the armored vehicle and Espinosa imagines the devastating consequences, which he in fact witnesses upon arriving at the scene. In other words, the three initial reenactments show variations of Espinosa's binding to the notion of a plausible robbery at the administration and to variations of the heist as he gathers information.

With the last reenactment, which occurs when Espinosa tries to imagine and then succeeds in shooting Sosa, the function of the repetition/reenactment becomes more significant since the satisfaction of envisioning a scenario of emerging victorious is reinforced by providing Espinosa the courage to kill, which he vehemently opposed in the past. In lay terms, Espinosa resorts to the behaviorist technique of imagining an event (repeatedly) in order to find the wherewithal to perform a challenging action. But the final challenge seems overwhelming, for Sontag refers to Espinosa's aversion to hunting at the very beginning of the story. More importantly, the information may seem incongruous given that both men are taxidermists.

Following Deleuze, by linking the present to the past only to return to the present and thus making sense of the information gleaned at the cabin where Dietrich was holed up, the flashbacks reinforce the linear progression of narration. Yet, by repeating the process and involving a multiplicity of circuits, Bielinsky arrives at an even deeper state of the situation as he reinforces psychological causality. Furthermore, since the events foreshadowed in the flash-forwards may or may not take place, they introduce forks that break causality, thus generating suspense (*Cinema 2*, 46–48). Although the recurrence of the device casts doubts on the verisimilitude of the events, the final panning shot of Espinosa's workshop, which ends with a close-up of Dietrich's dog's icy blue eyes, significantly reasserts the veracity of events.

Like Hitchcock's films, which require constant interpretation with signs planted to distract the investigator, *El aura* turns on clues, not all of them ultimately significant. Such is the key Espinosa retrieves from the dying robbery suspect: that key is useless because it doesn't open Dietrich's cabin. Moreover, since the third man in the armored vehicle ultimately preempts the use of the key to open the safe, it may be conceived of as a "demark": rather than referring back to other terms in a customary series such that each can be "interpreted" in light of the others, a demark suddenly appears in conditions that take it out of its series or set it in contradiction with the series (*Cinema 1*, 203).

Bielinsky inscribes the generic formula of the noir film, despite the improbabilities of the plot and the action, as the set of relationships becomes more complicated and the stakes higher as the plot line evolves. When Sosa and Montero interrogate Espinosa, for instance, Julio helps by stating that Dietrich had mentioned a friend from Buenos Aires. Later, when they are alone, Julio asks Espinosa whether Dietrich will return. He is quite candid about his rationale, for he states that he is only joining in the heist to obtain enough money to distance himself from Dietrich. In other words, there would be no point in taking the risk if Dietrich were not to return. Given that Sosa killed Julio, Espinosa could have saved his life by telling Julio that Dietrich was long dead. An example of significant repetition with variation occurs immediately afterward when Espinosa tells Diana that Dietrich will not return. Finally, according to Hitchcock's unspoken contract, the crime has always been done for the innocent man who, thereafter, is innocent no longer (*Cinema 1*, 201), which allows for another instance of repetition. Even as Dietrich plans the heist to settle his debt with Urién, Montero and Sosa collaborate to cancel their debt with El Turco. Dietrich's plot is delivered to Espinosa, who is innocent no longer due to the accidental killing. Moreover, repetition with variation reinforces the pattern of exchange, for after the final shoot-out, Montero and Sosa deliver their crime to Espinosa.

In her widely influential *Shots in the Mirror: Crime Films and Society*, criminologist Nicole Rafter describes the double movement of the classic Hollywood tradition as challenging the status quo only to reassure us that justice has been done (213). However, the postmodern sensibility epitomized in Tarantino's movies relies as much on intertextuality as on our ability (or lack thereof) to know and understand the world and the significance of our lives and actions (Conard, 101). Along these lines, Bielinsky subverts the modernist/noir belief in a metanarrative of crime and punishment that inscribes and subverts the classic Hollywood formula by foreclosing the resolution: no information is provided to clarify the mystery of the corpses and/or of the armored vehicle. In the second edition of her book (2006), Rafter includes a chapter on an alternative tradition of films of moral ambiguity in which justice is achieved only through irony (213). This would seem to be the case in *El aura*: despite the death of innocents such as Julio and the three guards, the villains get their comeuppance. To the extent that Espinosa legitimizes the possible heist by telling Sontag that "todos roban" (everyone steals), the leitmotif of *Nueve reinas*, Espinosa is amoral. Thus, Bielinsky's neonoir protagonist becomes an accurate reflection of the times. Carlos Saúl Menem's administration (1989–1999) was notoriously corrupt at all levels, including the judicial branch, as shown by the investigations into the bombings in 1992 of the Israeli embassy in Argentina and in 1994 of the Asociación Mutua Israelita Argentina (AMIA) Jewish community center in Buenos Aires. On the other hand, the devastating ensnarement of middle-class finances in the *corralito* (2001–2002), especially during Eduardo Duhalde's administration (2002–2003), widened the waves of corruption.[5] Thus, the generic conventions of noir provide an excellent framework to allude to the grim effects of contemporary social ills.

While the recurrent reenactments would lead us to believe that the
events took place in the protagonist's fertile imagination, this notion
is dispelled by the presence of Dietrich's dog in Espinosa's workshop.
Within the postmodern vantage point of neonoir, the haphazard timing
of the protagonist's epileptic attacks, posited at least in their onset as a
quasimystical cum existentialist experience, undermine the noir Cartesian
notion of the all-knowing subject. Still, the sense that Espinosa neither
seems to carry the booty with him nor even deigns to open the armored
vehicle would lead us to believe that the thrill lies in the intellectual accom-
plishment of a perfect heist—which would reinscribe the mathematical
precision of Hitchcock's best films.

CHAPTER TWO
SLIPPERY CRIMINAL PLEASURES

Intermediality and Voyeurism
in Jorge Furtado's *O homem
que copiava*

Brazilian director Jorge Furtado's *O homem que copiava* (*The Man Who Copied*, 2003) follows the classic Hollywood noir conventions, with a couple of murders, a protagonist crazed by greed, and a deceitful woman who ensnares him. Emphasizing the protagonist's voyeurism and placing most of the action in his bedroom are reminiscent of Hitchcock's *Rear Window* (1954).[1] As in Orson Welles's *The Lady from Shanghai* (1947), the audience identifies with the protagonist through the use of voice-over. The tight articulation of Furtado's plot, like Bielinsky's in *Nueve reinas*, follows Hitchcock's formula; as such it ascribes to Deleuze's concept of the action-image insofar as the aim of the film is to depict the exposition of a rationale (*Cinema 1*, 200). However, Furtado's film also subverts noir conventions because the denouement does not lead to a restoration of the moral order. As an alternative neonoir, the protagonist lives in such a corrupt world that his deeds pale by comparison and he is not finally punished (Rafter, 213). Perhaps the film's greatest asset is the unexpected ending that forces the audience to reconsider previous assumptions as it reinscribes noir generic conventions such as the deceitful dame and the focus on mental process, since the plot is once again laid out as a rationale for action.

O homem que copiava opens with a paradox. The cashier calls the manager when André (Lázaro Ramos) does not have enough money to pay for the scanned items. In the meantime, customers who are waiting in line behind André grow restless. The pity we feel for the self-conscious, awkward young man turns into puzzlement at his insistence on buying matches. That puzzlement widens into bewilderment when he uses them to burn a stack of Brazilian bank notes. The film begins in medias res and subsequently uses a voice-over to naturalize the plot as an autobiographical account of André, a black, lower-middle-class high school dropout who feels condemned to abject poverty. Teenage André daydreams of becoming a famous soccer player. When he is fired from his job as a supermarket bagger, these dreams come to an abrupt halt. His next position, as a copy-machine operator, is no more glamorous than his previous one, but he is spared the physical work of bagging groceries. After giving us a brief explanation of the operation of the machine, André wryly notes that the audience is as competent to operate it as he is. In all, he emphasizes the mechanical nature of his job; he also offers a critique of process of reification typical of industrialized societies.

André's father walked away when the boy was four. As a nineteen-year-old, André shares with his mother (Teresa Texeira) the rent and an installment plan to pay for the TV set. With little cash to spare, it takes André a year to buy a pair of binoculars. He figures he would need ten years to save enough to buy a car. André spends the evenings drawing cartoons in his bedroom while his mother watches soap operas. After she retires, it's his turn to use the television. With the volume down, he concentrates on the changing images and the movement of light as he flips through the channels. At about eleven o'clock he trains his binoculars on his neighbors. This habit at once emphasizes André's voyeurism and calls attention to the scopophilia of the cinematic apparatus. By having the audience share his point of view, the subjective shot sutures the spectator into his voyeuristic practice as he imagines the daily lives of his neighbors when he moves from window to window: his spying is an extension of zapping, or channel surfing.

André is particularly intent on watching Sílvia (Leandra Leal), a girl about his age who lives in an adjacent building, return home.[2] Reminiscent of *Rear Window*, each window of her apartment resembles the frame of a cartoon, suggesting the fragmented information André gathers about her (Rocco, 28). He gradually follows her to work and later to lunch until they establish a relationship. Utterly besotted, André despairs when he discovers that Sílvia's father, Antúnes (Carlos Cunha Filho), not only steals her money but also spies on her as she showers. At this point André becomes obsessed by the need to secure cash to elope with her.

André quickly realizes that he cannot reliably resort to his acquaintances. His co-worker Marinês (Luana Piovani) is equally underpaid. Indeed, she figures out that selling her strawberry-blond hair would be more profitable than her current job. André turns to her acquaintance Cardosa (Pedro Cardosa), who is equally destitute. Though André refuses to become a drug dealer like his friend Feitosa (Júlio Andrade), who is in and out of jail, the arrival of a color copier leads André and Cardosa into counterfeiting. The two become partners in creating and planting false bills at lottery-ticket venues. The process increases after André learns about the depravity of Sílvia's father; however, following Cardosa's suggestion that André obtain real money to marry her and leave, the teenager remembers the possibility of robbing the neighboring bank.

Cardosa agrees to drive André to safety but finds that because he doesn't have spare change, or any money for that matter, he cannot park the car sufficiently close to the bank. So, after shooting a guard in the leg, André literally runs away with the bags of money. When Cardosa finally meets André, the two robbers exit by bus. Ironically, they must rip open a bag of money, as neither of them can pay for the bus tickets. Following the time-honed conventions of cops-and-robbers films, André checks the newspaper's coverage of the heist and comes across the composite description of the robber, as the genre demands. The shifting of the genre toward comedy occurs when he also learns that they won the lottery. Fear of being recognized leads André and Cardosa to ask Marinês to collect their prize, thus bringing her into the secret.

After proposing to Sílvia, André invites her hobbling father to dinner. The action prompts anagnorisis, and the father attempts to blackmail André into handing over the stolen money. Following Sílvia's revelation that she is deadly opposed to sharing their fortune with her stepfather, the couple plans to murder him and return some of the stolen money to the bank. The movie ends in a *mise en abyme*. In an attempt to construct a happily-ever-after ending of Hollywood film, Sílvia restages the best period of her mother's life, when she visited Corcovado with her boyfriend, Sílvia's biological father, by writing him and asking to meet them at Rio's most emblematic tourist site.

Furtado's *O homem que copiava* may be read as a morality play that denounces the internalization of instrumental rationality in consumer society.[3] "Instrumental rationality" may be defined as the practical reasoning to which people resort to solve problems or perform tasks efficiently. Since the factors involved are regarded as variables but the question of limits is elided, the automatic behavior stemming from instrumental reason overrides the process of mutual understanding. Instrumental rationality appears in the behavior of the protagonists, who struggle to escape their lower-middle-class status. The film's action highlights their willingness to take risks in the pursuit of happiness. With this focus, the film suggests that these social actors bypass ethics as they perform (and/or condone) heinous acts.[4] More importantly, Furtado resorts to the voice-over, usually a framing device that underscores characterization as it mediates the backstory and exposition (Sommer, "Initial Framings," 398), to seduce the audience into accepting violent actions. Furtado's vivid portrayal of the protagonist's awareness of exclusion successfully draws the audience into accepting the violent acts as inevitable.

André's awareness of exclusion also stems from having experienced the heavy hand of hegemonic instrumental rationality. His track record is obliterated by a small mistake when he is fired from his job as a supermarket bagger for a lapse of attention—he was daydreaming about being the Pelé of his generation—and for not being sufficiently contrite or solicitous when the client complained. André failed to comply with consumption's ideology of personal service, which privileges consumer gratification (Baudrillard, *Consumer Society*, 159).[5]

Furtado's film depicts a society in which modernity's foundational paradigm, that of individual self-construction, hinges on consumption. Because André was expelled from school, he can only aspire to menial jobs such as supermarket bagger or photocopier operator. In contradistinction to the traditional mechanisms of social placement, according to which human beings could only live up to the standards ascribed to their social class (Bauman, *Work*, 27), André is desperate to break from the cycle of abject poverty. He strengthens his resolve by identifying with the hegemonic ideology of consumer society, which promises instant gratification and constant happiness. Furtado shows us that his characters do not conceive of poverty in terms of material deprivation and bodily distress. Rather, they suffer because they cannot enjoy the standard of living they aspire to experience. This social and psychological condition explains their willingness to take calculated risks (Bauman, *Consuming Life*, 44, 92).

The film's focus on consumerism occludes its generic fluctuation, for the teenager's personal narrative soon leads to counterfeiting and a bank robbery, circumstances whose depiction triggers neonoir generic conventions. Thus, Cardosa, André's partner in dumping counterfeit bills, agrees to aid and abet him in the heist as long as it does not turn violent. Similarly, André's co-worker Marinês joins the bank robbers André and Cardosa on condition that her role be restricted to distracting Antúnes while the two boys set up a gas cylinder to explode when his refrigerator door is opened. Sílvia's voice-over, disguised as a letter to her biological father, provides a rationale for her actions since it allows her to admit that Antúnes molested her repeatedly upon the death of her mother, when she was only eleven years old.

André seems keenly aware of the expropriation of his labor; his fetishization of currency and luxury items allows for a displacement of the traditional Marxian model into an analysis of advanced capitalism centered on the concept of the symbolic code.[6] After successfully planting the first counterfeit bank note, André muses, "Imagine all the things you could buy with that money" ("Imagina o monte de coisas que dá pra comprar com esse dinheiro"), "Imagine how you'll be treated after buying all these things" ("Imagina agora como vão te tratar depois de comprar o monte de coisas"). He concludes, "And now imagine having all those things" ("E agora imagina ser o otário com um monte de coisas").[7]

All his imagination and identity hinges on consumerism. Through a series of references to the discourse of advertising that allude to the colonization of the unconscious, the close-up reinforces affective identification, ironically, with objects (Deleuze, *Cinema 1*, 87). André only purchases

Figure 2.1
Self-worth measured through conspicuous consumption.

drawing paper and a powerful telescope, while Cardosa and Marinês acquire sport and formal apparel to show their adscription to a society structured like fashion, constantly searching for novelty and seduction (Lipovetsky, 36). This is especially evident in their quest for distinction through the consumption of luxury items such as the leather dress, the Mercedes, and the reservation of the presidential suite. Yet these examples of conspicuous consumption are typical of Brazilian society.[8] A society of consumers not only interpellates its members as consumers but, more importantly, judges them by their consumption (Bauman, *Liquid Life*, 82). Furtado stresses the societal impact of consumption as a measure of success to explain the protagonist's willingness to take risks, which reinforces the generic conventions of neonoir.

Most relevant for Latin American cinema is Furtado's deployment of intermediality, namely, cartoon panels, animated cartoons, television clips, and self-reflexive sections. Pastiche includes graphic images that become animated. This technique is reinforced by intertextuality, anchored in the texts that André photocopies, as well as self-reflexivity.

Further neonoir conventions appear toward the end of the movie as a voice-over. Sílvia claims to have set André up to free her from her stepfather when she realized he was spying on her. To this extent, the audience confronts the type of ambiguity flaunted by Borges's "El sur," a fiction that allows for two readings that appear to cancel each other out. In an exclusive disjunction, both propositions cannot be true; the reader is left with the tension resulting from the desire to choose and the apparent impossibility, given that both options seem equally valid (Dixon, 6–8). Therefore, titillating moments like the time Sílvia walks past the window in her underwear allow her to ascertain that André is aiming his binoculars at her. The audience discovers that she plants the idea of going to Rio at the very beginning of the movie by throwing a postcard into André's working area. On another occasion, trying to figure out whether she is being pursued, she runs to take the bus, with André in tow. Unbeknownst to André (and to the audience), she begins to have lunch closer to his worksite. This chain of premeditated interventions dizzyingly undermines the audience's assumptions by debunking the narrative previously provided by André's voice-over. The surprising plot reversal results from Sílvia's subverting the audience's expectations about the sexy Marinês, who was set up as a foil against homely and wholesome Sílvia.

Much of the action of Furtado's film takes place in André's bedroom,

where he draws, aims his binoculars, and meets friends, exactly like
Hitchcock's *Rear Window*. Instead of simply commenting on his personality, André's room seems like a literal representation of his thoughts and
desires. A collage of images completely obscures the walls. Yet, the
images also point at a social condition, given that life is represented as
the ongoing accumulation of spectacles (Debord, 12). As such, the walls
of André's bedroom conjure up a descent into the unconscious. As per
Jameson's comment on the colonization of the unconscious (44–54), the
images range from cabaret girls to soccer players. It is worth noting, however, that the collage emphasizes parceling. For instance, a row of cabaret
girls' legs are detached from their respective torsos, and one torso is
positioned in the opposite direction. Other fragments include images of
hand-drawn legs and skirts, a set of huge lips, an eye, and bottles of liquor.
Two parceled columns that appear to meet toward the bottom of the wall
reinforce the expressionistic atmosphere.[9]

After work, André retires to his room to draw cartoons. Although these
cartoons are a good venue to project his artistic talents, André has not
yet succeeded in being published. Pastiche also plays an integral part
in André's cartoons. Furtado shows us the image and then proceeds to
animate the cartoons. In so doing, Furtado shows us that hypermedia
are processed as reality (Rocco, 29). By resorting to intermedia, as the
play between media, Furtado provides more in-depth characterization,
which allows him to portray contemporary youth more realistically while
commenting on how these new technologies affect our interests and the
nature of our communities (Semali and Pailliotet, 15). André's cartoons

Figure 2.2
André as cyclops: Metonymic punishment for blinding Mairoldi; represented through intermediality as a TV cartoon.

Figure 2.3
Self-portrait: André as cyclops, or life represented through cartoons.

seem to be infused with details of real life, as the frames that would appear in a printed publication transition into TV animated cartoons. As André retells the traumatic event that led to his expulsion from school, we watch an animated cartoon of rather schematic drawings. We witness the protagonist's furious response to Mairoldi (Furtado's voice), a fat, white classmate who laughs at the possibility that André's father would return after a seven-year absence. At this point, the cartoon character that stands for André hits Mairoldi on the head. As the screen fills with red and an ambulance appears, we discover that Mairoldi has lost an eye. After the incident, we return to a frame of André that becomes animated when his eyes are displaced into one huge eye in the middle of his forehead like a cyclops—a metonymic punishment for his deed.

While the teachers and the principal are drawn as monsters, the mother figure is a rather primitive assemblage of a picture of Eleanor Roosevelt that André comes across at work. He finishes off the image by drawing a coat and legs. The proliferation of media goes hand in hand with the attempt to erase their mediation. Similarly, the audience learns about André's fatherless childhood through his recollections, represented as cartoons shown on television, and through his subsequently animated drawings. In other words, the audience watches a cartoon version of his life (Rocco, 30). As André retells the story of his sad childhood, he delves into the sheets of the past and focuses on peaks of time, memorable moments that stand out almost as traumatic events. The circuits involved in the process of recollection become all the more complex as André transfers his memories of those events into drawings and proceeds to animate them.

Obsessed as he is about money or the lack of it, André ponders the history of paper as currency that he learns as he copies a text about a Chinese emperor's order to exchange rice for paper bills. Then, André draws his own dollar bills that feature Marilyn Monroe and Mao Tse-Tung. While Monroe's picture epitomizes commodity fetishization, Mao Tse-Tung's represents capitalism's most ardent critique, as Furtado speaks against the values imposed by the oppressing force of money.[10] Pastiche also appears when André's voice-over mentions that Sílvia lives in a building named Santa Cecilia: a pastiche of images then depicts the saint's travails, as a paper image of her is juxtaposed against an elongated building where the Romans supposedly attempted to cook her. Since Santa Cecilia was miraculously spared, her persecutors decided to behead her, as shown through two swords that appear out of nowhere, accompanied by four sets of wings around her head, which are promptly weighed down by images of beheaded pork and poultry.

At that point, however, we notice that the representation of the saint bears some resemblance to Sílvia, which may be an intimation of her suffering at the hands of her perverted stepfather, Antúnes. When André considers punishing Antúnes, we return to the setting of Santa Cecilia's beheading. Resorting to pastiche, we see André's head in the garb of a Roman soldier and Antúnes's taking the place of the saint's, foreshadowing the denouement. All this deployment of pastiche, cartoons, and intertextuality paradoxically subverts the apparent linearity of the film, mimicking multimedia's nonlinearity and interactivity, which in turn mirror the spectator's associative thought processes (Shelton, 78).

Figure 2.4
Animated pastiche depicting Santa Cecilia's fate.

The remarkable effectiveness of Furtado's screenplay owes much to his using a range of techniques that reinforce the protagonist's innate decency, the seemingly inescapable plight of his poverty, his ardent imagination, and his skill as an artist. These techniques are combined with a plot that is set with the precision of Hitchcock's films. The voice-over draws the audience to empathize with André's predicament. The constant interplay of different media includes, for instance, a small statue of a winged saint clad as a Roman gladiator in silver armor and a greenish cape and wielding a golden sword; as André buys it for his mother as a birthday present, it becomes a topic for conversation intended to distract the cashier as he plants a counterfeit bill. André casually mentions that it is supposed to be a guardian angel but that his boss argues it must be Saint Gabriel on account of the sword. After admitting she doesn't know much about angels, the cashier guesses it must be an archangel. But the cashier sitting beside her says it must be Saint Michael because of the armor. As soon as he leaves the store, André invokes the angel as he recites a prayer: "Guardian Angel, meek and mild, look on me, your little child. Bless me now the day is done. Amen" ("Santo anjo do Senhor, meu zeloso guardador / se a mim me confiou a piedade divina / me reza, me guarda, me ilumina. Amém"). The prayer endears André to the audience for his innocence and embattled state.

Intertextuality is incorporated into the screenplay by way of a copy machine. As André fills the various orders he wonders about the meaning of the texts, and some become leitmotifs. Perhaps the most poignant is the reference to Shakespeare's marriage sonnet—"When I do count the clock that tells the time . . ."—that ricochets through the movie, weaving the play of difference and deferral typical of *différance*, as it allows for character development and foreshadows a happy ending. In other words, the sonnet is presented initially as an example of André's habit of reading the material he copies, only in this case he doesn't understand the poem. Worse still, as the customer returns, he cannot read the last line. As André doesn't understand the meaning of "hirsuto" (hairy), the sonnet becomes a topic of conversation. The theme of marriage is woven into the plot because André imagines himself proposing, as Sílvia tells him the definition of the term. To the extent that Shakespeare's advice is to "breed, to brave him when he takes thee," that is, reproduction defies the onslaught of time, Sílvia has the power to redress her mother's unhappiness.

According to the diegesis—the world the audience constructs from events, spaces, and characters explicitly presented or inferred—André not only recreates traumatic events of his life in cartoons that become animations but also relies on this medium to think about his future, especially when he worries because no girl would possibly want to live with, marry, or have children with a Xerox operator. The movie poignantly juxtaposes André's musings with representations of women reminiscent of cartoons of the 1950s. Furthermore, André's voyeurism becomes self-reflexive as he draws circles, such as those of binoculars (voyeurism again), into the cartoons. André's emotions are also portrayed by way of TV images of visual slapstick. When Sílvia shows her distaste for beer, the image of a cream pie flattened on André's face suggests his feelings. Just before the heist and in an allusion to his state of mind, the audience is offered some rather dated TV images that depict a man tightening his tie just before jumping off a bridge into the sea. Intermediality is particularly apt, for the cartoons that André draws recall the storyboards of a movie, and they evoke the concept of cognitive frames, which may be described as culturally formed metaconcepts. As Werner Wolf explains, the cognitive frame operates as a basic orientation aid that assists us in our journey through our experiential universe, supports our cognitive activities, and usually anchors interpretation (5).

These frames provide foreshadowing and propel the action. A geometrical drawing provides resolution of the danger posed by Feitosa. Let us recall that for fun, André and his friend Feitosa often jump off a bridge onto the sand. While Feitosa jumps off the four flights of stairs from what appears to be a two-story free-fall from the bridge, André does so from half that distance, so Feitosa bullies André, calling him a coward. André buys the gun he uses to rob the armored vehicle at the bank from Feitosa. The counterfeit bills with which André pays him land Feitosa in jail, and Feitosa's plight becomes all the more dire when his handprints are discovered on the gun. Upon his release, Feitosa threatens to kill André, his mother, and his girlfriend unless he hands over the stolen money.

The meaning of the drawing of vertical lines resembling a triangle is evident in retrospect when we learn that André has stuck sharp poles in the patch of sand where Feitosa usually lands as he jumps. In the next frame, the triangle of parallel lines becomes soaked in red. Then a character drawn with bare sticks for arms and legs appears impaled and bleeding. Only after all that does the movie show a passing image of Feitosa impaled, lying on the sand. Therefore, the initial drawing of the poles prefigures the action and sheds light on André's stream of thought in that there appears to be no distinction between so-called real-life events and the stories he tells through his cartoons. These devices underscore noir generic conventions as evil characters get their comeuppance. Allusions to generic conventions of noir are seen in stylistic references like the experimental parallel takes of Sílvia's bedroom, naturalized as hinging on the angles of the wardrobe mirrors facing her window, which may be read as an intertextual allusion to the final mirror scene in Orson Welles's *Lady from Shanghai.*

While the previous examples show how these frames become models for future interactions, the slippage between "imagined" and "real" events, reminiscent of the Derridean notion of iterability, is typical of Furtado's aesthetics.[11] For instance, André's voice-over mentions that he was watching television when his father left for good. The traumatic event is engraved in the four-year-old's memory. The cartoon he was watching showed a house depicted as if the exterior walls were invisible. This image, in turn, conjures a contemporary one. As photocopier operator, he recalls having seen a book cover with a similar illustration. In other words, the images André encounters at work trigger recollections from different points of the past, generating circuits connecting them. As André refers to his mother's habit of taking a glass of water when he goes to bed, the mother's mechanical actions are shown by removing the back of the refrigerator to place the camera, located inside, as the image/frame of the original cartoon.

The self-reflexive comments of the voice-over offer a slight variation of this technique. Perhaps the most vivid, because the short scene is

Figure 2.5 Paneled view of Sílvia's room, reminiscent of Orson Welles's final scene in *The Lady from Shanghai.*

interpolated early on and the female character does not reappear, is the purported dialogue between André and an unnamed girl who appears to lose interest in him when she discovers he is a Xerox boy. Though the dialogue remains on a realistic level and she says *legal* (cool), André's ironic voice-over passes judgment over their polite exchanges: *muito legal* (very cool). At that point André mentions that he works with illustrations and has even sent some material to a magazine. But his voice-over questions the term "material." That's when André realizes that drawing cartoons doesn't work as a pick-up line. Toward the end of the film, however, this sequence is cancelled out by Sílvia's assurance that she always wanted to marry a photocopier operator.

Repetition is a major device deployed to analyze recent events; for instance, by way of a flashback that immediately replays the preceding scene, André analyzes the "Obrigada você" (I thank you) of Sílvia's first exchange in terms of intonation and eye contact to determine whether she is interested. Later, André proposes to Sílvia, and the verisimilitude of the scene is promptly undercut, set up as a figment of his imagination, as a flash-forward, the function of which may be similar to protagonist Espinosa's in *El aura* as it allows the protagonist to prepare for an emotionally draining action in the near future. A similar scene recurs soon after appearing to be "real," as in Bielinsky's *El aura*, where difference and repetition appear in the rehearsal that foreshadows the heist.

Conversely, Furtado uses the doubling of repetition, whether visual as in the cartoons or in the replayed scenes (André's musings regarding Sílvia, passing the counterfeit bills, the heist, and the collaborative planning of Antúnes's demise), in order to offer other plausible endings to the plot. Sílvia's admission that she engineered much of the action of the plot by leading André on as soon as she realized he was peeping on her is a prolonged flashback that restages and reinvents the plot as an indirect reflexive relationship. As Deleuze explains, such relationships occur when the contact of a real situation is expressed as a fictitious action that will merely prefigure a project or as a real action to come that does not immediately give rise to a corresponding action (*Cinema 1*, 181–182). In other words, Sílvia manipulates André to escape the abusive relationship with her stepfather. To rescue her, André engineers the heist, an indirect result of her action. All the generic conventions of noir emerge from Sílvia's admission of having led André on, her insistence on murdering Antúnes, and her rigging the refrigerator to explode when her stepfather opened it.

As befits Holt's indication that noir must involve certain realism in the stylized crime and the moral ambiguity of characters (25), moral turpitude appears in all characters, even (*cherchez la femme*) Sílvia's mother, who was having an affair with the artist who moved to Rio while she was engaged to Antúnes. While the representation of impalement and the foreclosure of the scene of the explosion would certainly allow for thinking of *O homem* as noir, the greater likelihood is that the film would be considered neonoir, for the text refers to visual or narrative aspects of the noir of the 1940s and 1950s but is set in the present (Wager, 124). Along these lines, the neonoir femme fatale is no less the dangerous object of desire; rather than paying for her crimes, she prospers (Holt, 27).[12]

To conclude, Furtado's *O homem que copiava* inscribes the generic conventions of film noir: stylized crime realism, moral ambiguity—especially related to the woman—and a superb plot line that illustrates a rationale for action, like the best of Hitchcock's movies. However, Furtado's film subverts the conventional noir restoration of the moral order. While in the most canonical neonoir films the woman prospers from crime, *O homem que copiava* is closer to an alternative neonoir, since the protagonists live in such a corrupt world that their misdeeds pale by comparison, so they are not finally punished. André plots the murder of his friend Feitosa only after the drug dealer threatens to kill him, his mother, and his fiancée, so the impalement becomes an act of self-defense. While Antúnes blackmails André, asking him to deliver all of the stolen money, André is leery of killing him even though Antúnes is a pervert. André sees Antúnes robbing Sílvia's money from her handbag and presumes that the stepfather masturbates as he peeps through the keyhole when she showers. On the other hand, though Sílvia insists on murdering Antúnes, she is shown to be terrified that he will not allow her to marry André. Only when Sílvia tells André that her stepfather sexually abused her upon the death of her mother does André agree to murder Antúnes. Most important for Latin American cinema, Furtado's baroque neonoir movie incorporates collage, cartoons, animation, and TV scenes, the discourse of advertisement, intertextuality (through the texts copied), and an equally rich sound track. While animation enriches characterization, the voice-over interpellates the audience in an attempt to naturalize the violent actions, suturing them into the road to happiness promised by consumerism.

CHAPTER THREE
ENDLESS QUEST

Chasing Sex, Lies, and Money at the Gates of Hell in Heitor Dhalia's *O cheiro do ralo*

Noir conventions such as murder and a final reversal that reinstates order appear in Heitor Dhalia's *O cheiro do ralo* (*Drained*, 2006). The film also incorporates neonoir conventions such as the dangerous dame whose crime not only goes unpunished but also leads to her self-realization.[1] In *O cheiro do ralo*, the typical flawed protagonist of noir movies turns into a morally ambiguous, perhaps delusional, neonoir character whose fixations allude to psychoanalysis. Dahlia's alternative neonoir focuses on consumerism, for like Furtado, Dhalia offers a critique of commodity fetishization. Dhalia and Furtado coincide as well in deploying voice-over to seduce the audience into condoning, or at least understanding, the actions of their respective protagonists. And like those of Bielinsky and Furtado, Dhalia's film underscores the clockwork of causality typical of Hitchcock's films. Thus, the plot becomes an exposition of a reasoning, which Deleuze analyzes by way of the concept of the action-image.

Faithful to the stereotypical Brazilian fixation with *bundas* (derrieres), *O cheiro do ralo* begins with a subjective shot of a woman's buttocks.[2] The camera subsequently follows the male protagonist, Lourenço (Selton Mello), as he strolls past a series of warehouses painted in bright colors. When an old man approaches him attempting to sell him an antique watch, we learn that Lourenço owns a second-hand store and that his clients' desperation has turned the store into a kind of pawnshop. A muted voice-over articulates Lourenço's obsession: "I could spend a week watching that butt" ("Poderia passar uma semana só olhando para o seu rabo") (11).[3] This sentiment serves to explain his daily presence at the diner where the waitress with the attractive bunda works.

After he cancels his impending wedding based on the argument that only fools believe in happiness, Lourenço's struggle for power and money, which he conceives of as aphrodisiacs, taints his interactions. There are times, however, when Lourenço revels. Toasting with champagne, he gives money and cigars away, ostensibly to fete the soldier who saved his father's life but in fact to celebrate his freedom on the day he was to wed. Lourenço's conscious attempt to avoid feeling pity for his clients results in constant verbal abuse. His lack of self-control peaks with his gratuitous physical abuse of the old man whose offer of the watch opened the plot's cycle of negotiation. Unrepentant, Lourenço plants a gun by the man's apparently unconscious body and bribes the security agent to ensure that he will support the story when Lourenço tells the police the old man attempted to rob him. The plot also follows the gradual deterioration of a drug addict who has nothing left to sell but a voyeuristic approach to her body, which excites Lourenço as he masturbates. Ironically, the self-destructive drug addict becomes the femme fatale insofar as she recovers her dignity by murdering Lourenço, thus putting an end to his abusive behavior.

O cheiro do ralo adapts a 2002 novel by Lourenço Mutarelli.[4] Fluctuating between the indirect style of the simple past and the present of dialogues and the narrator's monologues, the novel consists of nine chapters: "Tudo o que o mundo tem a lhe oferecer" (All the World Has to Offer), "O portal" (The Portal), "Voltando" (Returning), "Ciclo" (Cycle), "Estive no inferno e me lembrei de você" (I Was in Hell and Remembered You), "O jogo" (The Game), "Ausência" (Absence), "A imensa bunda e o buraco" (The Huge Butt and the Hole), and "O buraco e mais nada" (The Hole and Nothing Else). The chapters follow a pattern of repetition with variation. Lourenço always tries to shortchange his clients.[5] In the film version, the need to condense the story line and the need to generate revenue led to a certain simplification to ensure that the audience would follow the plot (Seger, 2–7). Therefore, only one of the titles of the chapters appears verbatim in the movie. Other titles have been slightly changed, "Tudo o que a vida tem a lhe oferecer" (All Life Has to Offer), or synthesized, "A imensa bunda e mais nada" (Just the Huge Butt). "Estive no inferno e lembrei de você" has material from the previous chapter ("Voltando").

Similarly, secondary plot lines like the chaste love affair between the protagonist and the married woman are eliminated (48–51, 85–88). The suppression matters because it establishes a counterpoint between Lourenço's insulting words toward his girlfriend—"Só os ingênuos acredita- vam em felicidade" (Only fools believe in happiness) (12)—and the feeling experienced while kissing the married woman: "Acho que foi a experiência mais incrível que provei em toda minha vida. A sensação de amor que eu sentia, irradiava muito além de meu corpo" (I think it was the most incred- ible experience I ever had. The feeling of love I experienced even radiated from my body) (88).

The omission of most of the novel's erotic scenes may be explained in terms of film distribution. Both the novel and the screenplay register Lou- renço's fiancée's violent reaction to his calling off their wedding, as Louren- ço successfully takes the kitchen knife she was wielding at him. Yet in the novel the episode is followed by Lourenço's reification of her, since while he subjects her, he forces his face into her butt, a scene followed by cun- nilingis and masturbation (13, 19–20). The scene comes to an end abruptly when he tells her, "Nada tem para me dar" (You have nothing to give me) (20). Likewise, when the bunda becomes "uma coisa" (a thing), the waitress tries to comfort Lourenço by way of fellatio (136). The novel cancels out these and a similar panoply of erotic scenes by resorting to parody, which diffuses sexuality, referring to the events through a process of mechanical dissociation: "E como no canal pornô da TV acabo. Imitando engranagem" (And, as in the porno channel, I come. Like clockwork) (135).

In the novel, the cliché of the married woman's dream is similarly downgraded to the generic conventions of a commercial featuring her and Lourenço: "Corro em câmera lenta. Nos abraçamos e giramos, giramos, giramos . . . Aí meu pensamento enquadra meus dentes. E num zoom se aproxima . . . Entra uma voz muito grave. A voz diz: KOLINOS" (I run in slow motion. We hug and turn around and around and around . . . At that point I think of a shot focusing on my teeth. As the zoom approaches . . . a deep voice says, Kolynos [toothpaste]) (90). It is unfortunate that these scenes were omitted from the screenplay.

Gambling, which defines Lourenço's obsessive behavior, usually works because his clients are desperate. The paratactical articulation of the respective exchanges is underscored by the anaphoric constructions of the novel, such as "A vida procura viver./ A arte imita a vida./ A vida imita a vida./ A arte imita a arte" (Life tries to live/ Art imitates life/ Life imitates life/ Art imitates art) (18), as well as in the thirteen variations of "esses livros" (those books) in a scene at the doctor's office (72–73) and in the summary, "Ele entra e ele rasga dinheiro/ Ele entra e sai carregando uma coisa pesada . . . É relógio, alfinete, é faca . . . É o azar, é a sorte/ É a porta que bate" (He comes in and tears up the money/ He comes in and leaves carrying a heavy item . . . It's a watch, a pin, it's a knife . . . It's bad luck, it's good luck,/ It's the slamming door) (138–139). Thus, the paratactical construction of the novel is both experimental and postmodern.

The profuse intertextual references in the novel result in dissemination.[6] "Rosebud," the name of the sled in Orson Welles's *Citizen Kane*, becomes a leitmotif (17, 28, 117), associated as it is with the quest for the bunda and alluding to the nostalgia of Welles's character's frustrated life. The protagonist's intellectual pyrotechnics underscore his desire to "escrever um livro" (write a book) (123), which self-reflexively alludes to the text itself. The reference to Sidney Lumet's film *The Pawnbroker* (*Homem do prego*, 1961) as well as its protagonist, played by Rod Steiger (110), underscores the structure of mise-en-abyme. The novel ends with Lourenço's epiphany: "O que eu realmente buscava não estava ali . . . O que eu buscava, era só a busca" (What I was really searching for was not there . . . What I was searching for was the quest itself) (134). His sudden moment of illumination is connected to the reference to the Borgesian paradox about the eternal nature of promises in general—they undergo constant metamorphosis and can only be kept insofar as they are not fulfilled. Thus, the allusion to Borges reinforces the novel's self-reflexive mise en abyme (135).

Considering that the process of adaptation is similar to translation, Charles Fillmore's system of scenes-and-frames semantics might be productive. Fillmore argues that prototypes were experiential in that the process of using a word in a novel situation involves comparing it to past experiences to judge whether the similarity warrants the same linguistic coding. While defining the linguistic coding as "frame," "scene" encompasses visual scenes, familiar layouts and kinds of interpersonal transactions, institutional structures, body image, and, in general, sets of actions, experiences, or coherent beliefs or imaginings (61–63). Following Fillmore, as contemporary Brazilians, both Mutarelli and Dhalia along with their collaborators and other production workers share a range of identifiable social, linguistic, and semantic codes. As their audience, we might expect to see these codes articulated in the film.

Mutarelli is free to consciously avoid descriptions in the novel, while film's dependence on images leads to reification. By Mutarelli's choosing to simply name but not describe the props, his novel offers a certain freedom of adaptation, though the selection of props also may have been haphazard or driven by chance. For instance, many different models fit the description of an antique watch. At times the film overrides references made in the novel. Despite its broken lid, the watch is supposed to be musical. The film shows a watch with no lid, and the music is transferred to a jewelry box. Since the movie is set in Brazil we might expect the sale of items of African or indigenous origin.[7] Yet, perhaps because the action takes place in southern Brazil, a region settled since the mid-nineteenth century by many Germans, Italians, and other Europeans, ethnic references are largely absent from the novel and the movie. Another reason for this lack may be the need to underscore the seedy nature of Lourenço's business.

The frog condenses references to witchcraft and ghosts, associated as it is with the destructive forces of African *ndoki*, aimed at destroying the victims by consuming their psyches and internal life forces. The function of ndoki witchcraft is to collect debts, in this case, the shame of being jilted (McElroy, 350–351). The novel refers to a kind of voodoo practice in which a doll stands for the victim, represented by Lourenço's picture, "um boneco de madeira . . . todo marcado. Por pontas que alguém lhe enfiou" (a wooden doll . . . marked all over by pins that someone stuck in it) (104). Though we know the scene was filmed because the wooden object appears in the paratextual material ("The Making of *O cheiro do ralo*"), it was not included in the final cut.

Moreover, the movie avoids the topic of the ghost (*vulto*) that Lourenço felt when he learned that his fiancée attempted suicide (21). In Mutarelli's novel the ghost is associated with hell: "O cheiro que aspiro vem do inferno./ O vulto é o cheiro também. Porra eu estou assustado" (The smell I inhale comes from hell./ The ghost and the smell too. Hell, I'm scared) (29). Belief in the ghost is shored up by the maid, who claims to have seen "o vulto sentado aí no sofá" (the ghost sitting there on the sofa) (51). Despite its recurrence (74) and its association with his fiancée's long, blond hair (52, 100, 110), Lourenço tries to deal with his fear by resorting to a psychoanalytic argument: "Eu sei o que Freud falou sobre o medo. Sei o que falou dos fantasmas. Os fantasmas são a culpa. Mas eu desconheço esse sentimento" (I know what Freud said about fear. I know what he said about ghosts. Ghosts are our guilt. But I don't know that feeling) (29).

The items in Lourenço's pawnshop belong to a (retro) Euro-American ethos suggested by mannequins, ancient deep-sea diving gear, TV sets, bicycles, paintings, music systems, and Hollywood movie posters, among them Steve McQueen's *Twenty-Four Hours of Le Mans*. The nostalgic retro look is reinforced by the characters' costumes in the film, since the action could take place any time from the 1950s on and perhaps even earlier were it not for the iconic references to TV sets.[8] The palette ranges from mustard yellow to a sickly green that connotes fear and the lack of upright moral qualities. In shades of brown, Lourenço's clothes underscore the connotation of the drain. Precisely the lack of descriptions in the novel regarding characters and mise-en-scène makes the adaptation all the more interesting.

While the novel closely follows Lourenço's first-person stream of consciousness, the film sparingly uses voice-over. The omission of his interior monologue may be explained as performativity, since showing is more effective than telling. Such omissions may have taken place to avoid ambiguity (Seger, 7). Both versions of *O cheiro do ralo* focus on the protagonist's thinking process. In every one of the exchanges Lourenço attempts to discover his opponent's weakness. That he prefers to make his clients suffer rather than profit from them is particularly apparent in the exchanges regarding the attempted sale of a gold fountain pen whose elderly owner grovels to the extent of offering to do whatever Lourenço asks.

Lourenço's emotional detachment stems from a conscious strategy of self-preservation that is a primary motif for the protagonist in noir. He cannot feel sorry for his clients, for he can only profit when shortchanging them. The chronicle of his interactions reveals that Lourenço engages in a kind of duel that consists of imitating his interlocutors and upending them at their own game. According to the paratextual material of the film titled "The Making of *O cheiro do ralo*," some of the most offensive scenes were discarded. In one of them, an elderly man with a severe case of Parkinson's disease sells a golden cage with two porcelain birds (the novel mentions an embalmed canary). As Lourenço pays him a pittance, the very ill man's head continues to bob up and down. In other omitted scenes a young man cannot play the flute he intends to sell, and a youth begins to sing and goes on to hum a tango as he tries to sell vinyl records of Carlos Gardel. These rather pathetic scenes are included in extra material on the DVD as an acknowledgement of performances that did not make the final cut despite the hard work of the respective actors. In these cases, Lourenço knows the value of the items should be considered apart from the histrionic abilities of their owners, but he prefers to humiliate these prospective sellers instead.

Dhalia's adaptation of the novel downplays the focus on the intellectual disquisitions of the tormented protagonist, structuring the plot instead by deploying the generic conventions of noir. Intertextual references to Raymond Chandler, James Ellroy, and Paul Auster, who are known for the morally ambiguous characters of their dark crime novels, set the tone, for moral turbidity taints most of the film's characters. Lourenço's girlfriend (Fabiana Guglielmetti) slaps him repeatedly while they are having dinner but becomes incensed upon being jilted, arguing that the wedding invitations are at the printer's. She appears brandishing a kitchen knife at Lourenço's office and leaves other mementos such as a message stuck with a knife to Lourenço's front door. After her botched suicide attempt, Lourenço finds a shoebox at his front door. He opens it and is terrified by the toad that hops out of it because its lips are sewn, a sign of black magic. Having killed it, Lourenço retrieves the message, "I was in hell and remembered you," which he attributes to his girlfriend's blind rage.

As per noir conventions, in addition to the murderous rage of the jilted girlfriend Lourenço faces other dangerous women, notably the drug addict who ultimately kills him. Yet, in contradistinction to noir conventions and reinscribing neonoir variations, the drug addict's revenge goes unpunished. Following the generic conventions of the alternative neonoir, the murderer's action pales in comparison to the moral turpitude of her victim. Indeed, the film shows the progressive physical deterioration of the drug

Figure 3.1
Lourenço takes advantage of the drug addict.

addict. At first, she sells a solid-gold jewelry case, including some items inside it.

At the end, the woman only has an old kitchen plate to sell. Therefore, her addiction forces her to agree to be paid for lowering her pants so Lourenço can see her naked, which excites him. Though she becomes increasingly emaciated, ragged, and shaky, she usually fights back. Her attitude toward Lourenço also deteriorates. She tells Lourenço he looks like the guy in an ad campaign, and she is interested in the glass eye he shows her that he passes off as a memento of his father, who died in World War II. Later, she vents her anger at his lie. She accuses Lourenço of forcing her to sell him all of her belongings, but he is adamant about setting the record straight. She succeeds in startling Lourenço by telling him he has a hole for a face. When Lourenço doesn't want to enter into a financial transaction, she undresses and publicly accuses him of having sexually abused her. The clients sitting in the waiting room rush in, and the mob beats Lourenço up. The security agent tells the police she is Satan. Though she has the habit of entering unannounced, her unexpected shooting reestablishes her connection with hell: Lourenço dies next to the drain, which he considered the gates of hell. Thus, the drug addict's act of murder results in her recovering her self-respect and independence by disposing of her abuser. But unless she kicks the habit she will soon be among the dead.

Lourenço's flaunted rationality is undermined by the frequency of his concerns about the ghosts of the items stored in the warehouse because he believes that the affective charge of their previous owners lives on in them and that they may thus exert a noxious effect on him. Lourenço feels increasingly sick. He ponders the problems posed by the diner's fast food that force him to use the backed-up restroom but also reflect it through his symptoms. However, the argument involves cycles of memories that lead back to sheets of the past as he acknowledges his obsession for the bunda, which is thus tied to the drain and through a convoluted reasoning to the gates of hell. In conclusion, these fears hardly enhance Lourenço's rationality.

Dhalia adds a tropical touch to noir and neonoir conventions through Lourenço's obsession with the bunda, the musical score, and the homage to Lourenço Mutarelli, the author of the novel. By Mutarelli's playing the part of the *segurança* (security agent), the homage becomes even funnier since, as mentioned in the paratextual section "The Making of *O cheiro do ralo*," Brazilian security agents tend to be big and sweaty—the complete

opposite of the slender Mutarelli clad in deep-red polyester.[9] While such
adaptations imply systematic suppression (Leitch, 99), Mutarelli's inclusion led to developing the action to provide depth to characterization. As
an example, the director adds a sequence in the waiting room in which a
client sells the security agent a pack of antique cards with illustrations of
nude women for a pittance. He convinces the prospective client by assuring him that Lourenço will not be interested because the boss is both gay
and stingy. Shots added in the movie suggest the security agent's complicity with the secretary and his aversion toward the drug addict. After the

Figures 3.2 and 3.3
Though run-down, the drug
addict takes revenge.

mob attacks Lourenço for allegedly raping the drug addict, the security agent replaces the secretary at the reception.

Dhalia's *O cheiro do ralo* offers a more traditional indictment of the expropriation of labor, which is significant because noir thrives in periods of crisis. The hedonism of Dhalia's *O cheiro*, in contrast to the moralism of Furtado's *O homem que copiava*, attests to a critique of consumer society. The reification of people, articulated in the services they perform in exchange for money, is evident in the scenes involving the addict (Sílvia Lourenço), the married woman (Lorena Lobato), and the waitress (Paula Braun). The addict turns to Lourenço because she needs money. Occasionally, when she has nothing to sell, he asks her to turn around and show her buttocks.[10] The exchange with the married woman is set as a crescendo of monetary transactions since she requires payment for each step of the striptease. While the addict feels abused, the married woman happily engages in a game for which she is generously compensated. These instances lead to masturbation and fellatio, respectively, and both show Lourenço's drive for control.

Despite his obsession with the bunda, Lourenço's exchanges with the waitress are similar. When she suggests they have a beer after her shift, he stalls because he is leery of commitment. Lourenço only grudgingly acknowledges that what is really significant cannot be bought: "Of all the things I've ever had, those that were worth anything, the ones I miss the most are the things you can't touch, the things that are out of reach of our hands, the things that don't belong in the material world" ("De todas as coisas que eu tive as que mais me valeram, as que mais sinto falta . . .

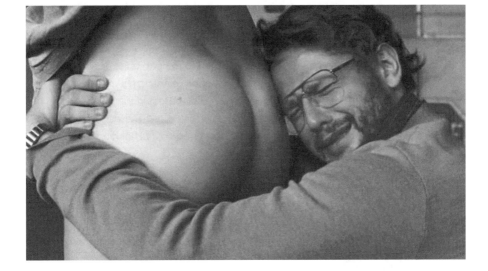

Figure 3.4 Commodification of the bunda.

Figure 3.5
The eye's multiple connotations self-reflexively include the scopic drive.

são as coisas que não se pode tocar ... são as coisas que não estão ao alcance das nossas mãos, são as coisas que não fazem parte do mundo da matéria"). Here Lourenço offers a variation on the theme of consumerism, in that his obsession with the bunda clearly points at objectification. Verisimilitude is stretched, as is fundamental to parody, when Lourenço asks the new waitress to turn around to ascertain that he is not speaking to the owner of the bunda with which he is obsessed. The waitress finally consents to Lourenço's proposition to pay to see her bunda because he offers her a secretarial position as well as the emotional attachment implied by his avowed need to have her close by. Ironically, when she does strip, Lourenço weeps. A close-up of Lourenço crying while he hugs the bunda shows that it has been reified.

Even though Lourenço is diegetically dead, the movie ends with a shot of the bunda from his point of view, after which the credits roll.

The interpolated stories of *O cheiro do ralo* show a pattern of repetition with variation, underscored by the use of a fixed camera and reinforced by the panning of a mobile one. Faithful to the capitalist principle of maximizing profits at any cost, Lourenço shortchanges his clients but for the few exceptions that confirm the rule. His interest in the prosthetic eye, which acquires symbolic value, drives up the price. Whether it stands for the Panopticon, his father, or himself, Lourenço enjoys flashing the eye because it is so disturbing.

While most clients take his abuse, others score moral victories. Morelli, the owner of a Stradivarius, proves to Lourenço that he is the one who

Figure 3.6
The prosthetic eye finally
sees the bunda.

smells bad, since he is the only one to use the stinking bathroom. Following this line of thought, repetition with variation includes the multiple aspects of Lourenço's obsession. Most exchanges make reference to the stench from the backed-up drain—a leitmotif relative to capitalism's worship of filthy lucre, since money, the alienated by-product of labor, equals feces—and to the bunda. Even as the quest for the bunda becomes intertwined with the stench, Lourenço acknowledges that the quest is the only reason for him to eat at a place where the food doesn't agree with him. Conversely, another object, the prosthetic eye, is endowed with power. Once Lourenço acquires the prosthetic eye he flashes it to test the interlocutor's reaction. The owner who sells it to him says the eye has seen it all, but Lourenço thinks otherwise because it has not been exposed to the bunda. Lourenço asks the waitress with whom he is infatuated to bend down, and he flashes the eye at her backside. Upon being discovered, he wonders whether the waitress is offended by the eye or his offer of money to see it.

The Brazilian expression *olho da bunda* reinforces the interrelation between voyeurism and sexuality by bringing about the idea of viewing as penetration as well as the interdiction of sodomy, even in terms of heterosexuality, since the practice precludes reproduction. The psychoanalytical equation of money with feces explains Lourenço's obsession with the backed-up drain.[11] The moral indictment of usury sheds light on the interconnection between the drain and hell, and the eye's rich symbolism ranges from the western connotations of knowledge to a self-reflexive reference to the voyeurism of the cinematic apparatus.[12] Either way, the expression *olho da bunda* opens up the paradoxical nature of the limit between the inside and the outside, the drain and the body. Thus, *olho da bunda* refers to the in-between, the cavernous outside and inside, epitomized by the throat and the ear (Derrida, *Margins of Philosophy*, xx). Moreover, the tubes (veins, arteries, intestines) that traverse the body establish a similarity with the drainage system.

Yet, when a client observes that the prosthetic eye is the eye of God, Lourenço promptly denies it, saying it is the eye of the other. According to Lourenço, the drain communicates with hell, so the paradoxical limit between the inside and the outside suggested by the expresssion *olho da bunda* explains his final moments as he drags himself to the latticed cover of the drain, which resembles the iris of an eye and thus reconnects the different layers of rich symbolism. The drain is connected with the capitalist alienation of labor and with usury as filthy lucre. In terms of the religious condemnation of usury, the drain symbolizes the gates of hell. The stench of the drain foreshadows a crescendo. The drain takes on a life of its own when it overflows. It commands Lourenço's attention when he unsuccessfully attempts to fill it up with sand and cement. As its latticed cover is reminiscent of an eye, its connotations expand to include the Panopticon and God's eye, reinforcing the religious overtones. Finally, the expression *olho da bunda* allows for the incorporation of sexuality, the paradoxical site where the inside and the outside meet, in the object of Lourenço's quest.

Lourenço's compulsive behavior suggests the endless repetition of trauma. But approaches to trauma differ. According to Freud, the traumatized individual repeats the repressed material as a contemporary experience.[13] According to Georges Bataille, however, not only does violent trauma constitute the self, it also integrates individuals and society through erotic or sacrificial violence (in Boulter, 154). Considering the sacrificial nature of the ending and the syncopated rhythm resulting from narratives structured in serial but static repetition (ibid.), *O cheiro do ralo* appears to subscribe to Bataille's thesis.

Unlike *O homen que copiava*, *O cheiro* partakes of the five characteristics that Deleuze identifies in the postwar new image (*Cinema 1*, 210–212). Both the novel and the film follow a voyage form, since despite the routine, Lourenço seems to have embarked on a path of moral degradation. Despite the structure of repetition with variation resulting from the daily exchanges with his clients, their sheer variety allows for a dispersive situation that is all the more evident in the novel, given that the strong intertextual component reminds us of the Barthesian death of the author. By omitting secondary plot lines to construct a linear plot, Dahlia in the movie regresses into the logic of cause-effect of realism.

The movie and the novel faithfully depict the protagonist's progressive moral deterioration. In addition, the links between the discreet parts of Lourenço's venality are weak. The security agent, the married woman, and the waitress-secretary all engage in commercial transactions that render their characters dispensable, while Lourenço's lack of interest in their history or emotional lives robs them of interiority. Clichés appear not only in filmic representations of such attitudes to life as the fatalistic accep-tance of events in "A vida é dura" (Life is hard), but more importantly, every character becomes a cliché. From the venally adulterous married woman to the helpless retiree, from the desperate drug addict to the callous youth who invokes class attitudes to sell a rake, the characters are set up as archetypes. The slim plot line hinges on the repeated transactions.

In contradistinction to the ambivalence regarding the meaning of the drain, which only weakens the narrative, Dhalia structures the movie in a paratactical juxtaposition of exchanges. These transactions follow a pattern of repetition with variation that highlights the protagonist's train of thought as he devises different strategies to bilk his clients. Lourenço's demise reads like a chronicle of a death foretold: he severs emotional ties, and his interpersonal exchanges become increasingly reified and violent. In sum, by offering a scathing critique of contemporary Brazilian mores, Dhalia's *O cheiro do ralo* remains faithful to the attacks on neoliberalism that are typical in the Cinema da Retomada.

PART TWO
ROAD MOVIES

CHAPTER FOUR
THE PARADOXICAL EFFECT OF THE DOCUMENTARY

Walter Salles's *Central do Brasil*

As one of the most successful and financially viable of the films I discuss in this book, Walter Salles's melodramatic *Central do Brasil* (*Central Station*, 1998) apparently follows the industrial Hollywood model, and it has earned many awards. The generic conventions of the road movie signal the transition between the classic Hollywood model, which Deleuze defines as the movement-image, and the unscripted allure of the journey, as per Deleuze's time-image.[1] The inclusion of generic conventions of the documentary (interviews showing multiple points of view, attention to historical time, shooting on location, long takes in real time) and especially of the observational documentary allows for fusion with the conventions of fiction films (shorthand for the generic category of "drama," which relies on in-depth development of realistic characters dealing with emotional themes that lead to inner conflict or conflict with others or society in general). In addition to the similarities between the road movie and the postwar image, *Central do Brasil* underscores the fusion between conventions of the documentary and neorealism. Finally, the affective reaction elicited by the conventions of melodrama is reinforced by the pull of the close-up in the series of interviews. Thus Salles's film presents a synergy that arguably dates from the impact of the legacies of the documentary and neorealism on the New Latin American Cinema and Cinema Novo.

Figure 4.1
Intensive (passionate) face: Ana's anger at Josué's father.

Central do Brasil opens at Rio de Janeiro's main train station, as Dora (Fernanda Montenegro), a retired teacher who makes ends meet by writing letters for her illiterate customers, sets up business at her folding table. Among her clients is Ana (Soia Lira), intent on writing her estranged husband because her nine-year-old son, Josué (Vinícius de Oliveira), wants to meet him.

Unbeknownst to her clients, Dora entertains her neighbor Irene (Marília Pêra) by allowing her to decide which letters, if any, Dora will mail. A few days later mother and son return, requesting to change their message. The boy irritates Dora by sticking the metallic point of his top into her table, so Dora is relieved to seem them leave. As they cross the street Josué accidentally drops the wooden top he had been playing with. Letting go of his mother, he runs toward the sidewalk to pick it up. His mother hesitates, and she is run over by a bus. When Josué reappears at Dora's stand, she refuses to let him change the letter once again, fully aware that he is penniless. On the following morning, Pedrão (Otávio Agusto), the security agent at the station, notices Josué and suggests selling the boy to an organization that places orphans abroad—in fact, an organ-trafficking business—and splitting the earnings. Dora complies, returning with a huge, brand-new TV set. Sensing the crime, her close friend and neighbor Irene warns Dora about the real nature of the organization. After a restless night, Dora locates Josué and cunningly manages to escape with the boy in tow.

At this point, the generic conventions of the roadie take over, since Dora must travel to the arid Northeast to deliver the boy to his father. The first leg of the journey takes place in a bus. After Dora lulls herself to sleep by sipping wine, Josué takes to the bottle and becomes disruptive. Publicly shamed, Dora decides to let him continue on his own, leaving instructions with the driver and placing all her money in his knapsack. Far from being asleep, Josué follows Dora, leaving the knapsack behind. Distraught, Dora stops several vehicles and they continue their journey with a wholesome truck driver, César (Othon Bastos), who fears Dora's affection and leaves them stranded a couple of days later. Desperate, Dora exchanges her watch for another ride, and the pair mingles with pilgrims on the way to Bom Jesus do Norte. Upon arrival at the shrine, exhausted and hungry, Dora berates Josué, who flees into the crowd. Dora chases him into the sanctuary, where she faints. On the following morning Dora awakens on Josué's lap. At this point, he takes charge by setting up the letter-writing business, which affords them the means to eat, rent a room, and even buy some clothes. Dora takes Josué to his father's ranch, only to discover that the father has moved into a neighboring development. Once again, after arriving at the address where they expect to meet Josué's father, Dora and Josué learn that he has left, ironically, hoping to find Ana in Rio. Seeing that they had been making inquiries about his father, one of Josué's stepbrothers invites them home, where they meet the other brother. Dora delivers Ana's letter, which remains by the last one they received from their father. On the following morning, Dora leaves. Josué runs out just in time to see the bus depart. The film closes with the voice-over of a changed Dora recalling their adventures in a letter to Josué.

Adhering to the generic conventions of the road movie, the female lead's hardened heart changes during the journey, influenced by the pilgrims and by the boy's and her misadventures. Salles engages in cultural critique as he establishes a counterpoint between the amoral and violent environment of Central Station that condones killing a youth for stealing a Walkman as well as selling orphans to organ traffickers and the pristine landscape of the Northeast that allows for redemption through religion, good deeds, and hard work. While Josué's quest for his unknown father propels the action, the road movie affords him a number of possible father figures (the evangelical driver, the peasant who purchased his father's ranch, the worker staying in the house Josué's father won in the urban development) who invariably disappoint him. Thus, the traditional father figure is superseded by the filial connection established with his brothers.

Usually in road movies, dissatisfied or distressed characters embark on a journey that results in an open-ended, meandering plot structure. Dora's harrowing rescue of Josué predetermines their flight, pursued as she is initially by the agents of the organ-trafficking organization and later by the security agent of the station who enticed her into selling the boy. The episodic plot structure favors the depiction of alternative lifestyles based on trust and sharing. Such lifestyles appear in the experiences with César, the evangelical truck driver, as well as in scenes of sharing food with the pilgrims on the truck and of Josué's brothers. The typical frame compositions that incorporate vehicles' windshields or side windows to suggest the driver's point of view, particularly evident in scenes of the truck driver, underscore the distance traversed during the journey by showcasing the landscape. More importantly, they allude to Josué's desperate need for a father figure, especially when César allows Josué, who is sitting on his lap, to drive.

The generic conventions of the road movie feed into the characterization of the Deleuzian time-image organized around the open possibilities offered by a voyage. In contradistinction to the movement-image, based on a clockwork type of plot, the time-image favors a rambling journey, and its episodic nature results in the condemnation of the traditional plot. The episodic plot, in turn, allows the protagonists to explore different social organizations. The aleatory nature of the journey, depending as Dora and Josué do on the kindness of strangers to get a ride, reinforces the dispersive nature of the situation and the deliberately weak links. Thus, rather than focusing on causal relations, the new aesthetics explores the situation itself, emphasizing the dispersive nature of reality. Moreover, the protagonists record reality rather than react to it.

The episodic structure of the film's plot is reinforced by the conventions of melodrama.[2] Melodrama is commonly defined as a dramatic narrative with emotional effects marked by musical accompaniment. The orchestration of dramatic situations tends to be complemented by a tug on emotions (Elsaesser, 172). Melodrama may include shock tactics, illustrated in the film by the letters and the pent-up violence unleashed in the execution of the youth at the train station. By drawing on emotions, melodrama elicits an affective response, and it most often reinforces the digressive nature of the plot line (Roston).

Dora's remorse for having sold Josué to an organ-trafficking organization is conveyed with much emotion, which is further developed in her subsequent ploys to rescue the child. The horror of her action is brought home when Dora realizes that the blond little girl they met upon arriving at the so-called agency is nowhere to be seen. The plot turns on sudden reversals of fortune—a lost knapsack, an unredeemable bus ticket, and César's departure. Melodrama blatantly plays on the audience's sympathies, as is evident every time Josué prepares to meet his father. The final parallel scenes with Dora sobbing as she writes to Josué and the child crying as he chases the bus in which she leaves attest to the end of their sojourn and the appeal to the audience's feelings. By focusing on the problem of organ trafficking, a late modern version of slavery's inhumanity' that reduces the body to market value, *Central do Brasil* traces Dora's journey from the gravest fault, underscored by the new television set she purchases with her earnings, to redemption. While such an abhorrent crime may lead the audience to resist accepting Dora's implication, she, like most other bystanders, condones the execution of the petty thief, which should further move the audience into horror at the naturalization of violence. Melodrama allows Salles to posit an ethical imperative, thereby generating active thinking and feeling in cinema (Gutiérrez-Albilla, 153).

Melodrama traditionally flourishes during periods of social and ideological crisis (Elsaesser, 167). Indeed, *Central do Brasil* alludes to the devastating results of the imposition of neoliberal economic policies.[3] The ambiguity typically found in melodrama appears when Dora and Josué's siblings miss their respective fathers, but they do not deny their bad memories. The film reinscribes the nuclear family only to subvert it, for Josué's father is missing and Dora's is long dead.

While Salles's previous experience in the documentary led to scouting for locations, modifying the script accordingly, and resorting to hidden cameras, his experience in advertising resulted in breath-taking photography. The documentary scene opens with a close-up of a sobbing middle-age woman, Nobre, who proves her "exceptional talent as an amateur actress" (Nagib, *Brazil on Screen*, 40) by saying, "Querido, o meu coração é seu. Não importa o que você seja ou o que tenha feito, te amo. Esses anos todos que você ficar aí dentro trancado eu também vou ficar trancada aqui fora te esperando" ("My darling, my heart belongs to you,

Figure 4.2
Intensive (passionate) face: Socorro Nobre's
heartbreak about her beloved's imprisonment.

no matter what you've done, I still love you. While you're locked in there, all
those years, I'll be locked out here, waiting for you").

After a contrasting shot of the throngs of people passing by the station, the camera then focuses on a scrawny old man, apparently riddled
with Parkinson's disease. The man's face fills the screen as he states halt-
ingly, "Seu Zé Amaro, muito obrigado pelo que você fez comigo. Eu confiei
em você e você me enganou. Até a chave do meu apartamento você car-
regou" ("Zé Amaro, thanks a lot for what you did to me. I trusted in you and
you cheated me. You even ran off with my apartment key"). Thus, in retrospect, we learn that the woman, earlier, was dictating a letter. The pathos
of her voice is supplanted by the sarcasm evident in the man's accusation
of the betrayal of his trust. This tension is exacerbated when the nine-
year-old protagonist of the film appears with his mother, who now dictates
a third letter: "Jesus, você foi a pior coisa que já me aconteceu. Eu não tô
te escrevendo pra te dar satisfação da minha vida. Só escrevo porque o
teu filho Josué pediu. Eu contei pra ele que você não vale nada, mas ainda
assim o menino pôs na idéia que quer te conhecer" ("Dear Jesús, you're
the worst thing to happen to me. I'm only writing because your son Josué
asked me to. I told him you're worthless, and yet he still wants to meet
you"). As in many other cases, Dora, the retired schoolteacher who writes

letters for a living, interrupts the mother's monologue by requesting an address. This act reminds viewers of the larger social network. Next comes a young man of mixed race who dictates, "Meu tesão ... Sentir o seu corpo junto do meu, carnes se unindo naquela cama de motel, nosso suor se misturando. Eu ainda me sinto, me sinto me" ("My hot pussy ... Your body against mine, rolling around in the motel bed, our sweat boiling, me, still ... I still feel").

This montage of voices and situations that implicate the characters in one another's lives and in larger social networks is extremely effective. The addressee's physical location is absent in this scene of sexual desire, and the next sequence stresses the lack of a precise address when a young girl offers, "Terceira casa depois da padaria, Mimoso, Pernambuco" (Third house after the bakery, Mimoso, Pernambuco). Each scene works with the leitmotif of the address, reducing the information of each element in the series to a close-up and a destination. Thus a middle-age man states, "Cansanção, Bahia"; a very sweet old woman smiles and says, "Carangola, Minas Gerais"; a young girl says, "Município de Relutaba, Ceará"; and the last middle-age man utters, "Muzanbinho, Minas Gerais."

The documentary approach of the initial scenes is underscored by the faces of the nonprofessional actors, ranging from Vinícius de Oliveira, who was a shoeshine boy, to those who asked Dora to write letters for them when she set up her table on the first day of the shoot (Shaw, 163). The initial letter-writing scene was shot with a small, generally concealed, camera (James, "Heartbreaks," 15), pointing to the ethical considerations inherent in the observational mode. Since the filmmaker should be unobtrusive, to what extent does the film respect the lives of others? Or, as Nichols asks (39), does it use them to prove someone else's discourse? That concealment is consistent with other characteristic features, namely, synchronizing of sound and long takes, presenting the voice of the observed in indirect verbal address, emphasizing impartiality by means of close-ups, suggesting intimate detail and lived experience as it illuminates the behavior of subjects within social formations during periods of personal crisis (Burton, 4). Since the interaction between observer and observed is apparently kept to a minimum, documentary aspects are indirectly woven into the picture, in that, for example, nonprofessional actors Nobre and de Oliveira follow a script that is not too different from so-called real lives. In other words, these are social actors representing themselves (Nichols, 42).

Deborah Shaw argues that the initial contrast between the crowd scenes and the customers at Dora's table prevents character development;[4] Nichols's characterization of the observational documentary, though, proves that the infusion of documentary techniques exerts an affective impact on the audience. In other words, by presenting fiction as conveyed through the conventions of observational documentaries, Salles elicits an affective reaction of the audience, which is expected to care about the plight of the nordestinos. To an extent, Lúcia Nagib appears to agree with Shaw, insofar as Nagib argues that the range of peculiar racial features and regional variations contributes to a portrayal of the country as devoid of prejudice. Furthermore, Nagib adds, the representation of Brazilians as a cheerful and sensual people despite their suffering ultimately obstructs political action (40). Yet, these assertions can be countered by emphasizing the affective impact of the close-ups, due to which the scant development of their stories becomes all the more frustrating. Moreover, despite and because of their sanitized representation, the close-ups draw us into caring for the illiterate who pay Dora to write for them.

Salles incorporates the conventions of the documentary into the screenplay as well as the style. According to Salles, the rawness, honesty, and beauty of the letters dictated by the correspondents exerted a significant influence on the script because they conveyed a need to be heard and brought an incredible emotional power to the story (James, "Heartbreaks," 15). Naturally, ethical concerns would explain the omission of the content of so many letters. The fusion of fiction and conventions of the documentary is particularly apparent in the sequences representing public expressions of devotion, since Salles acknowledged in a 2004 interview in *The Guardian* that they rewrote the screenplay when they became aware of the religious processions typical of that region of Brazil.[5] Fittingly, as the film crew decided to work with real pilgrims rather than develop a reenactment, the pilgrimage scene became the thing itself, shot over the course of a night in a single take (James, "Heartbreaks," 15). Adhering to Burton's requirements (4), the shot had synchronous sound, and the interaction between the observer and the observed was minimal because Walter Carvalho, the cinematographer, relied on the natural light of the candles held by thousands of pilgrims (Shaw, 165). In other words, Salles was aware of the impact of the fusion of documentary techniques that ironically both emphasize the illusion of objectivity and draw an affective reaction from the audience.

Figure 4.3
Reflexive (surface) face:
Grateful bride's bliss.

The observational mode is particularly relevant to describe *Central do Brasil* because such features as the apparent unity in determining the observer's location and especially that location's three-dimensional fullness coincide with the aspects of classic narrative fiction and the historical world that Nichols regards as crucial to the overlap between fiction and film (38, 107). What Nichols does not anticipate is how these traits can be present in the pseudo-documentary sections. Thus, the second set of close-ups and the gleeful messages of the pilgrims at Bom Jesus do Norte are set against the drama of the initial letter-writing scene. As in the first set of close-ups, the ontological status of the talking heads is unclear. Are these real letters? Are these nonprofessional actors performing their own stories? Or performing those of others? Similarly, as in the initial section, while some offer a story, the elision of the content of some messages generates suspense. For instance, a young man states, "Criselda, Criseldinha, vim lá de Itabaiana . . . Até aqui, a pé pela estrada" ("Criseldhina, I've come here from Itabaiana. I walked all the way. Along the road"). A young bride says, "Tou aqui em Bom Jesus pra agradecer a promessa que fiz do Benício aceitar casar comigo" ("I'm fulfilling the vow I made to come here if Bernicio agreed to marry me").

A mature woman wearing a blue polka-dot dress beams with satisfaction: "Obrigada, Bom Jesus, pela graça alcançada de o meu marido ter

Figure 4.4
Reflexive (surface) face:
Happiest man on earth.

largado a cachaça" ("Thank you, Jesus, for answering my prayers. My husband has stopped drinking"). The audience may wonder why an emaciated middle-aged man rocking with laughter says, "Leontina Emerentina . . . Já posso ser o homem mais feliz do mundo" ("Leontina Emerintina, I am now the happiest man in the world").

However, in a melodramatic turn, another middle-aged man worries about his son: "Já faz quatro anos que ele já saiu" ("It's four years since he's left"). To the extent that the series of close-ups conjures the conventions of observational documentaries, it encourages viewer belief. Ultimately, observational documentaries afford the viewer a sense of looking in, overhearing the experiences of others, witnessing the rhythms of daily life, examining spatial relationships among people and their possessions, and hearing the "grain" that distinguishes one native speaker from another (Nichols, 42).

A montage of fragments follows these messages, mirroring the initial shot at the station. A young girl says, "Lembrança para minha mãe [Love to my mother], Maria Adalgiza Bezerra." A man wearing a cap addresses his letter to "Josefa Maria da Silva" in "São Bento do Una." A girl offers a dedication "pra meu noivo [to my fiancé], João Pedro da Silva" in "São Paulo." And two brothers wearing almost identical straw hats address a letter to their father, "José Alves da Silva." The section ends with a bang as the last client takes his hat off, almost bragging, "Obrigado, Menino Jesus, pela graça alcançada, de ter feito chover esse ano lá na roça. Vim a Bom Jesus e soltei dez foguete colorido em sua homenagem. Sebastiano" ("Thank you baby Jesus, for answering our prayers. Thank you for bringing us rain. I came to Bom Jesus and set off ten colored rockets in your honor. Sebastiano"). In sum, the details of these letters reinforce the delight on people's faces, the object of the close-up. The suppression of the content of a number of letters in both series of close-ups whets the audience's curiosity but also places those letters under erasure.[6] As we expect each subject to dictate a letter, the fragmentary nature of these texts underscores the elisions that preclude interpretation.

Two more instances of close-ups complement the letter-writing sequences. By presenting the ride among pilgrims in the back of the truck through a panning shot, the real time of documentary is invoked even as the illusion of the documentary develops from a montage of shots focusing on the conventional behavior of pilgrims. Some chant, others pray, some eat, and still others remain silent. In contrast to the pan and montage of the scenes in which Dora chases Josué through the tide of pilgrims, the camera focuses on different individuals whose chants are typical of the traditional repertoire of Catholic pilgrimages. While Salles's selection of chants appears to emphasize the virtue of prayer and the admission of guilt, he underscores the typical negotiation established between the pilgrim who requests a favor and the sacred figure who may or may not grant it. Thus, a woman prays, "Obrigado, obrigado, Jesus, eu tô te pedindo, te orando, com todo o meu coração. Jesus, com toda minha alma, Jesus" ("Thank you, thank you, Jesus. Here I am, Lord. I beg of you. I'm praying with all my heart, with all my soul, Jesus"). A Franciscan follows, "Abençoa o meu povo" ("Bless my people"). A male pilgrim follows, "Me perdoa, Senhor, que sou um pecador. Pelo sangue de Cristo, Senhor. Olha as minhas dificuldades . . . o meu sangue na veia . . . no meu corpo" ("I'm a sinner, Jesus. Pardon. For the blood of Christ, look at the hardships I must bear! I suffer in my flesh, my bone, my blood, in my body").

As in a structure of call and response, these individual chants are set against other voices, "Viva a Virgem Santíssima!" ("Hail Mary"). This pseudo-documentary device also appears in shots within the sanctuary under the guise of representing Dora's point of view as she is about to faint.

The affective impact of all these scenes matters as it is heightened

Figure 4.5
Dora faints due to hunger
and overexertion.

by the techniques deployed in observational cinema. This deployment of
unmediated and unfettered access to the world ironically depends on the
absent presence of the filmmaker (Nichols, 43). Indeed, the exploration
of the contemporary sertão is so compelling because of the constraints
involved in the representation of an identifiable historical reality.[7] The
documentary technique draws an affective impact from the audience that
is further reinforced by the effect of the close-up.

The power of the close-up is a matter of some dispute among film critics. Minh-ha acknowledges the partiality of the close-up (34), and Deleuze
notes variations in its affective power. The film's opening close-ups show
intense faces that convey desire or power through an overriding emotion
such as sorrow, irony, annoyance, or sexual arousal. The audience's interpretation of these facial expressions is reinforced by an awareness of the
content of the respective letters, but the audience can only surmise the
emotions conveyed by the close-ups of the subjects for the letters pared
down to an addressee or a destination. Thus, even though the audience
cannot establish a link between a subject's facial expression and the content of his or her message, the sense that most characters are beaming
with satisfaction and their messages refer to the fulfillment of their vows
would allow us to consider these close-ups in terms of Deleuze's reflective
faces expressing different degrees of happiness, bliss, or admiration. As in

the first series of letters dictated, these close-ups on the back of the truck and at the pilgrimage stress one main aspect of each subject's behavior; in other words, the close-ups emphasize the myriad facets of desire, and the series emphasizes both the poignancy of the plights of those dictating the letters and the passionate beliefs of the pilgrims.

The affective power of the close-up is underscored by montage. In the drama of Eisenstein's *Battleship Potemkin*, perhaps the most memorable scenes are the close-ups of the people of Odessa who show their adhesion to the mutinous sailors and their horror at the massacre by the czarist soldiers marching down the stairs. Salles's film deploys a similar serial aspect in the pseudo-documentary scenes of *Central do Brasil*. The serial close-ups of the pilgrims on the truck and at Bom Jesus do Norte metonymically allude to the pilgrims' needs, expressed through chanting and praying. However, the multiple renderings of desire are replaced by different manifestations of happiness and gratitude in the close-ups of those requesting a letter to render their appreciation for the favors granted.

Directors may transfer their penchant for the close-up as a reflective or intensive surface to things, thus converting them into icons. That would seem to be the case regarding the close-up of the letters that Josué's parents wrote to one another: these are placed beneath the picture of the two as a couple, a placement that is ironic since the letters failed to reach the respective addressees and instead signal the frustrations of the past. As the letters finally arrive at the home of the siblings, they imply closure and signal a new beginning along the time-worn melodramatic convention of "the changing of the guard," that is, passing the torch so the next generation will carry on. Yet, while the diegesis establishes a clear-cut line between good and evil, Josué suspects that Dora may have added the words about his father's wish to meet him. Therefore, the truth/falsehood dichotomy is deconstructed by the Derridean supplement, that is, the pious white lie.[8]

There are several ways to link neorealism and the documentary in *Central do Brasil*. In his interview with Andrew, Salles acknowledges the shared features as an unintended influence of documentary practices. For instance, by including the stories of the people the crew met on the street, Salles's practice was no different from that of Italian neorealism. Furthermore, observational filmmakers first posited their kinship with fiction in relation to Italian neorealism (Nichols, 42). The beauty of the images and the documentary tone of *Central do Brasil* arise from its being shot on location, another shared feature of the two movements.

In contextualizing the movie, *Central do Brasil* continues the rich
tradition of Latin American films focused on the situations of poverty-
stricken children. A good many of these feature neorealist elements such
as the use of nonprofessional actors and outdoor locations. The tradition
unquestionably opens with Luis Buñuel's focus on the Mexican underclass
in *Los olvidados* (*The Young and the Damned*, 1950) and Birri's collaborative documentary *Tire dié* (*Toss Me a Dime*, 1960). In Brazil, Salles's film
has been compared to Héctor Babenco's classic *Pixote* (1981), a bleak
portrayal of the predicament of children living on the street.[9] Additionally, the shared neorealist detachment allows for gaining insights into
the protagonists' subjectivity through an objective examination of their
gestures (Traverso, 183). Likewise, Fernando Meirelles's *Cidade de Deus*
(*City of God*, 2002) exposes the ever-present violence in Brazilian favelas.
In Colombia, director Victor Gaviria's *Rodrigo D no futuro* (*Rodrigo D No
Future*, 1990) and *La vendedora de rosas* (*The Rose Seller*, 1998) dwell
on the impact of drug trafficking among the underprivileged, while Barbet
Schroeder re-creates the plight of Colombian minors as hit men in *La
virgen de los sicarios* (*Our Lady of the Assassins*, 2000). In sum, the influence of neorealist concerns is evident in the film production of the 1990s,
since the plight of children continues unabated.

Beyond the neorealist aspects of film production in the 1990s—among
them the penchant for nonprofessional actors, shooting on location with
natural lighting, and the focus on the underclass, particularly children—
the fusion of generic conventions of fiction (drama) and the documentary
resurfaced in Brazilian film production of the 1990s. In *Central do Brasil*
the fusion is a consequence of Salles's intertextual references to Cinema
Novo.[10] Indeed, Salles has acknowledged the influence of dos Santos's
Vidas secas, which deals with people thrown off their lands into a life of
nomadism and exile (Cowan, 72). As evidenced in Salles's interview with
Andrew in *The Guardian*, the inscription and subversion of Cinema Novo
is evident in his portrayal of the backlands, presented as a quest for
the father, which involves that of national identity, and illustrated by the
similarity between father (*pai*) and country (*pais*). Yet, in *Central do Brasil*
the land takes precedence over the ever-receding father figure. Salles's
sertão is very different from the deserted land in dos Santos's *Vidas secas*.
Perhaps the renewed engagement with classical narrative structures and
the visual glamour associated with industrial cinema may be attributed to
the contemporary imperative to appeal to national and international audiences (Traverso, 176).

In conclusion, Salles's *Central do Brasil* weaves fiction film with the conventions of the documentary. By dwelling on illiteracy, senseless violence like the killing of the youth at the station, and organ trafficking, Salles focuses on stories taken from the raw. By deploying conventions of the documentary to recount fiction in instances such as Dora's trance during the procession with the camera spinning around her, Salles alludes to the Cuban synergy between documentary and feature films. This synergy, in turn, is underscored by the observational mode of the documentary that conveys their textual and referential similarities. By creating the illusion of transparent access, Salles's work exerts a powerful affective impact on the audience. Furthermore, the affective draw of the observational documentary is reinforced by the deployment of the close-up in the pseudo-documentary sections of *Central do Brasil*.

While these techniques speak to Salles's indebtedness to the documentary, neorealism, and Cinema Novo, the affective impact emphasizes the audience's frustration at the melodramatic denouement. Even though the fraternal reunion implies a happy ending, Josué's brothers are squatting in a government house. Their apparent well-being is fragile, for their prospects are determined by the nature of the development, which Salles considers perilous, given the entrenched inequities arising from the land-ownership structure (in James, "Heartbreaks," 15). Salles adds that these developments tend to be isolated, as the lack of work opportunities turns them into ghost towns within five or six years.

The dire poverty among the nordestinos whom Dora and Josué meet on their way, set in the context of the high rate of illiteracy, is suggested by the clients at the station. Escape from the urban dystopia brought about by neoliberalism and the preceding rural-to-urban migrations remains all the more tenuous as the representation of the sertão remains fixed in the past.[11] To that extent, Salles's portrayal of the nordestinos as homage to dos Santos's *Vidas secas* suggests that the inscription of Cinema Novo ultimately backfires: it underscores the sense that there is no exit. The lack of investment in infrastructure, industries, and projects that would allow for self-reliance leaves nordestinos ultimately at the mercy of nature. Therefore, rural exodus can only continue unabated. Nonetheless, the affective impact resulting from the fusion of the fiction film and the observational documentary, reinforced by the subjective engagement of the close-up, intensifies the audience's empathy toward the nordestinos, thus calling for a more urgent resolution of their plight.

CHAPTER FIVE
TWIN PIQUES

The Double Discourse of Carlos Sorín's *El camino de San Diego*

Carlos Sorín is an important transitional figure whose work bridges the gap between the most representative directors of the previous generation and those associated with the New Argentine Cinema.[1] Sorín departs from the idea of cinema as a revolutionary tool as well as from the industrial model that focuses on issues of the middle class in Buenos Aires. Instead of reinforcing the stereotype of Argentina as the leisure class in Buenos Aires that European and Argentine audiences have come to expect, Sorín tackles the problems of the have-nots, of ethnic groups, and of Argentines living in other regions.

With the possible exception of *El gato desaparece* (*Missing Cat*, 2011), Sorín's cinematic production is synonymous with the road movie. As such, he will probably be remembered for expanding the Argentine visual and narrative imaginary to encompass Patagonia and northeastern Argentina. Though Sorín has been critiqued for inscribing an identitarian imperative that refers to a description of a national ethos, this imperative is hard to shake off in an aesthetics that deploys neorealist and documentary features such as nonprofessional actors, on-location shooting, and long takes. These techniques reinforce the link with the features of the New Argentine Cinema, which thrives on presenting protagonists as witnesses of rambling plot lines.

Such an expansion of the national imaginary appeared in Sorín's first film, *La película del rey* (1986), which was inspired by the difficulties that prevented Juan Fresán from finishing *La nueva Francia* (1972). Fresán's film focused on a Frenchman, Oreille Antoine de Tourens, who around 1861 proclaimed himself king of Patagonia. Sorín's film self-reflexively alludes to the roadie in terms of the hardships involved in the transportation and accommodation of the cast and crew of *La película del rey*. Surreal final shots of mannequins standing in for actors in the wind-swept land stress the quixotic nature of the project, and humor pervades *La película del rey*. The grotesque is evident after the high-pitched priest who runs the orphanage where the cast is staying blesses their meager breakfast and the plump prostitute bursts out laughing. Such moments of pathos following irony typify the self-reflexive *La película del rey*, as is poignantly reinforced when the camera focuses on the wistful face of an orphaned Mapuche boy framed by the window as he looks out, suggesting that at his early age he already has a deeper knowledge about the ways of an original people who may or may not have chosen a French king than the urbanite and inexperienced director.

Sorín's *Historias mínimas* (2002) presents three stories set in the arid area of Santa Cruz. It shows a neorealist influence like what we have seen in Salles—nonprofessional actors, on-location shooting, and long takes. In one of the intertwined stories, the protagonist, Don Justo Benedictis (Antonio Benedicti in real life), a retiree well past age sixty-five, has lost his dog. He hitchhikes two hundred miles to the place his dog was last seen. His quest is fueled by guilt. He believes his canine companion abandoned him because Benedictis failed to check on a dog that he accidentally ran over. Another, separate story line follows a traveling salesman who is intent on seducing a young widow by bringing a decorated birthday cake to her son, René. Wondering whether René can also be a girl's name, the salesman has the decoration changed from a soccer scene to a turtle. When the salesman sees his intended with another man, he gobbles up the cake, only to discover that the purported rival was in fact her brother. The third story line follows two women who are preparing to compete in a grotesque television program reminiscent of the 1950s to be broadcast by the local channel. Since the woman who wins the electric appliance does not have access to electricity, she agrees to exchange her prize with the greedy competitor who won the professional makeup case.

Sorín's next film, *Bombón, el perro* (2004), is also set in wind-swept

Patagonia. This story centers on fifty-two-year-old Juan "Coco" Villegas (Juan Villegas), a mechanic recently laid off from a gas station where he worked for twenty years. Villegas attempts to make a living by carving handles for knives from different types of wood and bone while he looks for another job. The situation evokes sympathy from the audience, for he is a protagonist who cannot compete with globalization, as represented by cheap imports coming from Brazil. Most striking in Sorín's *Bombón* is that Villegas is completely isolated: he hasn't seen his wife in twenty years. His daughter, who addresses him as Tucumano (from the northern province of Tucumán), yells at him for having turned up with a dog. While Villegas seems buried in contemporary anomie, he displays a traditional code of honor. He refuses to count the money at the bank, for instance, and he declines to check whether all of his belongings have been packed. He notably leaves his first job as a watchman without being paid because he empathizes with his predecessor on the job when the former employee returns drunk but promises to make good. Given Villegas's dire economic straits, his adherence to a code of honor to the extent of placing it above market relations is impressive.

Villegas travels, trying to sell his wares. He comes across Claudina (Claudina Fazzini), whose Mercedes has broken down on the way to the provincial city of Comodoro Rivadavia. Villegas tows the car about a hundred miles to the house of Claudina's mother, who is short of cash but repays the favor by giving Coco a pedigreed dog. Enter Bombón le Chien (named Gregorio in real life): despite Villegas's well-grounded reservations, Bombón commands attention. Walter Donado, the caretaker of a racetrack who plays himself, offers to supply his know-how as a dog handler as long as he and Villegas split the dog's hypothetical earnings. Indeed, when Bombón takes first and third prizes at his first show, Villegas discovers that offers to breed the dog are the real business. However, the dog's low libido puts an end to the two men's expectations.

Villegas remains in Bahia Blanca, which offers better prospects to find a job, while his friend takes care of the dog. When the ersatz Middle Eastern singer Susana (Rosa Valsecchi) tells Coco that dogs consumed by sadness die, Villegas returns just in time to track down Bombón, who escaped earlier that day. The search through a shantytown where people are rumored to eat dogs turns into a denunciation of substandard living conditions. Undernourished, whimpering dogs alternating with dead ones foreshadow a tragic ending. Villegas finds Bombón at a brick factory.[2] Significantly, the sounds that lead him to the dog are not those of distress but rather a result of Bombón's sexual performance, as Villegas peeps at the dogs coupling. Since Villegas was emasculated by the lack of a job, a place to stay, and a love interest, by overcoming his libido problems Bombón offers him the proverbial second chance. Insofar as Villegas might live off Bombón's services, the dog represents masculinity as a K-9 supplement in the Derridean sense.[3]

As is typical of roadies, the film follows Villegas spending most of his time traveling through the deserted landscape in his battered Estanciera (an Argentine Willys station wagon produced from 1956–1970). This travel is chronicled in a series of pan shots and close-ups that reinforce the affective pull of the film, working in combination with the audience's identification that arises from a diegesis of widespread intraclass economic crisis and the resulting need to barter. The economic crisis reinforces the romantic commonplace of Patagonia as a new frontier, a setting in which one must rely upon the generosity of strangers. Sorín describes the film as a fable. Despite this observation, even a cursory glance at the cast shows that the names of the characters are for the most part the actors' real names, in accordance with vérité traditions of using or seeming to use nonprofessional actors, location shooting, and a bare story about the working class in a state of extreme deprivation (Kolker, 17). *Bombón* subscribes to the tenets of neorealism but modifies them by accentuation of stories reflecting personal and social crisis, by melodramatic turns such as the dog's escape, by the use of comedy, and by the overriding function of music that guides the audience's reactions. From the moment Villegas and Donado make their pact, the film moves forward in accordance with the expectations of the buddy road movie. The reserved, polite, and almost obsequious Villegas encounters his Sancho Panza in the *gordo chanta* (stocky trickster) Donado.[4]

Most of Sorín's cinematic production but especially *Bombón* and *El camino de San Diego* are suffused with elements of the long tradition of the *grotesco criollo*, a theatrical style that arose during the transition between the generation of 1894, influenced by (Rubén Darío's) *modernismo* and *posmodernismo*, and the avant-garde generation of 1924.[5] The crisis at this juncture leads to a perception of the social order as alienating and unfair as well as an indirect challenge of its foundational myths (Kaiser-Lenoir, 8). The initial scene of the movie when the protagonist has to deliver the most valuable item of merchandise to bribe the security agent at the oil-drilling station who admonishes him for trespassing sets the stage for the film's commentary on public corruption, a theme that handily corresponds to the grotesco criollo. In a plot that explores the seedy world of dog shows and the market that sustains it, promoting food, vaccines, care, and fashion, Sorín's film stresses the grotesque in terms of individual lack of opportunities. The two men share the melodramatic ups and downs of a Laurel and Hardy team, even in vaudeville or burlesque aspects such as the encounter with the ersatz belly dancer whose performance only becomes more jarring when a tipsy Donado follows her, imitating a simulacra of a simulacra, and this leads to a brawl and lands him in jail with a black eye.

Sorín inscribes and subverts the main structural features of grotesco criollo texts as they are structured on trials that the subject cannot overcome. As is often the case in buddy movies, the second-rate protagonist's fate depends on someone or something else, in this case the dog's masculinity, rather than on his own resources. Moreover, while Villegas is sensitive and intuitive and seems aware of his predicament, his friend Donado illustrates the typical lack of awareness of the protagonist of the grotesco criollo. As Pelletieri suggests (56), that lack of awareness stymies any chance of real communication. Donado is a self-assured and almost cocky *porteño* (from Buenos Aires). He brags about his abilities but is incapable of taking care of the dog. His failure leads to Bombón's escape. Ultimately, the dialogic juxtaposition of the two men's ideologies produces an unresolved tension that only the plot's finale is able to bring into equilibrium. The dialogic tension between these characters propels the melodramatic turns of the diegesis.

In *La ventana* (2009), Sorín returns to the idea of a voyage set in the *pampas* just north of Patagonia, in a film that chronicles an elderly writer's last journey. As in more recent neorealism, ambiguity pervades key aspects of the film. Little information about the protagonist's life appears, for example, with minimal continuity in how each of the major characters—his housekeeper, maid, physician, and son—relates to him. Knowing that the protagonist, Antonio Larreta (1922–), is an established Uruguayan actor and writer, winner of the 1980 Premio Planeta for the novel *Volavérunt*, adds a self-reflexive twist to the film and underscores the concept of the active spectator that Sorín expects. Despite the beauty of the location and the counterpoints of the different perspectives, the sudden arrival of a group of bicycle-riding Spaniards undermines verisimilitude. As an unlikely deus ex machina, the bicycle riders who challenge high pampa grass by riding the hilly slopes locate the unconscious protagonist and thereby save his life. Their presence exposes the perils of co-production: the serendipity of the events, that is, the unlikely presence of the loud Spanish tourists, can only be explained in terms of the exigencies of international funding.

Finally, *El gato desaparece* (*Missing Cat*, 2011) marks a change as Sorín follows the thriller's generic conventions. The plot centers on an academic who is institutionalized due to a violent bout that prompted a legal process; he eventually returns home medicated, and the film conveys his wife's mounting fear.

Like *Bombón*, Sorín's *El camino de San Diego* (2006) is a roadie that presents the protagonist through his interplay with the environment, this time in northeastern Argentina. The structure of the buddy movie allows Sorín to compare belief systems, social classes, and (for the first time) nationalities. The film opens showing Tati Benítez (Ignacio Benítez) at work as a lumberjack. An extreme fan of Argentine soccer luminary Diego Maradona, Tati practices the star's footwork, knows all the trivia, and sports a tattoo of the soccer player on his arm and another one of Maradona's famous number 10 on his back. The latter tattoo creates a spectacular effect when he removes the striped T-shirt he wears that also bears the number 10. Tati's fanaticism is evident when he attempts to baptize his baby daughter with Maradona's name. After another baby girl, Tati's wife finally gives birth to a boy who could carry the idol's name. Soon after that, Tati loses his job. Taking a friend's advice, Tati begins to apprentice with a Guaraní carver. But life changes when, looking for wood, Tati recognizes an image of Maradona on the root of a fallen tree. After having the number 10 carved into the massive statue, Tati ponders delivering it to the recently inaugurated Boca Juniors museum.

Tati learns that Maradona has entered intensive care, presumably as a result of his long-standing drug addiction, and the pressure intensifies to hand-deliver the carving. Archival television broadcasts evidence the massive convergence of fans at the clinic, testifying to the historical reality of the events in which Tati is an anonymous actor. Wondering whether to deliver the carved root, Tati consults Señora Matilde (Silvia Fontelles), a self-made seer who advises him to go. Desperate, his wife (Paola Rotelo) asks the pastor (Hermano Otto Mosdien) to counsel Tati against taking the trip, but the pastor ultimately gives his benediction. As Tati leaves the forest, a coatí, golden butterflies, and his parrots all bid him farewell. This panoply of omens corresponds to Sorín's intention to represent Tati's life in Pozo Azul in the context of a fable, yet the leave-taking signals a clear shift in the plot as the film begins to adhere to the conventions of the road movie.[6]

The thousand-mile trip from Pozo Azul, a hamlet in northeastern

Figures 5.1 and 5.2
End of the forest fable. Courtesy Wandavisión.
Tati on the road. Courtesy Wandavisión.

Misiones province, to General Rodríguez, thirty-four miles west of Buenos Aires, involves several stages. Tati takes a bus from Pozo Azul to Oberá. There he gets a ride to San Javier in the back of a truck.

As his luck persists, Tati manages to convince an ambulance driver to take him to Paso de los Libres. By mistake he takes the bus to the Gauchito Gil sanctuary, where he meets Waguinho, a Brazilian truck driver who leaves him close to Maradona's country estate.

A local bus picks Tati up from the highway. On the last leg of the journey Tati walks some seven blocks in the company of a blind man who intends to sell lottery tickets to the crowds camped at the gates of the soccer star's residence.

As Tati dreams about meeting his idol in a green, well-lit area, the golf links at the property in General Rodríguez may thus foreshadow the realization of Tati's desire. Wondering how to deliver the carving, Tati pro-

Figure 5.3
Waguinho's truck, a symbol of power.
Courtesy Wandavisión.

Figure 5.4
Tati and Waguinho: Unlikely buddies.
Courtesy Wandavisión.

ceeds to the security booth. Reluctantly, the employee stores the gift in the booth for a long time, but it suddenly disappears. Anguished, Tati runs toward the gate only to realize that someone is taking it into the property. Shortly afterward, Maradona leaves the premises in an ambulance. Tati agonizes, wondering whether his idol received the gift. Though Sorín slowly erodes Tati's confidence in meeting D10S (God, spelled with Maradona's number 10), the object of Tati's quest, the ambiguity of an employee's tepid reassurance that Maradona might have taken the carving since it does not seem to be in the residence allows Tati to rejoice. As the fans disperse, Tati tells the blind lottery man whom he earlier helped that he hopes Maradona will like the carving. Feeling grateful, the man gives him a lottery ticket, assuring him that his luck will turn. Despite all the hints that allow the audience to realize that Maradona did not become aware of the carving, the movie stresses the hope of magical thought by focusing on Tati's anticipation of a different future, as suggested by the ascending circles in the flight pattern of a flock of birds.

As per the generic conventions of the roadie and certainly underscored by the grotesco criollo, the journey allows for social critique. Sorín's film emphasizes the effect of the unabated economic crisis, especially but not exclusively on the poor. For instance, throughout the film the camera focuses on missing teeth or flashy dentures to suggest the widespread lack of access to periodic dental care and, by implication, chronic poverty. On the bus to the Gauchito Gil sanctuary, a passenger tells Tati that her husband has been unemployed for nine months. Given that the bus is full, we are to imagine that many others have suffered the same fate.[7] Later, the truck driver is stopped by *piqueteros*, unemployed protesters who take to the streets to demand better living conditions.[8] By stopping at a nightclub that is actually a brothel, Waguinho is presented as an oversexed but tender and hairy bear. His solidarity is underscored by giving sex worker Soledad (María Marta Alvez) a ride to Buenos Aires, where she has been told she can substantially increase her income. Uncertainty takes over when she learns that her friend has left without a forwarding address. This additional reference to the crisis further establishes its pervasive nature, that no aspect of life as represented in the film is untouched by the devastation of the Argentine economy.

One convention of the road movie is the unplanned visit that puts the traveler in the situation of the outsider, at one with the audience. Tati accepts the unplanned visit to the Gauchito Gil sanctuary since it happens to be on the way and he is offered a free ride. Sorín uses the opportunity to capture *costumbrismo* (local color) within the melodramatic pull of accordion music being played on the bus. Especially effective is the mise-en-scène of the Gauchito Gil costume—white shirt, black tie, *bombachas* (trousers buttoned at the ankle), and leather boots—worn as a sign of devotion to this figure by most boys and men on the bus. While the four-hundred-year-old tradition of Catholic pilgrimages serves as a frame for popular devotion, the huge expansion of the Gauchito Gil official sanctuary and the roadside sites of devotion to this iconoclastic figure that mushroom throughout the country suggest the exponential growth of unmet needs, since the standard of living plummeted due to the entrenchment of neoliberal policies, leading to the withdrawal of the welfare state and the 2001 economic debacle.

Popular devotion is underscored at the sanctuary. Yet Tati, unlike Salles's Dora in *Central do Brasil*, does not undergo a visible transformation. He is not plagued by guilt and seeking redemption. Rather, he is gullible, idealistic, and generous to a fault. Although he is unemployed and cannot feed his children, he still attempts to save the popular icon he idolizes, although Maradona seems to be a victim of his own success. Despite his doubts about Gauchito Gil's potency, Tati places his hand on the head of the statue and, as instructed, presumably asks for divine intervention, a wish apparently granted when Waguinho offers him a ride to Buenos Aires. Tati's quest would come to an end with the fulfillment of his most cherished wish—to meet Maradona (God)—in person; however, he only sees the car in which his idol is whisked away from the country estate.

That the figure of Waguinho represents the plurality of belief systems that characterize the Brazilian ethos is evidenced when he shows Tati his church. Two effigies of the Virgin Mary, among them Nuestra Señora de Itatí, alternate with three *orishás* whose images continue on the reverse side of the sun visors, and a *sapo fortuna* (fortune frog) appears, assuring work, money, and good luck. A photo of Waguinho's aunt, a *mãe de santo* (priestess), further displays these figures, which with all their weight in tradition compete for attention on the dashboard of Waguinho's vehicle.[9] Given this pantheon, we are not surprised when the ride allows Sorín to rely on the conventions of the buddy movie. Waguinho is ebullient and extroverted, while Tati becomes more doubtful and introverted, perhaps as a result of the journey's impact on him. The newly reflective and somber Tati finds a foil in the figure of Waguinho. The drive with Waguinho allows Sorín to embody the ideologies explored in the film.

In contradistinction to the rather secular nature of most urban middle-class Argentines, Sorín attributes deep faith to those who live in the Argentine northeast due to their proximity to Brazil.[10] The difference between the national foundational narratives would appear to support Sorín's thesis. The Brazilian syncretism of indigenous, Portuguese, and African peoples resulted in a premodern cultural logic, and the foundational Argentine narrative underscores the arrival of European immigrants who imposed their culture over the existing creole one, severing the connection with the previous syncretism and enforcing a modern cultural logic. Centralization, which leads to the metonymic transfer between Buenos Aires and Argentina, contributes to this phenomenon. Ethnicity, a factor that tends to be bracketed in the Argentine imaginary, lends further credence to Sorín's thesis.

Argentines have obliterated the legacy of people of African descent, even though they comprised more than 50 percent of the populations of many towns in the interior toward the turn of the eighteenth century and about 30 percent of the population in Buenos Aires by 1810. This cultural amnesia is all the more bewildering considering that people of African descent continued to perform their religious rites until 1893. In sum, a reconsideration of the influence of indigenous and African peoples would allow for a better understanding of ritual, aesthetic, and theological aspects of the cults of San La Muerte, Gauchito Gil, and San Baltasar that have been identified throughout the country.[11] Despite their strong anticlerical tendencies (of anarchist and socialist origins), the turn-of-the-century Germanic migrants to the Argentine northeast, to Montevideo, and to São Paulo reinforced the practices of a popular religion based on devotion to saints identified with specific problems—the predominant kind of Catholicism among contemporary Latin American popular classes (Korstanje, 80). The convergence of so many practices of popular religion (Virgin of Itatí, Gauchito Gil, San La Muerte, San Baltasar) in the province of Corrientes would suggest that despite the differences in the national foundational narratives, the Argentine northeast is a fertile ground for popular religious practices.

Tati's discourse on Maradona may be considered, in part, a popular response to the need for heroes. Salvational figures include popular culture icons such as Che Guevara, Gauchito Gil, and *cuarteto* singer Carlitos "La Mona" Jiménez.[12] During the long truck ride, Waguinho's typical Brazilian antagonism toward Maradona turns into a cautious and humorous devotion. The honking vehicles passing by attest to the general enthusiasm at the news that Maradona fled the clinic. Waguinho suggests that only a miracle would allow Maradona to be playing golf at his estate in General Rodríguez, and Tati may wonder if Gauchito Gil performed it. Maradona performs another so-called miracle when Waguinho offers to show the piqueteros the carving—on the condition that they let him pass with his cargo.

Melodrama reinforces the episodic nature of the plot. Maradona's commitment to a clinic triggers Tati's trip. His improper escape from the clinic to golf is well received by the public in general and drivers specifically, as evidenced by their honking. The lightning speed at which informal vendors must dismantle their stands and drive away prior to the arrival of the police also accelerates the action. The impending death of the 150,000 chicks that will run out of feed unless the piqueteros relent and let Waguinho get through the picket line is certainly melodramatic. And learning upon her arrival in Buenos Aires that the sex worker's friend not only is missing but has left no forwarding address is unsettling to her, to say the least.

Such an accretion of emotional upheaval leads to the affective reading of film that is reinforced by a series of close-ups. Unlike Salles, whose use of the close-up piques our curiosity about the life stories of the Brazilian nordestinos who ask Dora to write for them, Sorín's close-ups show men swapping stories about Tati. The audience learns, visually, about Tati's tattoos. Furthermore, as the men address the camera and, by extension, the director, the audience is sutured into the diegesis. Yet, paradoxically, by identifying with the gaze of the camera, the spectators unwillingly become complicit in a condescending view of the very protagonist with whom they are expected to empathize: despite their variety, the men's comments portray Tati as a simple-minded fanatic.

In the first third of the film, the close-ups of the men who provide information about Tati alternate with shots that illustrate the stories conveyed by a voice-over. Brief comments, such as the one about the framed ticket to the only game in which Tati actually saw Maradona play, are presented through short shots that almost resemble postcard images. Longer sequences show, for example, Tati bragging about having purchased an autographed picture of Maradona, which turns out to be a mere copy. Though the men poke fun at Tati's fanaticism, the close-ups of his calm face display his hope to meet the star. Another sequence, with voice-over, presents the instructions in Guaraní that the sculptor provides Tati, his prospective apprentice, telling him how to search for the soul of wood. This sequence suggests that Tati moves easily between cultures. Tati's intuitive and creative nature is evidenced when a voice-over mentions that he saw an image of Maradona in the root of a fallen tree. Self-reflexively, it adds, "¿Quién iba a pensar que eso le iba a cambiar la vida?" (Who would have figured it would change his life?). The introductory section ends with a three-dimensional sequence on Tati's parrots chanting "Maradona" repeatedly and in unison, like the fans, which produces a tear in the fabric of realism.

—

The blend of fiction with documentary that characterizes the films of Sorín and Salles proceeds from a script, even as Sorín relies on nonprofessional actors, shoots on location, and brags about being open to the unexpected. These neorealist features do not, however, leave aside the concern with the national, as is evident in the work of the politically inclined directors of the generation of the 1960s and 1970s and epitomized by Birri and Solanas. This is apparent in the ubiquitous references to crises, particularly to unemployment, adding as such an intertextual echo to *Bombón*.

Concern for the national constitutes crucial contextualizing information for the figure of Maradona throughout *El camino de San Diego* both at home and abroad in terms of an international and globalized audience:

El 17 de abril de 2004, Diego Armando Maradona fue internado en la clínica Suizo-Argentina de Buenos Aires afectado por una grave crisis cardíaca. Durante esos días la salud de Maradona conmovió a buena parte de los argentinos. Muchos de ellos viajaron cientos de kilómetros . . . para estar junto a su ídolo . . . Tati Benítez pudo haber sido uno de ellos.

[Experiencing cardiac arrest, Diego Armando Maradona was admitted to the Clínica Suizo-Argentina in Buenos Aires on April 17, 2004. During that time, a great many Argentines were concerned about Maradona's health. Many of them traveled hundreds of kilometers . . . to stand by his side . . . Tati Benítez could have been one of them.]

This concern about Maradona embodies a continuity of national identity because it reflects the preoccupation of the masses for the well-being of idolized popular figures. Evidence of such concern appears as well in Sorín's comments on the spontaneous outpouring of the masses in 1952 during Evita's last bout with cancer. Sorín worked on a script about two lumberjacks who carry a tree trunk to Buenos Aires hoping that their penance would bring about Evita's recovery. Since Maradona's illness triggered a similar outpouring of sympathy, Sorín changed the characters and updated the script, according to "Making of the Movie" and "Interview" on the DVD of *El camino de San Diego*.

Despite Sorín's thoroughly unidimensional protagonist, tenets of the aesthetics of the New Argentine Cinema, such as the presentation of protagonists as witnesses to rambling plot lines, otherwise pervade his work. Furthermore, the generic conventions of road movies reinforce the meandering nature of the plot. *El camino de San Diego* also shares certain features of Italian neorealism. While Sorín paradoxically inscribes and subverts the dispersive situation through the initial pseudo-documentary that includes a plurality of viewpoints converging on Tati, the voyage form is implicit in the generic conventions of the roadie. Moreover, the postwar condemnation of plot predetermines the weak links, which are mirrored in the typical rambling plot of the roadie.

The pseudo-documentary and neorealist overtones of the movie notwithstanding, the cast allows for light-hearted humor through intertextual connection with Sorín's previous film *Bombón*, since a number of nonprofessional actors who worked in *Bombón* make cameo appearances in *El camino de San Diego*. For instance, Tati meets Pascual Condito as the person in charge of the cash register at a gas station. But Condito, who plays the owner of the first dog to be serviced in *Bombón*, is in fact Sorín's distributor. Juan Villegas, the lead figure of *Bombón*, reappears as a pathetic owner of a photo store and recent widower. Juan Donado, Bombón's trainer, reappears as an ambulance driver, slimmed down but with the same porteño know-it-all attitude.

Like *Central do Brasil*, *El camino de San Diego* may be interpreted as a critique of neoliberalism. In contradistinction to Salles's aesthetically pleasing poor, Sorín portrays many toothless actors—a strategy also evident in the squalor shown in César Charlone and Enrique Fernández's Uruguayan film, *El baño del Papa* (2009). To this extent Sorín shows the acute, prolonged, critical deterioration of the living standards of the poor who, according to the director, have "lost it all." By following the tenets of the grotesco criollo, Sorín has Tati come to terms with the many interrelated aspects of the national crisis. Factories have shut down, unemployment is rampant, and many women take to prostitution as the only viable alternative.

Sorín's development of grotesco criollo is part and parcel of a double discourse. While unemployment is present in the introductory section set in Pozo Azul, the topic appears repeatedly during Tati's journey to Buenos Aires, as evidenced by the piqueteros and the sex workers. The audience becomes aware of the crisis and perceives the social order as alienating and unfair. Far from the call to action of New Latin American Cinema, as epitomized by Solanas's *La hora de los hornos* (1968), Tati's role is that of a witness who does not explicitly question the social order. In terms of the similarities among directors of the New Argentine Cinema, Aguilar notes leaving aside pedagogical or self-accusatory stances (20). In other words, most of the protagonists of the New Argentine Cinema are portrayed as self-centered witnesses who do not pass judgment: Tati certainly embodies this notion. As in *Bombón*, Sorín inscribes and subverts the main structural features of grotesco criollo texts, presented as a series of trials that the subject cannot overcome (Pelletieri, 56). As Tati cannot deliver the statue and does not meet Maradona, the ambiguity of the ending allows

Sorín to deploy the typical failure of grotesco criollo (Kaiser-Lenoir, 10), and he does so with such mastery that instead of taking in Tati's crushing defeat, moviegoers may believe in a happy ending, given the hope offered by the lottery ticket.

In effect, Sorín develops a double discourse that pervades the film. While the initial close-ups of the men passing judgment on Tati suture the audience into the position of the camera and therefore engage us in their condescending attitude, Tati represents behaviors shared by a significant sector of the population, including the men interviewed. Tati's search for spiritual guidance is undermined by humor in the case of the seer, since the pendulum does not reveal any information beyond what Tati volunteers. The sappy words of the priest are pervaded with ambiguity. Tati neither intended to visit the Gauchito Gil shrine nor is convinced of the popular saint's powers. His desire to actually meet Maradona is thwarted initially by the star's escape from the clinic and then from the estate in General Rodríguez. Furthermore, the timing between the delivery of the carving and the soccer player's exit forecloses the probability of his ever having seen it, far less taken it with him.

Perhaps the camera best symbolizes this double talk. The seer suggests that Tati have a picture taken when he delivers the carving. Since he doesn't own a camera, he has to find a friend to lend him one. After Tati sweet-talks the friend's wife, the friend agrees and peppers him with recommendations. The camera lacks film, so Tati needs to embark on a series of trips through which he meets Condito and arrives at Villegas's photo shop only to find out that the camera is so outdated that film is no longer produced for it. The quest does not end there but among the illegal vendors selling their wares on the side of the highway, offering, as in a picaresque journey, another look at the informal economy. After the sudden arrival of the police makes the vendors flee, Tati is exempted from paying for the so-called imported disposable camera.

The camera functions as a demark: it highlights the futility of the trip, in that Tati does not succeed in meeting Maradona. On the other hand, it is perhaps the only material reward he obtains in the trip. While the camera self-reflexively alludes to cinema, the pathos of the incidents surrounding it mirrors the ambiguous representation of the protagonist. When Tati embarks on the roadie section of the film he clams up and becomes a subaltern. Sorín seems to feel intellectual uncertainty about representing the masses. Very much like the new generation of directors, he is content with registering the other's presence without making explicit political statements. Nonetheless, the double discourse works so well because Sorín naturalizes the film in the conventions of neorealism. The director tells a credible story shot on location and played with astonishing grace by nonprofessional actors.

Though Sorín has been critiqued for attempting to describe the national ethos, this reification is hard to shake off in an aesthetics that deploys neorealist and documentary features. These reinforce the link with the features of the New Argentine Cinema, which thrives on presenting protagonists as witnesses within rambling plot lines, immersed in their experiences (Aguilar, 20). As Deleuze mentions with regard to the postwar image, neorealist characters are entranced by a vision, and Tati's single-minded purpose—and perhaps a high dose of fatalism—precludes any reaction to the symptoms of the crisis. The grotesco criollo enables Sorín to marry a documentary approach to the polished look of industrial feature films, specifically comedies. While the latter attract broad audiences at home and abroad, the documentary approach allows this transitional Argentine director to remain faithful to his vision.

CHAPTER SIX
ORPHANS' SOLIDARITY

María Victoria Menis's *El cielito*

The synergy of neorealist aspects such as shooting on location with nonprofessional actors and lyrical experimental sequences naturalized as dreams is significant in Menis's *El cielito* (*Little Sky*, 2004).[1] *El cielito* is based on a true story. It follows the experiences of Félix (Leonardo Ramírez), a transient who witnesses the failure of the marriage of Roberto (Darío Levy) and Mercedes (Mónica Lairana) and tries to save Chango, their baby boy (Rodrigo Silva). Menis's film offers social critique, set as it is in the midst of Argentina's 2001 economic meltdown. *El cielito* opens with Félix in his late teens or early twenties jumping off a train and following the tracks to the station where he meets Roberto, a middle-age unemployed mason who offers Félix room and board on the condition that he help Mercedes, a victim of domestic violence, on the family farm. Mercedes has a baby boy who tellingly lacks a proper name. She seems exhausted by the daily toil and is comforted by Félix's attention to the baby, which increases as time goes by.

Félix's arrival seems to offer Mercedes a second chance, and she opens up. However, her attempt to displace her attention from Roberto onto Félix fails.[2] Consequently, Mercedes becomes increasingly despondent and foreshadows her death wish.[3] Félix witnesses Mercedes attempting to escape with the baby as well as her suddenly giving up. As

Figures 6.1 and 6.2
Chango as Félix's fantasmatic image.
Félix at peace: Back with grandmother.

her depression sets in, Félix is also privy to her suicide attempt. Sometime later, Mercedes disappears. Roberto unsuccessfully searches for her in town, and the audience assumes she has drowned. Félix realizes that Roberto would rather drink himself to death than take care of the baby, so Félix takes Chango to Buenos Aires, where Félix is mugged and left destitute shortly after his arrival. Cadillac, a boy with street smarts, offers lodging to the unfortunate newcomers. At Cadillac's home, Félix meets the boy's sister, and she plays with Chango.

Félix notices when two men give Cadillac a boombox as an advance payment for a job he keeps to himself. Cadillac asks Félix to accompany him. Unaware of the nature of the job, Félix agrees. However, as Cadillac guns down a middle-age man, Félix realizes that he has been betrayed—his role was that of a decoy. Instead of running away, Félix freezes, and a furious neighbor shoots him dead. The closing scenes show Félix remembering his own infancy, safely held in his grandmother's arms. Chango's fate is uncertain.

El cielito shares certain generic conventions of the documentary: it is shot on location, it tells a true story through colloquial turns of speech, it engages in social commentary, and its cast includes nonprofessional actors. Location shooting provides a striking documentary tone in *El cielito*. It alludes to the passing of time, as in shots of old buildings that suggest the turn of the twentieth century.

These aspects of the setting all point toward the sociohistorical context of the *aluvión inmigratorio* (migratory waves) from 1881 to 1930, when more than three and a half million immigrants entered Argentina.[4] References to Río Paraná and shots of the river further remind an Argentine audience of the immigrant colonies of this definitive period in the nation's history. These and other allusions inscribe the plot at a precise period relating to the generation of 1880, associated with Positivism, progress, and modernity. However, Menis suggests that the ideology of constant and continued progress is no longer tenable.

Though all characters experience the devastating effects of the retreat of the welfare state, only Roberto, whose family has (at least for two generations) lived off the land, vents his frustration. Roberto admits he hates that lifestyle, which is why he worked at a factory. Perhaps his

Figure 6.3 Inscription of time in the buildings.

resentment stems from having lost his job when the factory closed, presumably because it was no longer competitive.[5] The impact of neoliberalism becomes more evident with the repeated failures of the sale at the roadside stall of fruit jams and preserves made at the farm. Even if their prices were competitive, the farm products fail because they do not reach large enough public venues, and, in the economic downturn, no one comes to buy produce at the farm. Given the myriad economic recessions in Argentina's recent past, the reference to the closing of the factory where Roberto worked is ambiguous.[6]

Since the documentary and neorealism share certain basic generic conventions such as shooting on location, social critique, and colloquial language, El cielito also partakes of conventions of neorealism. But, additionally, El cielito shares the neorealist fascination with the point of view of children. El cielito, like Salles's Central do Brasil (1998), follows the tradition of films about Latin American youth. Unlike the gritty realism of Buñuel's Los olvidados (1950), El cielito offers a salvational narrative. Where Birri's Tire dié (1960) follows a large cast of characters, El cielito follows a pivotal relationship, a pas-de-deux between two characters whose lives plummet to self-destruction. Like the portrayal of marginal children in Babenco's Pixote: A lei do mais fraco (1981), Menis centers the movie on the relationship between a teenager and a baby boy. Meirelles's Cidade de Deus (2002) depicts the vicissitudes of favela life, while the action of El cielito is largely set in the countryside. Where Gaviria's Rodrigo D no futuro (1990) depicts a somber protagonist overtaken by sorrow, the young protagonists of El cielito are full of life. Finally, unlike Gaviria's La vendedora de rosas (1998) and Schroeder's La virgen de los sicarios (2000), which depict the violence of a society in which narco-trafficking offers a way out of poverty, El cielito examines the violence of poverty and its effects on male self-esteem and domestic abuse, as well as the daily betrayals necessary for survival in the face of dire need. More somber than Salles's Central do Brasil (1998), El cielito juxtaposes the tight bond between the transient and the baby with the increasing estrangement of the child's parents.

While Menis's thematic experimentation appears to subvert the gendered construction of space, time, and roles, the documentary and neorealist focus on the place and its inhabitants explains their paradoxical inscription and subversion. The gendered construction of space is a persistent concern for Argentine women directors. Set in a rural environment, El cielito evidences the pervasiveness of gender roles over time and across cultures (Spain, xiv). Roles involve spatial institutions, which manifest through filmic depictions who is in charge of the reproduction of labor. The home is, in theorist Elizabeth Grosz's words, the site of endless repeatable chores that are usually erased in terms of social value or recognition. Thus, the affirmation and replenishment of others at the home is always already at the expense of the self (122). Within *El cielito*, it is evident that besides housework and chores around the farm, Mercedes is responsible for taking care of the baby.

From a western (masculine and thus putatively universal) perspective, time tends to be perceived as linear. Such linearity is usually associated with Positivism and the concomitant belief in unlimited progress. Roberto ascribes to this ideology in *El cielito*. These linear-structure activities appear in Roberto's having worked at a factory job, bonding with Félix because of their shared interest in boxing, and showing the younger man how to shoot.[7] Roberto is at odds with his more recent environment because work at the farm is cyclical, involving daily and seasonal activities such as raising livestock and picking fruit. Women's bodies (menses) remind them that time has a cyclical aspect, which is why some of them perceive it as discontinuous (Cottle, 187). In other words, the linear ideology pointing toward the future differs from the organic cycles of life—pregnancy, birth, and lactation that women experience even in industrial societies (Pfeufer, 21).

Although Mercedes is associated with nature, she is not in her original locus, as she tells Félix, "Acá en seguida crece todo, allá . . . Igual, la casa la hemos perdido. Yo me he venido y después, se han ido todos" ("Things grow easily here, over there . . . Anyway, we lost the house there. I came over here and then they all left"). Since Roberto despises farmwork, he delegates these responsibilities to Mercedes, who is expected to perform the daily household chores in addition to raising the baby.[8] As Roberto tells Félix when he shows him what to do, "El laburo no es difícil, toda mi familia lo hizo y siempre le dio de comer. Pero las cosas cambiaron. A mí no me gusta. Nunca me ha gustado" ("It's not hard work. My family always did it and lived well. But things have changed. I never liked this").

The interrelation of time and roles appears in the notion of "maialogical time," defined in terms of mutuality or interrelatedness in relationships like those of childbearing and breast-feeding (Pfeufer, 27). In *El cielito*, the actions involved in feeding, cleaning, and rocking Chango to sleep all remind Félix of his own childhood and especially of the deep connection with his grandmother. As he identifies with the infant and becomes aware of his predicament, Félix offers the baby protection. Thus, as Roberto drags Mercedes in to have sex, leaving the baby outdoors, Félix tells Chango:

Escúcheme una cosa, Changuito. Le voy a decir algo muy impor-
tante. ¿Usted se acuerda del día en que su madre me lo pasó?
¿El día en que se agarró de mi mano? Ahí yo supe muy bien lo
que usted me quería decir con eso. Pero quédese tranquilo. Yo
nunca lo voy a dejar solo. Nunca más usted va a estar solo.

[Listen Chango. This is very important. Remember the day your
mother handed you over to me? When you grabbed my hand? I knew
very well what you meant by that. I know you need me. But don't
worry. I won't leave you alone. You'll never be alone again.]

In *El cielito* the notion of maialogical time does not follow the expected mother-child relationship. Indeed, the film bears out the suggestion of the three types of fathering that coexist in Argentina: premodern (father-*patrón*), modern (classical father of Oedipal resolution), and postmodern awareness of the tension between these models that leads to a search for new gender positionalities (Burin and Meler, 332). Roberto epitomizes the premodern type, and Félix stands for an androgynous postmodern version predicated on harmony. As we are reminded in Burin and Meler (342), the postmodern version is defined as subjective, a social construct that transcends systemic duality, although it results from the constant interaction of opposites. Burin and Meler, however, fail to acknowledge indigenous configurations of fatherhood: among the nomadic Guaraní the father is responsible for carrying the babies during the journey. To that extent, Félix's subversion of the typical construction of hegemonic western masculinity and fatherhood hinges on ancestral indigenous traditions;[9] portraying these reaffirms Menis's emphasis on the generic conventions of the documentary and neorealism in showing authentic stories of a locale and its people.

The generic conventions of the documentary and neorealism likewise call for the inscription of social reality, as is apparent as Félix travels to Buenos Aires. He wakes up when the bus is stopped by piqueteros who have taken to the streets. The shots emphasize the presence of women and children. The close-up on the sign that reads "Bienaventurados los niños" (Blessed be the children) is certainly ironic, given the huge increase of population including children living below the poverty line. These shots suggest that far from being an isolated event affecting Roberto, unemployment is rampant. And the consequences of poverty, hunger, lack of access to health services and education, and so on are widespread. In other words, the particular becomes generalized, and the shots allow for a transition to the same social evils in Buenos Aires. Unrest and an impending sense of violence arise from a piquetero demonstration upon Félix and Chango's arrival in the city. As an alienated *cabecita negra* (rural immigrant of indigenous phenotype), Félix is unaware of the nature of the piquetero movement that might have offered him support.

El cielito offers a definite contrast between the modernist ideal of unlimited progress and the actual outcome of neoliberalism. Menis resorts to the conventions of the documentary in the scenes shot on the bus, conventions that then become dominant in the metropolis as the camera pans and Félix's travel takes him through the shantytowns that have become a permanent feature of Buenos Aires. The shots of men living and sleeping in the park evidence the increase in homelessness. These and other scenes date the movie as taking place after 2001 and attest to the devastating effects of globalized neoliberalism and the dismantling of the welfare state in a process that started under the 1970s military dictatorship and accelerated under presidents Raúl Alfonsín and Carlos Menem in the 1980s and 1990s (Bassi and Fuentes).[10]

The dream sequences showcase Menis's lyrical style as they provide the context necessary to infer Félix's motivation. Dream sequences are not a common feature of Hollywood movies, but Soviet cinema, German expressionism, and the French school have represented psychic phenomena to break away from the "American" limitations of the action-image. Dream images tend to be depicted by way of dissolves, superimpositions, special effects, and manipulations in the laboratory to produce the abstract images or, alternatively, by means of montage to produce an unhinging look that suggests a dream while still focusing on concrete objects (Deleuze, *Cinema 2*, 58). *El cielito* appears to partake of both options. On the one hand, images of lily pads, trees, a table, and a wrinkled woman are concrete. On the other hand, Menis restricts the chromatic palette to white, hues of blue, green, and red. Moreover, the shots are overexposed, and the alternation between certain shots lends them a rhythm that suggests the repetition and transposition of dreams. Despite the

Figure 6.4
Overexposure to suggest Félix's dreams about his grandmother.

simplicity of the montage, the recurrence of shots of water, lily pads, trees, and branches suggests a combinatoire that allows for the difference and deferral of différance.

While the recurrence and rearticulation of images bring back certain memories, the randomness with which they surface underscores Félix's growing awareness of his debt of gratitude toward the woman who raised him mixed, as is evident from the dialogue with Mercedes, with Félix's sadness at his grandmother's passing.

A brief summary of the montage show that dream states or states of extreme sensory motor relaxation allow for the surfacing of childhood memories that are essential to Félix's characterization (Deleuze, *Cinema 2*, 56). The first dream begins with shots of lily pads, trees, and marshes. The shot of a skinny woman, taken from the back and focusing from the waist down, is superseded by the startling close-up of a stick apparently endowed with a movement of its own, since the woman's hand its concealed as it moves branches around on the ground. Focusing on bugs displaced by the movement, the camera pans on the woman's legs as she walks into the water. Lacking context, the first dream sequence is ambiguous, as it could suggest Félix's interest in Mercedes, an interdiction barred by Roberto, his employer and the owner of a gun. What is certain is that we do not expect the scene to suggest anyone but Mercedes.

The second sequence is presented as daydreaming. Rocking the baby to sleep triggers Félix's recollection of his grandmother's lullaby. The dreamlike effect results from blending his voice into (presumably) hers as the camera focuses on arms cleaning a wooden table and a red tablecloth. Then it shifts to shots of gnarled hands sprinkling a powdery substance into a pot of water. As the hands clean string beans and drop them into the liquid, the camera rhythmically returns to the hands setting two places on a table while the child makes mud cakes and plays with water. The sequence ends with the reflection of a child's face in the water, which breaks into ripples as it is stirred.

Once again, the body parts appear parceled; however, the audience infers that Félix identifies with Chango.

A third dream sequence continues the previous tendency to provide social critique in a lyrical, experimental fashion on the part of the filmmaker. Like the first one, the third sequence appears as Félix sleeps, in this case on the bus to Buenos Aires. The dream is interrupted when piqueteros who seem to have blocked traffic awaken Félix. As he falls asleep again, a shadow turns into fabric waving in the wind. A close-up of eyes and nose is followed by one of a wrinkled face. Following the parceled effect, the camera focuses on an old woman's smile. The similarity between her wrinkled arm and the rugged tree trunk is not lost. In an upward swoop, the camera follows the branches into the sky. The direction is reversed as the camera follows the downward movement of a red cloth waving as it drops to the ground. A barefoot woman throws twigs into the cloth. She ties the cloth into a bundle, fastens the cloth onto her back, and walks away. In Guaraní culture, firewood symbolizes the hearth and therefore the home, which Menis presents metaphorically through these images.

At this point, there is no doubt that Félix remembers the frugal lifestyle of his grandmother, who took care of him. The last dream sequence sug-

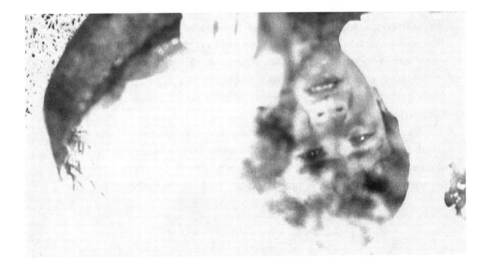

Figure 6.5 Deep memories surface: Félix remembers his childhood.

gests Félix's death. As he lies fatally wounded on the sidewalk, his gaze
fixes onto the branches above him. Then, a close-up of a hand stirring
something in a red bucket is juxtaposed to one of an old woman with a
baby about Chango's age on her lap, revealing Félix's wishful return to the
comfort offered by his grandmother.

In addition to the above generic conventions of the documentary and
neorealism, El cielito shows five characteristics of the postwar new image
forged by Italian neorealism: the dispersive situation, the deliberately weak
links, the voyage form, the consciousness of clichés, and the condemnation of plot (Deleuze, Cinema 1, 210, 212). The protagonist of El cielito is
placed in an ongoing situation but remains unaware of its causes; as such,
the repudiation of plot, the concomitant dispersive situation, and the deliberately weak links are evident. El cielito exemplifies the Italian neorealist
emphasis on the seer and no longer the agent (Cinema 2, 3), an emphasis
that has had a lasting impact on the New Latin American Cinema. Accordingly, Félix takes on the role of witness. His ride on the train ends as the
employee who checks tickets approaches. Félix witnesses the roadblocks
as signs of civil unrest on his way to Buenos Aires. Once at the metropolis,
he discovers he has no options with a baby in tow.

Lastly, the consciousness of clichés appears in Roberto's abusive behavior, which may also be attributed to the widespread (Hispanic) custom
of adding sexual services to the duties of female employees. Ambiguously,
Roberto refers to Mercedes as his mujer, his woman, a term that encompasses the connotation of wife. This lack of consideration extends to his
issue. As a white male, Roberto might feel superior to Mercedes and Félix,
both of whom appear to share indigenous traits—Aymara and Guaraní, respectively. Argentine racism against Bolivian immigrants may be a factor
in Roberto's domestic abuse as well, since Mercedes sings "La cantuta," a
Bolivian lullaby, as she rocks the baby to sleep by the riverside.[11] Roberto's
intense homosocial bond, abusive behavior, and addiction to alcohol are
attempts to conceal his extreme vulnerability;[12] Félix, in contrast, identifies
with Mercedes due to their shared indigenous backgrounds and rural exile.
Félix cares for the baby because he identifies with Chango's predicament,
which mirrors his own.

Besides the use of dream sequences, Menis's signature style is defined
by the treatment of time, as can be illustrated by the categories that Deleuze deploys in his study of cinema. The crystal-image splits the present
into two directions, one launched toward the future to make the present

pass and the other falling into the past to preserve it (*Cinema 2*, 81). By its very nature, each instance of domestic abuse reminds the victim of previous occasions and projects the event into the future. For instance, Roberto rapes Mercedes repeatedly. The more aloof she becomes, the more he beats her. By bearing witness, Félix allows for a disjunction between present as past—the habit and the future—the possibility that he may set her free. However, Félix does not intervene. The river suggests timelessness, while the notion of sheets of time, defined in terms of a coexistence of circles (99), is particularly evident in the farm. The hollow trunk of the ancient tree, the style of the house, and its weather-beaten walls attest to the passing of time.

Roberto remembers that for generations his people managed to eke out a living at the farm. Mercedes gives a further example of how the past persists when she reads aloud one of the recipes of Roberto's grandmother as she tells Félix how Roberto's father taught her to make preserves. When Félix remembers scenes of his infancy in the care of his grandmother, it is not specific recollection-images that surface but rather fluid, malleable sheets of past that are happy (56).

Lastly, the Deleuzian notion of peaks of time, defined as the possibility of treating an episode as a single event that provides the basis for the implication of presents (100), appears when Félix witnesses two of the most dramatic instances: Mercedes's aborted flight and her failed suicide attempt. By escaping her predicament, the former offers the possibility of a future. Though Mercedes teeters on the brink of taking a leap of faith, reality—her limited choices with a baby—sets in and she succumbs to the routine of the past. Some time later, Félix watches Mercedes move to

Figure 6.6
Ancient tree witnesses
the passing generations.

and fro, about to plunge into the river, for freedom paradoxically implies annihilation. As she wavers between an oppressive present/past and an unknown present/future, the dog nudges her back to reality. Although (and because) Mercedes becomes increasingly alienated from the baby as the cycle of abuse spirals and Félix begins to take her place, the night he is awakened by the bawling baby is highly significant, since it is the first time Chango is ignored by both parents. Mercedes lies fully dressed in bed appearing to be asleep, and Roberto drowns the infant's cries by increasing the volume of the TV. At this point Félix takes on full responsibility for Chango. He is aware of the baby's helplessness, and the dream sequences establish his identification with the baby in terms of his own past.

In sum, the documentary effect of *El cielito* is supplemented by the sequences attributed to Félix's dreams and recollections. Those dreams and memories ultimately disrupt the linear structure of the plot both as journey and as bildungsroman. Despite the distancing effect arising from the chromatic choice, the rhythmic structure of the repeated overexposed shots of lily pads, trees, and the old woman all take on a lyrical quality reminiscent of the echolalia of poetic language. Precisely because the audience lacks a context or the referent for those memories, the shots carry an affective charge heightened by their beauty. Their aleatory nature suggests an apparent randomness kept within the bounds of repetition with variation. To that extent, these images are analogous to a vocal or kinetic rhythm.[13] This preverbal stage reinforces the unconscious process of Félix's memories of having been a baby himself. In addition, this process introduces Félix's final regression to the (grand)mother and sheds light on his motivation.

Though the dialogue is sparse and we are not privy to the character's thoughts, we could argue that through Chango, Félix vicariously relives his childhood, the only happy period of his life. However, as proven by lack of empathy (and generosity) of the passersby when Félix has to resort to begging with Chango in arms because he has been mugged, racism prevents porteños from acknowledging that a teenager may be taking care of a baby who is not his own son. Chango becomes an albatross, much as his mother feared.

From an allegorical standpoint, Félix represents the *guacho* (orphan) *gaucho* (mestizo), and as such, he stands for all Argentines. Like his compatriots, Félix has been betrayed by neoliberal policies. The closing of the factory and lack of jobs traumatizes Roberto. Given the crisis, few drivers stop to purchase the preserves that Félix attempts to sell by the roadside, and in terms of price, farms cannot compete with established industries. The lack of social services deprives the characters of much-needed assistance: rehabilitation clinics, subsidized child care, safety nets to combat domestic abuse. Thus, as Menis suggests, "En una Argentina devastada . . . la vida no es más que una supervivencia" (In a devastated Argentina . . . life is reduced to survival).

Yet, perhaps Menis's greatest success lies in the aesthetics of the film. By focusing on time, the film succeeds in highlighting the dire predicament of the growing masses of impoverished Argentines for whom the land no longer affords sustenance. To conclude, besides inscribing and subverting gendered constructions of time and space, the movie disrupts hegemonic representations of roles, and the inscription of (Roberto's) abusive behavior notwithstanding, it reinscribes fatherhood by means of a gentle and caring male character like Félix. Most tellingly, Menis recreates the ancestral practices of the Guaraní, and the film's aesthetic features elicit an affective response.

PART THREE
DRAMA

CHAPTER SEVEN
SCULPTING TIME

Inés de Oliveira Cézar's
Como pasan las horas

Inés de Oliveira Cézar's focus on time is a recurrent element in her corpus and in experimental film generally as it evidences the transition between films centered on action and those around an open-ended journey.[1] Rather than depicting a rationale, these films trace the mystifying allure of time. Time is central to Oliveira Cézar's cinematic production: her oeuvre may be defined, following Tarkovsky, as sculpting in time, as it shows sustained experimentation regarding the nature of repeated actions in recorded time and myth. *Como pasan las horas* (2005) is like Victoria Menis's *El cielito* in that it centers on the paradoxical inscription and subversion of the gendered construction of space, time, and roles.

In Oliveira Cézar's *Como pasan las horas*, action, gender, and formulations about time converge in developing an account of a dramatic day that changes the course of "family" life. The film opens with a piano lesson. The middle-age René (Susana Berco) sits alongside her student, Agustina (Agustina Muñoz), whose muttered words "miedo" (fear) and "muerte" (death) set the tone of the piece and foreshadow the action. Once René has returned to her home, she greets her son, Santiago (Agustín Alcoba), and husband, Juan (Guillermo Arengo). In a separate scene René discreetly rejects her husband's approaches and is noncommittal about spending the following day at the beach. Over breakfast Juan engages in

playful bantering about life in a one-room apartment; his words and actions allude to a muted disagreement. The movie then branches into two
plot lines. While father and son go to the beach, René takes her terminally
ill mother, Virginia (Susana Campos), out of hospice and drives her home.
In the meantime, Juan stops for a meal; he stops again later because he
thinks he has a flat. On both occasions, the boy Santi, who seems to be
four or five years old, leaves the battered Ford to explore the surroundings,
and Juan asks him to promise to never venture out again. At the beach,
father and son walk playfully in straight or diagonal lines along the sand.

The boy and the middle-age man meet two fishermen. Later, they
look for cockles and build a sandcastle. Since the boy does not want to go
swimming, Juan suggests that they take a nap. Santi plays close to Juan,
who appears to be sleeping. The passing of time is suggested by a shot
of the waves at sunset, followed by a shot of the child clutching at Juan
to protect himself from the wind. Surprised to see them sleeping on the
beach, the returning fishermen attempt to wake Juan up. As the cell phone
rings they speak to René. The camera then alternates between shots of
mother and daughter driving down to the beach and of a fisherman rocking Santi as he sings a lullaby against the backdrop of the sea.

Como pasan las horas inscribes and subverts the pervasiveness
of gender roles over time and across cultures. Though the time span of
Como pasan las horas is only one day, René dutifully prepares breakfast
for husband and son and begs Juan not to feed Santi on the way to avoid
the boy getting an upset stomach. Moreover, adhering to the gendered
construction of space, René and Virginia settle in the house; given the
latter's terminal illness, the two women cherish their time together in what
becomes a nurturing space (Grosz, 116).[2] In accordance with gendered
construction, Juan and Santi stop by the family's beach house but spend
the day outdoors by the sea, whose presence foreshadows death, since
from a symbolic perspective oceans stand for both the origin and the end
of life (Cirlot, 298).

To develop the consistent inscription of real time in *Como pasan las
horas* the camera takes Santi's point of view and focuses on the passing
trees to suggest the speed of movement on the way to the beach. These
shots are complemented by others, taken looking backward but keeping
the child's point of view, as when Santi looks at the changing colors of the
pavement. He naturalizes them by experiencing nausea. The inscription
of real time also appears in the depiction of Juan and Santi playing at the

seaside, especially when Santi waits by his father, as well as in such moments as when René and Virginia make a toast, in a clear debt to the influence of Tarkovsky. In the Russian filmmaker's words, the director's work is defined as "sculpting in time," which is achieved by discarding what is not integral to the cinematic image (63–64). Despite the lack of background information about the characters in *Como pasan las horas* and the fact that each action needs to be executed for the first time before it can become habitual, it would appear that Juan and Santi have spent time at the beach before, usually accompanied by René, as suggested by Santi's two inquiries about her whereabouts. Therefore, despite its habitual nature, their day at the seaside is unique, as opposed to René's activities, including the piano lesson, which appear to be cyclical, recurring.

Perhaps influenced by the director's background in theater, *Como pasan las horas* follows the neoclassical unities of time, place, and plot. The desolate beach and the bare tree branches suggest winter. The function of the sparse background information on the characters lends them a certain universality, for viewers register them less as individuals than in their respective subject positions within the family, that is, as parents, children, lovers, thus allowing for a broader identification. Further, the movie is dedicated to Susana Campos (Virginia), who was Susana (René) Berco's mother in real life. Since a brain tumor would take Campos's life soon after the film was shot, the plot line of the dying Virginia being tended by her daughter René reflected the two actresses' predicament as a mise-en-abyme.

The notion of maialogical time, defined in terms of mutuality and interrelation, is fleshed out in the depth of the relationships between René and Virginia and between Juan and Santi. That sense of time as interrelation also arises in the tender care of the fishermen who find Santi. Like Menis's contesting of gender roles, in *Como pasan las horas* the notion of maialogical time does not follow the expected mother-child relationship. On the one hand, Juan rather than René is the parent who interacts more with Santi (in their conversation about Tom and Jerry, the boy's birthday, and so on).

Furthermore, though he presumes Juan is asleep, the child tells his father how much he loves spending the day with him: "Papi, yo siempre quise ser un dinosaurio. Hasta que pude hacerme humano. Me encantan los dinosaurios. Y la arena también siempre me gustó. Pero a mí siempre me gustó más estar con vos" (Daddy, I always wanted to be a dinosaur.

Until I became human. I love dinosaurs, and I always liked sand, too. But I always liked to be with you more).

On the other hand, René and Virginia take turns mothering each other. Virginia offers advice when René admits her disenchantment with Juan. She admonishes her daughter for living in a hurry, assuring René that Juan loves her and adores Santi. Instead of thinking it over, René quibbles: "Si uno supiese cuál es el tiempo de cada cosa" (If one only knew the time for each thing). Laughing, Virginia agrees, "El tiempo, si uno supiese" (The time, if anyone knew). René is shown as tender and caring toward her mother as well, helping her walk, preparing dinner, and relishing their outing.

The plot in *Como pasan las horas* supports the assertion that Santi's last day with his father will forever link the present and the past. Deleuze's notion of sheets of the past describes numerous interactions. For Virginia and René the actions of going for a walk, having dinner, sitting on the porch, and so on constitute a repetition of activities performed and enjoyed repeatedly in the past. Repetition leads the actors to relive their memories of past actions. To the extent that they recall habitual actions, the present is suffused by the past, defined and owned, claimed as a fusion of that repetition (Deleuze, *Difference and Repetition*, 74). Given the denouement of the film, future habitual actions such as building castles in the sand will become suffused with the past and particularly with the last occasion the boy played with his father. Preoccupation with the passing of time, which arises from the acknowledgement of Virginia's impending demise, allows mother and daughter to go beyond their own lifespans.

Figure 7.1
Maialogical time as mutuality and interrelation: Juan and Santi. Courtesy Inés de Oliveira Cézar.

Figure 7.2
Maialogical time: René and Virginia.
Courtesy Inés de Oliveira Cézar.

They transcend the immediate in singing ancient ballads about death and by repeating customs followed for thousand of years, such as spilling wine for the dead. In so doing they enjoy, relive, and keep alive traditions that span different periods and eras; moreover, as these actions are shown in real time, mother and daughter sculpt actions in time in Tarkovsky's sense.

The passing references to dreams in *Como pasan las horas* are significant as they articulate the dying Virginia's wish to be young again. Like Menis in *El cielito*, however, Oliveira Cézar features shots that convey psychic processes in numerous anamorphic, slanted takes that are supposed to suggest altered states of consciousness. The first of these, attributed to Virginia, appears at the hospice, while another set of anamorphic shots, presumably attributed to Juan, shows the windmill as well as many scenes at the beach, such as the view of him and the dunes, and the paradoxical, vertigo-inducing view of the pier suspended in high air.

Further anamorphic shots focus on the surrounding tree trunks as René and her mother go for a walk, producing a sensation of their certainty of the impending closing of a cycle. A final anamorphic shot focuses on the piano at Virginia's home: reinforced by Virginia's comment about her preoccupation with the piano once she passes, this shot echoes the initial piano lesson, which in turn recalls the unspoken recollection of the lessons that Virginia imparted to her daughter in years past.[3]

In terms of experimentation, Oliveira Cézar's movies embody five characteristics of the postwar new image. Repudiation of plot and the concomitant dispersive situation as well as deliberately weak links characterize *Como pasan las horas*, whose protagonists are placed in an ongoing situation with no awareness of the causes that led to it. Like Reygadas, Oliveira Cézar stresses the interval as the scenes of all three films appear to be structured paratactically; to that extent, the absence of transitions increases the suspense and shock of Juan's unexpected death. The neorealist emphasis on the seer and no longer the agent appears in the muted action of *Como pasan las horas*, which relates Juan and Santi playing at the beach while René and Virginia fondly remember old times. Overall, the movie is structured in terms of truncated voyages, as Juan and Santi's day at the beach ends unexpectedly, affecting the alternate story line and linking them again toward the end of the diegesis. As the consciousness of clichés appears in *Como pasan las horas*, the director rigorously avoids postcard images of the countryside in spring as well or of the beach in summer. Even the tantalizing symbol of the mirror at the beach house avoids cliché as it reflects the sea when Juan opens the windows and later reappears to suggest the passing of time through the darkening image of the waves. Rather, the darkening mirror foreshadows, implicitly, Juan's unforeseen demise.

Figure 7.3
Anamorphic shot: Juan passes by the windmill, his heightened perception conveyed by the slanted picture. Courtesy Inés de Oliveira Cézar.

Figure 7.4
Anamorphic shot: Juan and Santi at the beach. While the heightened perception encompasses both figures, it is no longer attributed to the protagonist's point of view. Courtesy Inés de Oliveira Cézar.

CHAPTER EIGHT
THE PAST ENGULFS THE PRESENT

Josué Méndez's *Días de Santiago*

Following an extended stint in the Peruvian armed forces, the protagonist of Josué Méndez's *Días de Santiago* (2004) returns to Lima.[1] Inquiring about financial aid for veterans, Santiago Román (Pietro Sibille) initially states, "Soy ex-combatiente. He luchado por mi patria tres años" ("I'm a war veteran. I fought three years for my country"). However, when Santiago goes for the first time to the nightclub where his classmates meet and marvels at seeing teenagers dancing, drinking, and having a good time in the afternoon, he recalls his past differently: "Seis años sin poder pasarla así, como cualquiera" ("Six years unable to have a good time like all the rest"). The screenplay offers two dates. During his military service Santiago fought against (alleged) terrorists (*tucos*), such as the members of Shining Path, and Ecuadorians (*morros*) amid the eruption of a border conflict. Although the film gives few specific time references, the allusions have historical parameters: Shining Path leader Abimael Guzmán was apprehended in 1992, and in 1995 Peru and Ecuador again clashed in their fifty-year border conflict.[2] Therefore, Santiago must have been in the service from approximately 1992 through 1995 and perhaps a couple of years earlier or later.

Disgusted with military life, Santiago retires to be at peace with his conscience; however, the civilian life to which he returns proves no less

harrowing. Santiago must come to terms with the mistrust of his wife, Mari
(Alhelí Castillo), who is afraid of his outbursts and seems unaware that
they are caused by post-traumatic stress disorder, PTSD. He also discovers the ongoing cycle of family violence in the life of his brother, Coco
(Erik García), who is caught in a marriage that compounds spousal abuse
with child neglect. Moreover, as his sister-in-law, Elisa (Marisela Puicón),
seduces Santiago, she asks him to kill Coco.

The biblical interdiction is echoed by another taboo, incest, when Santiago discovers that his father (Ricardo Mejía) sexually abuses Santiago's
sister, Inés (Ivy La Noire). About to shoot his father on the spot, Santiago
finally gives in to the entreaties of his mother (Lili Urbina), "No malogres tu
vida" ("Don't ruin your life").

In *Días de Santiago*, one of the first Latin American movies to focus on
the problems of combat veterans experiencing PTSD, Méndez offers social critique as he charts the difficulties of reinsertion into civilian life. The
Peruvian filmmaker develops an experimental aesthetics that consists
of alternating shots in color to suggest contemporary reality with shots in
black and white to allude to the protagonist's past. The combination reflects the paradoxical position of this psychic phenomenon, located on the
threshold between remembering and forgetting, between experience and
its absence (Huyssen, 16). Méndez stresses these aspects of traumatic
repetition in ways corresponding to the symptoms that the American
Psychiatric Association first codified in 1980. PTSD previously was called

Figure 8.1
Santiago is seduced and betrayed by his
sister-in-law. Courtesy Tropical Cinema.

"shell shock, combat stress, delayed stress syndrome, and traumatic neurosis" (Caruth, 3) and has been widely recognized in the United States, where there has been a boom in publications on PTSD addressing war veterans and their families.

Méndez's film joins a long tradition of Latin American cinematic representation of the trauma of war. Luis Alberto Restrepo's *La primera noche* (2003) chronicles the vicissitudes of the protracted Colombian civil war waged between guerrilla organizations and the army for more than forty years. Restrepo presents the perspective of a soldier who witnesses the carnage of the army against unarmed civilians, particularly his own family. Restrepo's work heightens the drama by beginning close to the focal point of the action and alternating sequences on the lives of the protagonists, moving from the massacre to their perilous escape to the capital and the main character's demise. Argentine film director Tristán Bauer's *Iluminados por el fuego* (2005) calls attention to the nation's dereliction of duty when he opens the film with the suicide of a veteran of the Malvinas/ Falklands War as a consequence of undiagnosed PTSD.

Méndez's experimental aesthetics is evident in an eclectic visual style. The Peruvian filmmaker notes in *Cinencuentro* that there is a balance in the photography: "La mitad del tiempo la fotografía es a color, la otra mitad blanco y negro" (Half the time the photography is in color, the other half in black and white). Méndez appears nonchalant about the choice to alternate color with black and white photography and justifies it by the

Figure 8.2
Santiago is invited to engage in illegal activities. Courtesy Tropical Cinema.

protagonist's search for order, balance, and harmony in a chaotic world. With the exception of Santiago's double rehearsal of the way to approach a girl at the nightclub (shown in color and with voice-over), the alternation seems to represent the counterpoint between actions (color) and thinking processes (black and white). This offers an experimental alternative to the more traditional deployment of flashbacks by way of parallel plot lines, which Restrepo's *Primera noche* used to represent trauma.

Following Méndez's acknowledgement in *Cinencuentro* that the voice-over articulates the memories haunting Santiago, we shall examine the interplay of alternating color and black and white sequences. As *Días de Santiago* begins, a silent black and white section shows a woman (Mari) staring at someone (Santiago) while she waits for a bus. Subsequently, in a color section, through Santiago's dialogue with his mother we learn that Mari is upset because he cannot find a job. We also learn, in black and white, that there is no government-sponsored program aimed at assimilating veterans in Lima and that Santiago works in construction but the job doesn't amount to much. In Santiago's conversations with his buddies and his father that appear in color, he has turned down job offers such as being a guard or a civil servant because he still believes in doing something useful. Confronting a similar dilemma, Santiago's platoon members (in color) consider returning to the jungle to open a bordello or venture into gold or drug trafficking.

The reconstituted group of army veterans opts for robbing a bank, and they fail miserably at the robbery. Rata, a maimed comrade, offers his car to Santiago. So, after Rata's suicide, Santiago becomes a cabdriver and searches for information on different degrees. He feels anger at being snubbed by a receptionist at one school, and he seems overwhelmed by the expense of a five-year or even three-year course of study. These scenes are in color.

As Santiago walks toward a bus stop (black and white), his voice-over admonishes some youths staring at a woman whose skirt is unzipped. The event triggers the protagonist's salvational ideology, "Uno tiene que ayudar" ("One has to help out"). Once Santiago is on the bus, the voice-over illustrates the continued impact of military training on the veteran's daily life: "Ves a todos y los distingues" ("You look at everybody and figure them out"), "¿Qué estarán pensando hacer?" ("What is it they wanna do?"), "¿Adónde pensarán ir?" ("Where do they wanna go?"), "¿Me estarán viendo también a mí?" ("Could they also be watching me?"). Then, some brash young men go by, pushing and shoving, and he admits, "Dan ganas de hacerles algo, pero no puedes, te controlas porque ya no estás allá, ahora estás acá" ("You wanna do something . . . but you can't. You control yourself because you're not there any more . . . now you're here"). These sequences show the extent that Santiago's personality has internalized the military way of life.

The voice-over continues in black and white, recalling the military training that naturalized behavior in the war zone, presenting a jarring contrast to the seemingly carefree behavior of civilians:

Uno debe pensar antes de actuar. Caminas por la calle y tienes que analizar. Sacar tu línea . . . armar tu estrategia porque en cualquier momento puede comenzar el hostigamiento . . . las trampas que te pone el camino. ¿Y cómo las vas a pasar? Tienes que andar mirando a todos lados. Preparado a todo. Siempre listo para reducir al enemigo con las manos, con la mirada . . . Le vas sacando la línea a todos, porque puede venir de cualquier lado. Atrás tuyo y te comienzan a mirar. Te clavan la mirada y no tienes dónde ir . . . Y se te empiezan a venir todos encima . . . se ríen en tu cara y te persiguen y te acuerdas de todo.

[One should think before he acts. Walk down the streets and analyze. Draw your line, develop your strategy 'cause the harassment starts at any moment . . . traps laid for you in the way. How are you gonna get through? You gotta keep looking around. Ready for everything . . . anticipating everyone . . . always ready to reduce the enemy, with your eyes, with your hands . . . You check them all out, 'cause it could come from anywhere. Behind you they turn around. They stare at you and you have nowhere to go . . . They come after you and laugh at you and you remember everything.]

As the voice-over continues, Santiago's military training overtakes him even though he is walking around the densely populated streets of Lima. Santiago shoves a man against a wall and pushes him to the ground. He grabs another one by the back, turning him over and flat onto the sidewalk. The voice-over becomes increasingly menacing: "Si lo tuvieras que hacer, ¿cómo lo harías?" ("If you had to do it, how would you?"); "Unas ideas terribles que se te vienen a la cabeza" ("Terrible ideas that come to your head"); "Las ganas de hacerle algo a alguien, a cualquiera" ("The need to do something to someone, anyone"). As he is about to bash the fourth victim's face in, the voice-over urges restraint: "Pero no puedes. Te tienes que controlar" ("But you can't. You have to control yourself"). Here everyone around seems to stare at him. Nonetheless, the fact that no one visibly reacts reinforces the idea that we are witnessing how, in Santiago's stream of consciousness, the repressed returns with a vengeance, engulfing the present through a reenactment of the past, a definitive quality of PTSD.[3]

For Méndez (in *Cinencuentro*), Santiago represents a generation that lost its youth on the battlefield: like so many veterans, he has struggled to adapt and survive in a society that neither recognizes nor appreciates his effort. This urban film accordingly focuses on the chaotic nature of life in the city, eschewing flashbacks: Santiago blocks memories off, and there is persistent avoidance of stimuli such as thoughts, feelings, or conversations associated with the trauma. In Santiago's continued experience of anxiety and increased physical arousal, he is repeatedly exposed to situations that remind him of the trauma. Even walking down the street leads Santiago to imagine he is automatically reenacting the trauma. In the voice-over he admits that his alienation—the predicament of the human condition—has become too heavy a burden. "Cuando estabas allá lo único que querías era volver. Pero vuelves y ya no puedes esperar más para que algo venga y te saque de todo. De acá, de allá, de todo" ("When you were there all you wanted was to come back. But you're back and now you can't wait for something to take you out. Out of here, of there, of it all"). In sum, Santiago experiences the sense of foreshortened future.

A series of unexpected reactions involving Santiago's gun, which is synonymous with sexuality, presents a leitmotif that begins with his pubescent sister dressed provocatively to attract male buyers into the family store. She asks Santiago for a ride in the car. As he drives her around, she opens the glove compartment, where she discovers, removes, and examines the gun. Silently, Santiago recovers it from her lap and returns it to the glove compartment. Later, in a more overtly sexual scene, the gun is associated with another woman, his sister-in-law, when she seduces Santiago. Elisa reminds him of the war as a way to naturalize her request to murder her husband, his brother. Finally, the gun is a topic of conversation when Andrea, a young classmate from the institute, kisses Santiago. Although he rebuffs her, she insists on getting close by asking to see his gun. But Santiago responds by pushing her violently back to her side of the car. On the following day, Santiago tries to make amends, but Andrea now holds back, as she realizes that he is not interested in a relationship. At this juncture, Santiago places the gun in Andrea's hands. Scared, she squirms around so that some passersby notice their struggle. They alert the guards at the institute, and Santiago's military training takes over, this time for real. Aiming the gun at her head, Santiago crosses the yard holding her hostage, making sure the guards have dropped their guns. Santiago leaves Andrea on the sidewalk as per the guard's request. The incident signals the end of his studies and illustrates another unconscious repetition of the past taking over the present.

Méndez's *Días de Santiago* explores fundamental tenets of PTSD: traumatic memories become dissociated and preserved in an altered state apart from the ordinary narrative flow of conscious experience, and they remain highly emotionally charged and continue to disrupt the individual's life functioning.[4] Santiago represents a case of how veterans may cope by foreclosing the traumatic events of war during the day, although memories haunt them at night. When they bury Rata, another platoon member insists that Santiago participate in a bank robbery. Santiago declines, adducing that he wants peace because he cannot sleep, and he guesses the others cannot either. Reinforcing this topic is a scene framed as a black and white shot of Santiago fully dressed in army fatigues lying wide awake on bedsprings. Following this scene is a color shot of Santiago training and/or enacting war memories as in a muted choreography atop a hill overlooking the city. The recurrence of the traumatic event is suggested as we witness a black and white shot of Santiago lying fully dressed in army fatigues on the bedsprings, eyes wide open, and we wonder whether he is awake or actually reminiscing. These shots appear to represent an apparently core aspect of delayed traumatic stress reaction—the repetitious cycling of intrusive recollections with denial and psychic numbing.

Santiago avoids conversations about the war, but recurrent, intrusive recollections appear as behavioral re-enactments, as evidenced by his actions as he walks through the busy Lima streets, and when he takes Andrea hostage after the gun episode. Though Santiago is seduced by Elisa's plea to be saved from her own husband, she ultimately fears him. His relations with Mari and Andrea register Santiago's detachment and the restricted range of his affect. Though apparent in the first long (black and white with voice-over) sequence on the streets of Lima, hypervigilance is evident when his classmates remark that he is taking a longer route, and he replies, "Siempre voy por una ruta distinta . . . Yo sé que alguien siempre me está siguiendo . . . Siempre hay alguien, atrás de uno siempre hay alguien" ("I always take different ways . . . I just know there's always somebody following me . . . There's always somebody right there behind you").

Santiago's search for meaning is anchored in two main beliefs: "La vida es una psicología" ("Life is a psychollogy" [*sic*]) and "Sin orden nada existe" ("Without order nothing exists").[5] The two slogans echo the discourse of order that the military has traditionally deployed to fashion the institution and to justify the drastic measures implemented during state terrorism in Latin America and elsewhere. Santiago's idea of order is based on this regimented routine, as is evident when he practices how to tell his wife what the daily life he has envisioned for them looks like: "Desde mañana vamos a dormir máximo hasta las siete. Vamos a preparar el desayuno en media hora" ("Starting tomorrow, we'll sleep until seven. We'll make breakfast in half an hour"). Santiago has even thought out their meals: "lunes, cevichito; martes, pollo; miércoles, frijol; jueves, fideos; viernes, quinoa; sábados, lo que tú quieras. No vayas a pensar que estoy tratando de imponerte algo. No. Y los domingos . . . nos vamos a comer afuera" ("Mondays, ceviche; Tuesdays, chicken; Wednesdays, beans; Thursdays, noodles; Fridays, quinoa; Saturdays, you do whatever you want. Don't think I'm imposing on you. And Sundays, we eat out").

In need of self-assurance, Santiago writes down his thoughts and rehearses his speech. He cannot accept dissent. So, when Mari interrupts him repeatedly, telling him to eat his bread, Santiago experiences an outburst of anger, evidenced by slamming his fist on the table . While his abrupt actions suggest vulnerability, his wife, who is a nurse, fails to interpret them that way or to read accurately the symptoms of his malaise. Further chauvinism precludes him from having his wife contribute to installment payments, and Santiago becomes infuriated at the salesperson who suggests he will not be able to make the payments for a refrigerator. As the couple's frustration mounts, his wife refers to his "mente enferma" (sick mind). Santiago slaps her, a sign of how his violence forecloses their chance of a life together. Like Espinosa in *El aura*, Santiago rehearses actions in his mind prior to attempting them. This is evident when he imagines how to invite a girl to dance.

A number of the protagonists of the films I discuss in this book evidence signs of trauma, among them Roberto and Mercedes in *El cielito*, the mother in Oliveira Cézar's *El recuento de los daños*, and the couple of elderly peasants in *Hamaca paraguaya*. Those who suffer trauma remain in a state of physiological preparedness for the return of the intrusive symptoms. Recovery depends on the progressive psychological mastery of the trauma. The defensive avoidance of symptoms operates to protect the individual from overstimulation or the fear of retraumatization (Flora, 7).

To the extent that the diegetic present is overtaken by its symptoms, PTSD becomes a primary structural device of the movie as sequences infused by Santiago's memories of the past alternate with interspersed reenactments of the war in the present. The actualization of the past in the present forecloses Santiago's reinsertion into society. His attempt to re-create the regimented lifestyle of the past in everyday life with his wife, the incidents with the gun, and the respect Santiago feels civilians owe him combine to deprive him of a normal life with wife, family, and friends. That same reactivation of memories also deprives Santiago of the chance to pursue a career that might allow for a more satisfying reinsertion into society.

The reappearance of the repressed in Méndez's *Días de Santiago* recalls Deleuze's peaks of the present, as when Santiago's mind returns, imagining, to warfront actions that became traumatic but suggests inappropriate ways of interacting, such as his planning how to demolish the enemy as he walks through the busy streets of Lima. That his reactions are triggered automatically is evident in his outbursts of anger, such as when Santiago shoves his brother out of the car. PTSD symptoms arising from intentional human action like combat, physical abuse, torture, and participating in violence and atrocities are considered the worst and are more difficult to treat because they are usually more complex and of longer duration. Victims often feel stigmatized, especially in the case of rape. Man-made traumas are more difficult to treat because they "cause people to lose faith and trust in humanity, in love, and in themselves" (Schiraldi, 7). That Santiago's symptoms stem from participating in the violence of a war is all the more relevant because they arise from his position as a perpetrator. In a meeting with his buddies Santiago considers how "allá éramos lo máximo . . . éramos los tigres . . . armados hasta los dientes destruíamos todo, decapitábamos tarrucos, enterrábamos a los morros, la pasábamos así, matando hombres, mujeres, niños, todos los días . . . acá ya no somos nada" ("There we were the best . . . We were tigers . . . Armed to the teeth we destroyed everything, decapitated terrorists, buried Ecuadorians. That's how it was, killing men, women, and children every day . . . Here, we're nothing").

Santiago's recollections show the numbing of soldiers immersed in

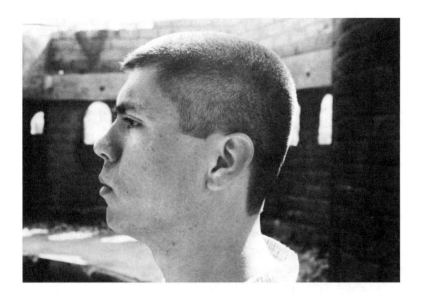

Figure 8.3
Santiago reminisces about lost power.
Courtesy Tropical Cinema.

conflict that allowed, or forced, them to inflict unthinkable violence on those in their path. Yet, despite the soldiers' apparent numbness, their harrowing deeds become etched in their consciousness only to torment them later.

Méndez addresses a two-pronged historical trauma, as the Peruvian army's war against terrorists was a civil war against Shining Path sympathizers, while the reference to the border dispute with Ecuador, an instance of international war, seems to have been waged against unarmed citizens. Rather than address national responsibility in these massacres, the film opens up the possibility of perpetrator trauma insofar as the very agents are willing to divest themselves from their implication in deadly practices (LaCapra, 79). The diegesis supports this thesis in that Santiago seeks to be discharged because he needs peace. Méndez's movie elides Santiago's actions at war with alleged terrorists or with neighboring Ecuadorians.

Since viewers are not privy to Santiago's thought processes when he re-experiences trauma, they cannot determine whether Santiago re-experiences the traumatic episodes literally. Therefore, Méndez's movie is not free from the current controversy surrounding trauma studies. On the one hand, in her introduction to *Trauma* Caruth maintains that psychic phenomena such as dreams, hallucinations, and thoughts are absolutely literal and thus cannot be assimilated to other associative chains of meaning (5). Therefore, she concludes, post-traumatic nightmares are re-experienced over and over again without modification (van der Kolk and van der Hart, 172). On the other hand, Leys contends (229) that despite the shared contention equating the traumatic symptoms with veridical memories, neither van der Kolk and van der Hart nor Caruth can prove that the symptoms are literal replicas. Indeed, trauma could not be curable if the exact same memories returned literally over and over.

Yet, Méndez's *Días de Santiago* shows that trauma is a structure of experience to the extent it is equated with being possessed by an image or event. Whether or not PTSD is a treatable condition or dulls with time, at the onset trauma is lived as a temporal delay that transports its victim beyond the initial shock (Caruth, 4, 10).[6] Therefore, the present is literally elided when the protagonist relives or reinstalls the past or when the past interacts with the present, as when Santiago walks through the streets of Lima imagining that he attacks the enemy among the passersby or when it becomes an automatic response, for example, in violent reactions toward friends and family.

In sum, Méndez's *Días de Santiago* places the problematic nature of trauma in the Latin American imaginary, where controversy persists about the role of the nation demanding unethical behavior from its soldiers. To that extent the film amplifies the graffiti Méndez came across in the streets of Lima that referred to condemning the consequences of oppression rather than its origin. The graffiti reads: "Se le llama salvaje al río que se desborda y no al cabrón que lo oprime" ("Rather than the jerk who stifles it, the overflowing river is called savage"). These words were complemented by a stark image of men about to break out of chains, and the graffiti and image appear in the movie. As Méndez's film offers a critique of the state's failure to provide adequate services for its veterans, he criticizes as abhorrent the practices that the state develops in order to counter the perceived danger of internal insurgency or the fear of losing territory at the border. Méndez's success is measured by the ability to show that PTSD haunts not just its victim but the perpetrators of state-sponsored violence. The alleged enemies of the state and those who purport to defend it are equally victims since they fall prey to PTSD. Given the traditional high profile of the military institution in Latin America, this is indeed a rather sober comment.

PART FOUR
EXPERIMENTAL AUTEURISM

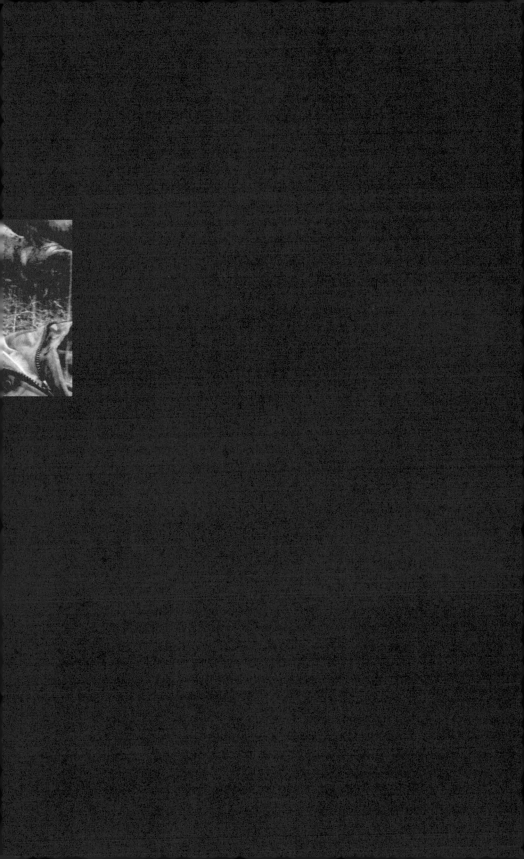

CHAPTER NINE
WHETHER OR NOT TO END ONE'S LIFE

Carlos Reygadas's *Japón*

In terms of auteurism, Reygadas's preference for "cine sensorial ... en que lo predominante es la emoción que se desprende de la imagen y el sonido" (a cinema of the senses ... in which emotion emanates primarily from images and sound) (in Romero, 180) is tantamount to a self-reflexive assessment, since the overarching effect of his three movies hinges on photography and music.[1] Like others in this study, the Mexican director acknowledges his debt to postwar Italian cinema: "I like Roberto Rossellini very much and the conditions in which he had to shoot, with the matter that was there. This was especially true of *Rome, Open City* [*Roma, città aperta*] (1945) and the situation was in some ways similar for me in *Japón*" (in Wood, *Talking Movies*, 190).

As Reygadas works with actors, he consistently holds information back to prevent them from intellectualizing the characters. Film critics usually mention Bresson's influence on Reygadas, which the Mexican director admits: "Bresson, though I am now influenced by him less and less, is also a master, especially for the way in which he works with actors and uses sound ... Tarkovsky was the one who really opened my eyes. When I saw his films I realized that emotion could come directly out of the sound and the image and not necessarily from the storytelling" (ibid., 190–191). These comments cast light on the revisionary nature of Reygadas's oeu-

vre, especially because the daring nature of his experimental movies positions him at the antipodes of the industrial (Hollywood) matrix, among
other current Mexican directors who have been successful both at home
and abroad. Where Guillermo del Toro's *El laberinto del Fauno* (2006) and
Alejandro González Iñárritu's *Babel* (2006) garnered Oscar nominations
for their adherence to generic conventions of horror and melodrama-
packed action movies, respectively, Reygadas focuses on feelings and
states of mind. He also participates actively in a Mexican cinematic tradition that stresses ideological differences. As opposed to del Toro's care-
ful orchestration of horror in the context of the Spanish Civil War and
Iñárritu's global interrelation of three simultaneous plot lines, Reygadas's
iconoclastic attitude is more attuned to the awareness of the New Latin
American Cinema, though not necessarily the commitment to espouse a
salvational metanarrative.

Japón opens with cars speeding through a tunnel. The camera follows
a highway through a variety of landscapes ranging from a wooded area to
lands cultivated with corn. Night goes by, and fog gives way to clarity.[2] The
trip ends on a dirt road, as suggested by the shaking images, in the midst
of an arid, mountainous landscape. As an unnamed, scrawny man (Alejandro Ferretis) walks through an area lined with agave he interrupts a hunting
party and asks the men for a ride down the cliff.[3]

When the hunters (among them Reygadas in a cameo appearance)
ask him the reason for his visit, the unidentified protagonist tells them he
wants to kill himself. His assertion ends the conversation.

Once in the village, he speaks to the indigenous community leaders,
who suggest that he find accommodations in a barn belonging to Ascen
(Magdalena Flores). Community members ask Sabina (Yolanda Villa), a
village woman, to accompany the man up the road and to ask Ascen to
honor his request. The unnamed man paints, listens to music, and smokes
pot. Provided with a cane, he climbs up the mesa to commit suicide only to

Figure 9.1
The unnamed protagonist asks an inquisitive
hunter for a ride. Courtesy Mantarraya.

discover the corpse of a castrated horse. The man blacks out, and when he regains consciousness, he returns to the village and learns that Ascen's nephew claims the stone foundations of the barn that also anchor her home, so he attempts to defend her well-being. Ascen, who shares indigenous phenotypes, is an octogenarian. Though the man is young enough to have been her son, he becomes sexually attracted to her. His interest is prefigured by a dream, a shot of her buttocks, and awkward moments when they hold hands. The mating of horses echoes the man's request to break intergenerational barriers by having intercourse.

Ascen finally acquiesces. The arrival of the townspeople, intent on demolishing the barn, interrupts the two as they attempt to have sex. Despite (or because of) their intentions, Ascen shows hospitality by offering the men pulque. After the heavy hewn foundation stones are loaded on two wagons pulled by a tractor, Ascen asks to accompany them on the ride down. The next morning Sabina, who introduced the man to Ascen, climbs up the road to tell him that everyone involved in the demolition of the barn has perished. The film ends with a long tracking shot that accounts for their strewn corpses.

While the camera shows the different scenarios, we assume retrospectively, though with no certainty, that it offers the man's point of view. For instance, when the camera is positioned at the front of a vehicle it focuses on the changing landscape and the passing of time to suggest the length of the journey. Though the audience does not see the vehicle, the camera focuses on a hand banging on a hood and pointing the way. Following the man's arrival at the mesa, the hand-held camera registers his perspective. The shaking image of the ground is almost dizzying, yet it is naturalized when we notice that the man, who is nearly lame, walks only with great difficulty, aided by a cane. A 360-degree shot of the mountainside subsequently allows for tracing the hunters' vehicle in its downward journey. The camera accomplishes this by following the movement of the

Figure 9.2
The protagonist's rebirth leads to sexual arousal and thus to an unexpected proposition. Courtesy Mantarraya.

front lights. The camera's alternation between the man's point of view and that of a distant observer emphasizes the beauty of the landscape, the changing light, and the cloud formations. The fog that fills the screen suggests that the man shot himself dead. Then the pouring rain awakens him.

That the botched suicide attempt becomes a rebirth is emphasized through camera work. From a helicopter the camera provides ever-widening and ascending circling shots of the man lying on the mesa facing the lush beauty of the gorge. The camera work accompanied by the crescendo of a chorale suggests the sublime, which by definition cannot be described.[4] The camera focuses on Ascen enthroned on the wagon; its parting shot zigzags from one side of the railway tracks to the other, showing the bodies that were strewn around as the excessive weight on the wagon caused it to go off the winding road and over the precipice. Fixed on the tracks, the lens zooms back a considerable distance until refocusing on Ascen, who stares ahead, unblinking, with lacelike blood criss-crossing her face.

Following Tarkovsky's technique, Reygadas's long shots allow for imprinting time "in its actual forms and manifestations" (63). The camera is as interested in the landscape as it is in the protagonist because the savage beauty of the mountains plays a significant role in character development. In contrast to the physically passive protagonist, the camera has agency. At odds mainly with himself, the protagonist does not seem proactive or efficacious even when he attempts to help Ascen. The film's morose rhythm arises from the combination of the protagonist's predicament and, following Tarkovsky, from the time inscribed in the shots (113).

This proactive role of the camera is key to Reygadas's auterism. As Clarke notes, *Japón* was initially shot on a 16mm camera, which allows for more mobility, and subsequently blown up to 35mm. The breathtaking landscapes are complemented by audacious camera work, as in the ascending circling shot of the man lying on the mesa, and in the way that Reygadas closes the film with a circling seven-minute shot that provides closure by swooping in on the fates of the various characters.

Figure 9.3
Contemplating suicide.
Courtesy Mantarraya.

Figure 9.4
Rebirth.
Courtesy Mantarraya.

Figure 9.5
Did Ascen plan the denouement?
Comeuppance or substitution?
Courtesy Mantarraya.

As a paratactical structuring device, montage is deployed to edit frames, shots, or alternating plot lines. In Reygadas's films the abrupt juxtaposition of scenes reinforces the importance of the interval, which results in a verfremdungs-effekt, because the need to fill in the blanks becomes obvious. By underscoring the intervals between scenes, *Japón* showcases Reygadas's auterism. The noise of a pig being slaughtered awakens the protagonist, allowing us to infer that he has spent the night at a butcher's shop. The initial zoom onto a shiny, black square with slits for eyes, crossed out with red, similarly produces estrangement until we discover that the square is a painting that offers information about the man's background, feelings, and habits, such as his close attention to the changing landscape. The interval reappears, first in the blackout following his botched suicide attempt and second in the traveling of the last scene that also shows Reygadas's allusion to the French sublime school, in which the interval defines the greatest relative quantity of movement in the content and for the imagination. The whole has accordingly become the simultaneous, the measureless, the immense, reducing imagination to impotence and confronting it with its own limit (Deleuze, *Cinema 1*, 48). In sum, Reygadas's paratactical structure hinges on the interval, and true to its nature, the interval appears to be elided.

While the scenes represent interrelated units, Reygadas's intense focus on landscape suggests its effect on the protagonist and reinforces the intimation of the sublime. The unexpected ending conjures the archaic poetic justice of Greek tragedies, as Ascen metes out death by getting the men so drunk that they remain unaware of the impending danger. Still, Ascen's regal descent into death is as unimaginable, as unfathomable, perhaps, as the man's opting for life, accidentally or not, or as Ascen's taking his place.

The attraction that the man, who appears to be from a cultured, urban, middle-class background (Clarke), feels for Ascen may stem from the

Figure 9.6 In the protagonist's dream, Ascen welcomes her younger self.

realization that city life is hollow in comparison to the woman's simple life, religious fervor, and willingness to discover new experiences such as art and marijuana. The attraction seems all the more unlikely because of Ascen's advanced age—which she states as a rationale not to have him as a lodger as well as her home's lack of running water. Reygadas resorts to a dream sequence to add plausibility to the attraction; thus, realistic shots of a bikini-clad young woman that affirm the hegemonic ideal of beauty become taboo when the young woman kisses Ascen on the mouth.

In other words, the object remains concrete, while the unhinging arises from the taboo (Deleuze, *Cinema 2*, 58). The audience may infer it is privy to an earlier avatar of the woman whom the man, as a painter, can appreciate. Breaking the taboo of intergenerational sexuality with the shots of a nude Ascen marks an attempt to expand the western imaginary in homage to the beauty of an old woman's body.[5] The sexual imagery is ambiguously connoted through showing horses. The image of the castrated horse at the top of the mesa may be read either as foreshadowing or as an intimation of the man's motivation. Though the camera shows the unnamed protagonist masturbating once he has given up on killing himself, in another scene he sees a horse mounting a mare, which suffuses the narrative as he asks Ascen to have sex.

In terms of the construction of characterization, Reygadas relies on the Kuleshov effect, which Reygadas describes in an interview by Peter Fraser as a method whereby actors receive practical spatial and temporal but not psychological information so the director's editing and the cinematic process construct the characters. Reygadas trusts the energy that the actors radiate by virtue of their mere existence, for he believes that a stronger sense of emotion comes through if they abstain from expressing emotions.[6] Faithful to Reygadas's style, he keeps the audience in the dark about the protagonist's possible motivations. Viewers never find out what drove the man to the village to commit suicide or, for that matter, why he did not carry through. Perhaps, and in accordance with the cliché, as an artist, he feels redeemed by the beauty of the landscape. Perhaps he is saved by Ascen's kindness and willingness to try new things. Perhaps Ascen reinforces the man's commitment to life by taking her life in stead.

The extent to which Reygadas's style includes neorealist features underscores aesthetic similarities in this set of influences, his oeuvre, and other directors working in the New Latin American Cinema. In addition to working with nonprofessional actors, ad-libbing many of the scenes, including the sex scene (Clarke), and shooting on location and with natural light, Reygadas includes the voyage, which begins in Mexico City and ends in the mountainous area of Hidalgo. Adhering to neorealist tenets, the character has become a kind of viewer who records rather than reacts (Deleuze, *Cinema 2*, 3). Reygadas uses the musical score to suggest changes in the protagonist's mindset at several points of the movie. On the few occasions when the protagonist tries to act, basically to defend Ascen's home from being destroyed, he fails. The dispersive situation arises from the examination of moral issues amid Reygadas's insistence on withholding crucial information regarding the characters' mindsets and/ or motivations.

Despite the clichés in presenting Ascen as a pious woman, her predicament is clear; the audience feels for the woman, who knows that the foundations of the barn anchor her home and that it will no longer resist the weather when they are removed. By giving them up, she signs her death sentence. Her acceptance may be attributed to the self-sacrificing role expected of women in Catholicism. The nephew's cheating is all the more galling because Ascen visited him when he was in prison. The implicit betrayal by the community that condones the action is also telling. Despite the ambiguity regarding Ascen's motivation to ride on the wagon, the denouement reads like the poetic justice of a Greek tragedy. Since Ascen's home is condemned when her nephew takes the foundations, her only option is death, either up on the mountain or on the wagon. Though the man never admits his motivation to Ascen, she appears to have inferred it and, as part of an unspoken pact, immolates herself in a perfect instance of the Derridean supplement. The resulting undecidability regarding the motivations of both the unnamed protagonist and Ascen allows for an allegorical reading of the film.

The condemnation of plot must be understood in the terms of the plot lines of action-image movies, as epitomized by Hitchcock, that rely strictly on causality and rationality. Rather than fleshing out any one character's reasoning, Reygadas focuses on mental processes and leaves the audience in the dark in an opacity reinforced by the paratactical articulation, the apparent juxtaposition of scenes, generally held together by the retrospectively assumed presence of the protagonist. The weak links between scenes underscore the importance of the interval in allowing for delayed reactions that includes an in-between, occupied by affection, which associates movement with a "quality" as lived state.

Affective films allow for a slippage since the event itself goes beyond its own causes, referring to other effects whose causes fall aside in turn. By flattening the third dimension, Reygadas connects the second dimension with the affect and with the fourth dimension of time and the fifth dimension of the spirit, which would explain the allegorical reading (Deleuze, *Cinema 1*, 107). The presence of the five characteristics that Deleuze attributes to the postwar new image links Reygadas's oeuvre to neorealism and to the New Latin American Cinema. Allusions to these movements provide continuity while assuring that this iconoclastic director can claim a representative place in contemporary New Latin American Cinema. Reygadas incorporates neorealist conventions typical of the New Latin American Cinema such as relying on nonprofessional actors and shooting on location, and his syncopated style challenges Hollywood conventions, creating alternative modes of production and reception.

CHAPTER TEN
CRIME AND SELF-INFLICTED PUNISHMENT

Carlos Reygadas's *Batalla en el cielo*

Reygadas acknowledges a displacement from the existential crisis in *Japón* to a social crisis in *Batalla en el cielo* (James, "Angels," 31). Like its predecessors in the New Latin American Cinema, Reygadas's *Batalla en el cielo* (*Battle in Heaven*, 2005) offers social critique in that it underscores economic inequality and rampant corruption throughout Mexican society. Examples of its shocking scenes appear when the film opens and closes with blow jobs. Marcos (Marcos Hernández) is beset by guilt because of the unexpected death of the baby he and his wife, Berta (Bertha Ruiz), kidnapped to exact ransom.[1] Marcos shares the news with Ana (Anapola Mushkadiz), the daughter of the general whose driver he has been for more than fifteen years. When Ana learns the secret she suggests Marcos get some consolation from her friends at the brothel where she, unbeknownst to her parents, works.

Given Marcos's impotence with another sex worker, Ana assumes Marcos wants to have intercourse with her, and she complies. When he returns home, Berta suggests the couple atone for their sins by going on a pilgrimage to the Basilica of the Virgin of Guadalupe, but Marcos seeks to assuage his guilt through strenuous activities such as climbing a mountain that is crowned by a set of crosses. When he realizes Ana doesn't care for him, he stabs her to death. After doing penance, he dies at the basilica.

Even though Marcos and Ana are dead, the movie ends with another blow job, which reinforces doubts about their ontological status. Are these scenes real? Imagined by Marcos? As we will see, the initial and final blow jobs suggest a circular structure, yet both scenes are diegetically out of sequence, and the attitudes of the protagonists differ. At the beginning, the camera focuses on a tear sliding down Ana's cheek; however, as the film closes, a beaming Marcos says, "Te quiero mucho Ana" (I love you so, Ana), and she replies, "Yo también te quiero, Marcos" (I love you too, Marcos).[2]

The deliberately weak links between the scenes lead to the ambiguity that pervades the film. Though the reappearance of the protagonist provides continuity, the abrupt shifts stress the interval. For instance, while the locale of the blow job remains undetermined, the next scene takes place in the wee hours of the morning at the Zócalo, where Marcos witnesses the raising of the flag, presumably because he works for the general, Ana's father, whose office is nearby. Afterward, we see Marcos standing against the blue metallic wall of the metro. Another cut leads us to a naked Marcos standing against the light-blue wall of the brothel. In the following scene, at night, Marcos is filling the tank at a deserted and aseptic gas station. Soon we see a Botero-like shot of Marcos's wife sitting by her son, Irving, who is sleeping on a yellow sofa. In the following scene the camera cuts to Marcos, who reappears at the Zócalo. It is dawn. Another cut takes us back to the so-called boutique. Then the camera leads us to the apartment of Ana's boyfriend, Jaime. At dawn, Marcos reappears at the Zócalo. Later that morning, he shows up at Jaime's apartment. After he kills Ana, information about Marcos and the agents who pursue him is presented through parallel alternate montage until the agents meet Marcos at the basilica. While the rain has a cleansing value, the bells toll for the dead in the Zócalo, reminding us of Berta's plans to do penance.

As in *Japón*, Reygadas uses the camera to follow quite closely the protagonist's point of view. Jostling to take the train, Marcos loses his eyeglasses. At the airport we see Ana through his eyes, that is, as in a dim blur, out of focus. The camera's point of view seemingly becomes independent when Ana and Marcos have intercourse.

The camera initially focuses on the open window before beginning a 360-degree pan that takes in two men installing a network dish. It then travels around the adjacent buildings, follows a long crack in the wall, and stops at a dripping faucet. The pan continues along the lovers' bodies to

Figure 10.1
Amoral Ana grants Marcos's wish.
Courtesy Mantarraya.

Marcos's erect member and to Ana's crotch. Lying beside him she says, "Vas a tener que entregarte, Marcos" (You'll have to turn yourself in, Marcos). Tavener's accompanying musical score suggests a funeral march and foreshadows a death pact.[3] The shot evidences Reygadas's interest in surfaces (bodies, walls) but also points at the function of the close-up, to draw the spectator in. While directors I previously discussed used the close-up for a series of faces or to suggest an ill-fated love, as with the letters of Josué's parents in *Central do Brasil*, the slow motion of Reygadas's circular pan suggests the passing of time and perhaps escapism on Ana's part, given that she is performing a service as a sex worker.

As an auteur, Reygadas takes an ironic stance. The irony that pervades *Batalla* allows for depth while also reinforcing intertextual allusions of the sort that heighten the neorealist aspects of Reygadas's oeuvre. For instance, when Berta tells Marcos how the baby died, their mechanical demeanor is reminiscent of wooden peasants in cuckoo clocks. In other words, there is a mise-en-abyme between the couple and the clocks sold at the makeshift stand in the metro.

Marcos is lost in thought at the gas station when a battered 1970s sedan pulls in. Slapstick humor arises from the surprising capacity of the automobile: eleven people march out of it. Furthermore, in a metatextual gesture, the female lead of *Japón* inquires, "¿Qué música es ésta, hijo?" (What is this music, son?). When Marcos goes to see Ana, Jaime playfully asks him if he woke up on top or under and proceeds to cut watermelon—after Frida Khalo, a symbol of femininity. While Marcos waits for Ana, he stares at a picture of a stallion—another obvious symbol—against the red wall. Finally, while Marcos is on his way to the basilica, a preacher assures him that he has been saved and as the proof, places a triangular bonnet— an allusion to the Inquisition—over Marcos's head. The preacher's speech becomes all the more playful as his words "No más mujeres, no más tetas" (No more women, no more tits) are heard in a shot of Marcos advancing on his knees, passing by two female officers enjoying an ice cream. As suggested by these images, the postwar cinema stresses clichés (Deleuze, *Cinema 1*, 210). By incorporating popular culture images that cross over internationally, such as cuckoo clocks and stallions, Reygadas reinforces audience appeal. Images like the watermelon naturalize the film in terms of its Mexican origin and stress its exotic allure for international audiences. Finally, in the image of the bonnet that harks back to the Inquisition, an institution that spread its nefarious power over Latin America, Reygadas reinforces the religious overtones of Marcos's quest for atonement.

This parade of deliberately weak links generates the indeterminacy and ambiguity that surrounds Marcos's demise. While on his knees, he falls head first at a street crossing; we notice that blood is beginning to stain the side of the bonnet that covers his face. Ironically, the bonnet allows Marcos to elude the police agents. At the basilica, bleeding profusely, Marcos kneels on a pew. His wife enters, sits beside Marcos, and touches him. Marcos's body falls sidewise. As on other occasions the stone-faced

Figure 10.2 Mise-en-abyme: Couple's mechanical demeanor is reminiscent of wooden peasants in cuckoo clocks. Courtesy Mantarraya.

woman stares at the camera like an Olmec idol, yet her tears parallel Ana's in the initial blow-job scene. Despite the foreshadowing effect of Tavener's music, Marcos's intentions are never clear. He seems to be overwhelmed by guilt and searching for atonement. The imagery in his bedroom is telling. The camera traces the blood that drips from Christ's side down to his loincloth, focusing on *jouissance*, the ecstasy of pain as suggested by his expression.[4] Though Ana seems amoral, the two are alike in their betrayal. Ana lies to her parents and to Jaime. Corruption may be rampant in the military and the police. The advantages of class, whiteness, and money set up insurmountable barriers to social advancement. Serving as a general's driver for more than fifteen years allows Marcos to scrape together a lower-middle-class income. By engaging in criminal activities that betray the trust of their close friend Viky, he and his wife victimize a member of their extended family.

All these weak links underscore the film's paratactical articulation, which is reinforced by iterability since the repetition of dialogue suggests the displacement of affection and structures the film as repetition with variation. For instance, Marcos assures his wife, "Vamos a estar separados pero te llevaré ahí dentro" (We'll be separated but you'll always be in my heart). Telling Ana that he's about to turn himself in to the police, he asks, "¿No te importa que quedemos separados?" (You don't mind us being separated?). In other words, he repeats the question Berta asked him, and ironically Ana repeats his, "No, . . . te voy a llevar ahí dentro" (I'll keep you in my heart).[5]

Figure 10.3
Ana's farewell since Marcos is purportedly giving himself up to the police. Courtesy Mantarraya.

Ellipsis, evident regarding the cause of the baby's death, reappears in the motivation for the kidnapping, Ana's murder, and the cause of Marcos's death. However, rather than being inherent to the plot, which moves from an action to a partially disclosed situation, the ellipsis belongs to the situation itself, because reality is lacunary as much as dispersive (Deleuze, *Cinema 1*, 207). As an auteur, Reygadas hints in the film at the partial and relative approaches to reality. *Batalla* explores the question of moral standards in a secular contemporary setting. Marcos, Berta, and Ana are guilty of greed and the betrayal of trust, but Ana appears unrepentant. Marcos and Berta sin further by causing the unexpected death of an innocent, but only Marcos seems to care. Guilt is always already subjective. While husband and wife struggle with it in different ways, they do so within a Catholic framework marked by an individual relationship with the deity, or its representative, for them the Virgin of Guadalupe.

This individualized moral struggle underscores the lacunary and dispersive aspect of reality in *Batalla* that may also result from Reygadas's method. The Mexican director "almost exclusively casts non-professionals, claiming that his requirement for the most natural performances necessitates a total lack of acting from real people who don't try to communicate meaning" (Wood, 189). As Reygadas works with nonprofessional actors, casting depends on their personalities. There is a certain citation of the documentary in that he does not tell them how to dress. The sense of a documentary also arises from the feeling of real time that certain scenes convey. Again following Tarkovsky, Reygadas's morose rhythm arises from the time inscribed in the shots, as is especially evident in the long pan around the building when Ana and Marcos are having intercourse and in the slow turn of Marcos's head as he addresses his wife at the stall in the metro when he inquires about the death of the kidnapped baby. His camera pans on nude bodies stirred much controversy, as critics adduced that the director had exploited nonprofessional actors. Yet those long sweeps on the surface of the bodies inscribe a variation of the close-up, characteristic of Carl Theodor Dreyer's style, that Reygadas fully articulates in his next film. Deleuze has noted that Dreyer's flowing close-ups, in continuous movement from the close-up to the medium shot, are primarily close-ups that reinforce an affective reading. Flattening the third dimension enables Reygadas to connect the second dimension with the affect. Although this may shock some readers who may wish to bracket the sexual scenes, this flattening should also connect with the fourth and fifth dimensions, that is, time and the spirit (*Cinema 1*, 107).

The scandal of an affair between Marcos, who has indigenous phenotypes and represents the lower middle class, and Ana, who is white and
belongs to the elite, undermines rigid Mexican class and racial divides,
adding to the controversy. While Marcos and his wife could be identified
phenotypically as sharing indigenous traits, in Mexico they would be
considered part of the lumpen-proletariat as *ladinos*—assimilated descendants from indigenous peoples. Reygadas runs counter to hegemonic
views by portraying obese women; some are like Viky, who sports shock-
ingly orange peroxide hair. In these views, the intimate scenes between
Marcos and his heavy wife are grotesque. Yet, even then it could be argued
that these scenes are taken to expand the Mexican imagery, as Reygadas
did when he included Ascen's nude body in *Japón*.[6]

Articulated as variations in cultural capital, Ana represents an amoral
present and Marcos a sinning but repentant past. The degree to which
each character sins remains unanswered, yet moral allegories emerge
from the interstices precisely because of the film's ambiguity. In other
words, echoing Deleuze's death knell of the action-image cinema, the
protagonist embarks on a voyage. In *Batalla en el cielo* that travel allows
for allegorical readings because the dispersive situation it presents is emphasized by deliberately weak links, resulting from Reygadas's intentional
condemnation of plot.

The extent to which Reygadas's style invokes neorealist features underscores further aesthetic influences and similarities between his oeuvre
and the New Latin American Cinema. The journey, typical of the postwar
image, begins with the accidental death of the kidnapped infant as Marcos embarks on a quest for atonement that leads to penance by way of
strenuous physical exercise and ironically, murder, given Marcos's inability
to come to terms with unrequited love, along with an archaic religious
desire to exact punishment for sins. The dispersive situation arises from
the frustrated examination of moral issues, given Reygadas's insistence
on withholding crucial information regarding the mindsets and/or the motives of the protagonists. Structured paratactically as a juxtaposition of
scenes, *Batalla* is generally held together by the retrospectively assumed
presence of the protagonist. As in *Japón*, Reygadas's *Batalla* underscores
the importance of the interval. The paratactical articulation is mirrored by
the ambiguity of characters' motives and clichés such as the picture of the
horse at the apartment of Ana's boyfriend, suggesting unbridled sexuality.
The ambiguity results in an affective reading that uncannily connects the
events with the spirit.

PART FIVE
EXPERIMENTAL AUTEURISM AND INTERTEXTUALITY

CHAPTER ELEVEN
THE MIRACLE OF FEMALE BONDING IN PATRIARCHAL SOCIETY

Carlos Reygadas's *Stellet licht*

As the last of a triptych of films centered on the attractions and revulsions in the social interdiction of taboo, Reygadas's *Stellet licht* returns to the question of guilt that he explored in *Batalla en el cielo*. *Stellet licht* could be seen as the reverse image of *Batalla*, for the taboos around crossing the sharply defined lines of race/ethnicity and class are transferred to a Mennonite community in northern Mexico.[1]

The action turns around adultery in *Stellet licht*, as Johan (Cornelio Wall), a farmer and father of seven, has told his wife, Esther (Miriam Toews),[2] about his ongoing affair with Marianne (María Pankratz), who runs a restaurant. Johan also confides in his close friend Zacarías (Jacobo Klassen), who repairs farming equipment; he furthermore seeks advice from his father, Peter (Peter Wall), a preacher. Though Mennonites wed for life, Johan is tempted to "make the necessary adjustments to correct his choice of a wife," a liberal attitude that also appears in his father's unwavering support, although the latter cautiously admits to his son that he also was in love with another woman at the time of his birth. The father nonetheless notes that he overcame temptation by distancing himself from the object of his desire.

Reygadas's *Stellet licht* adapts Carl Theodor Dreyer's masterpiece *Ordet* (1954), a film adapted in turn from Danish Lutheran pastor Kaj

Figure 11.1
Mennonite construction in northern Mexico.
Courtesy Mantarraya.

Munk's play *Ordet* (1932). Munk's *Ordet* depicts the primitive, hard farm life at Jutland and the religious feud between two families there: the Skraedders, who believe in divine grace, and the Borgens, who adhere to a hellfire message. In Munk's play, Johannes Borgen has a bout of insanity after a quarrel about religion, leading to the accidental death of his wife, Inger, in childbirth. Inger Borgen's resurrection from her coffin becomes a message of miraculous intervention. In Dreyer's adaptation, Johannes goes mad from overwork in studying theology: the focus shifts to Inger, his sister-in-law (Milne, 156–157).[3]

Transmutation best defines Reygadas's filmic adaptation, in which the action occurs in a Mennonite congregation in northern Mexico.[4] A middle-age father of seven, Johan suffers because he cannot stop himself from seeing his mistress, Marianne. His wife, Esther, initially feels hatred toward her rival and refers to her as a whore, but as the affair goes on, her rancor becomes pity. Esther appears to have a heart attack on the way to the doctor. After her dramatic death in the pouring rain, her husband becomes guilt-ridden and consumed by grief. During the wake, however, Marianne awakens Esther by kissing her on the lips.

According to Reygadas, "The other woman wakes up the wife in an act of compassion. Christ died on the cross for us. It is the same for her. She did this for the love of her man" (in Badt, "*Silent Light*"). But Marianne's

sensual kiss undermines heteronormative expectations: as her tear travels down Esther's cheek, the women's tragic bond is sealed, their apparent
rivalry undercut by their shared suffering. Esther's first reaction is a la-
ment, suggesting that she had in some way willed her death so as to allow
for her husband's affair. Marianne's kiss similarly mirrors Esther's sacrifice,
for she distances herself from Johan after every obstacle to their union
has seemingly been surmounted. The two women become complicit when
she tells Esther not to worry because Johan will cope. Reaction to the resurrection itself is elided. While the camera focuses intently on the body's
gradual changes (swallowing, eyelids flickering, and so on), the innocence
of the youngest daughters, who have been told that death is like sleeping,
naturalizes the event.

Figure 11.2
Redeemed and redeeming Marianne about
to resurrect Esther. Courtesy Mantarraya.

Unlike Dreyer's 1954 *Ordet*, which centers on securing the well-being of the family, Reygadas's *Stellet licht* a half-century later focuses on the collateral damage of the affair and the commiseration of the two women. Given that the protagonist is a middle-age man, one may in fact wonder if his plight is all the more pathetic as a Mennonite, saddled as he is with seven children. Despite his aging, saggy body, two women are ready to sacrifice themselves for him. Since Mennonite women's lives in this community are centered on the patriarchal family, Esther mentions that she feels unhinged: the affair has made her lose her anchoring in reality. On the other hand, Marianne appears to control Johan. She sends for him, decides to terminate the affair, and awakens Esther with the kiss, a taboo that seals a bond between the women even as it sidesteps the man they share.

The women eventually take over the film, and Johan becomes irrelevant. Much like the deformed image of Johan's family reflected on the bronze pendulum of the clock, Reygadas's *Stellet licht* inscribes and subverts the mechanism of the close-knit family that Dreyer portrays in his *Ordet*, for the affair lurks beneath the surface. In the course of unraveling the causality of Reygadas's film and considering the incidence of mental illness among Mennonite women (Dueck, 217), we could speculate on whether Esther's depression might have triggered Johan's affair (Žižek, 121).

In his reworking of the content of the earlier film, Reygadas's movie evidences his debt to Dreyer's style. An auteur, Dreyer is known for simplifying plot lines by reducing all actions, events, and props to a minimum. Dreyer's minimalism encompasses the movements of the characters, the repositioning of the camera, and the number of intercut shots in a scene. By paring events down Dreyer achieves a temporal retardation so as to emphasize the movement of his characters in the film's entire duration. Dreyer aimed at an evocative response: he expected the audience to imagine events beyond character's exchanges, actions, and so on (Carney, 72–75).[5]

Reygadas incorporates Dreyer's minimalism in mise-en-scène, plot, and movement of characters and camera into his depiction of Mennonite life, which is supposedly bereft of ornamentation. This is particularly obvious at the wake, where the corpse seems suspended in the whiteness of the sparse room. Reygadas stresses the habitual nature of the family's actions by having the image of the fixed camera gazing at the family during prayer before breakfast reflected on the bronze pendulum of the wall clock. Reygadas adheres to Dreyer's deliberate slowing down of character movements quite closely since most of the characters in all of his films appear to be sitting or still. Also like Dreyer, who tracks the entire duration of character movements, Reygadas has the camera follow Johan intently to reflect his mood. After picking up a piece of equipment at Zacarías's body shop where he discusses his love affair, Johan shows his joie de vivre at the imminent tryst by driving his truck in circles around his friend to the tune of the song played on the radio, "Volveré" (I Will Return). When Marianne calls the affair off, the camera offers a symbol by following the descent of a featherlike object—a red cedar leaf falling through the windowpane to the bedroom floor.

Dreyer's reduction of dialogue is particularly influential in Reygadas's movie. For instance, when Johan seeks advice from his father regarding which woman he should live with, the conversation moves away from the admission of guilt to the role of the devil (El Maligno), so Johan asks his father not to preach. Likewise, when Johan blames himself for having caused his wife's heart attack, his father attempts to deflect his remorse by stating the role of predestination. In other words, the intellectual discussion of ethics is bracketed twice, which is not surprising given Reygadas's previous films. As Reygadas relies on elision, it is up to viewer to endow the juxtaposed scenes with a sense of causality. This is particularly true in the scene at the pond in which bathing is followed by a shower, as suggested by the sounds of water coming from the open but dark doorways. Following Tarkovsky, the long shots allow for the inscription of time and set up the rhythm. A four-minute initial shot of sunrise, counterpointed with the final image of the sunset, sets up the characters' connection with their roots through images of the family house, childhood, and country (Tarkovsky, 193).[6] This is why the reflection of the family gathered at breakfast on the bronze pendulum of the clock is so significant: because it emphasizes the close-knit nature of family.

It is immaterial whether Reygadas is aware of the work of a film critic such as Carney, who argues for a transcendental reading of Dreyer's work, for Carney's reading of Dreyer's style casts a new light on all three of the Mexican director's movies. Moreover, Reygadas's interview by Badt on *Stellet licht* reinforces these views, even if couched in politically incorrect terms: "Most of the film is shot frontally and laterally because the place and the people demanded it; they are visually homogeneous and clean. They take the Bible literally, to take dominion over the land and propagate." But, as Carney has demonstrated, the transcendental reading is arrived at by breaching Hollywood conventions, making it all the harder for an audience to entertain such an oblique reading. To that extent, the movie offers another reading in which the Eden-like location of the pool enveloped in foliage and the angelic children thinly disguises the ugly truth of the father's affair.

Like the other Reygadas films, *Stellet licht* embodies the synergy between the fiction film and the conventions of the documentary—a legacy of the New Latin American Cinema, influenced as it was by Italian neorealism and the Cuban Revolution's emphasis on the documentary. As Reygadas was looking for an archetypal, placeless, and timeless setting, his rationale to portray the Mennonites grew from the uniformity of their society. He faced an obvious drawback in the Mennonite interdiction on the reproduction of human beings, even in paintings. Reygadas overcame this obstacle by relying on Germanic Protestantism, which implies that decisions are taken on an individual or family level, so the Mexican director spent time with members of the Mennonite community. During those four years he often visited actor Cornelio Wall Fehr's family. Reygadas's interest in the depiction of real locations, with the language and customs regarding dress, the architecture, and the tilling of the land (Romney, 43), all strike a cord with neorealism, as do the long shots, which also testify to Dreyer's influence.

In his adaptation of the New Latin American Cinema's penchant for re-counting fiction according to the generic conventions of the documentary (Bentes, 126), Reygadas underscores the textual and referential similarities between fiction films and observational documentaries. The affective impact of these scenes is heightened by the techniques deployed in observational cinema that convey the sense of direct access to the world by eliding the presence of the filmmaker. Pascal Mérigeau, who defines Reygadas's work as "poetic naturalism," contends that the Mexican director's aesthetics synthesizes the core ideals of the Latin American Cinema of the 1960s (in Amiot, 164), and Julie Amiot argues that Reygadas's international success results from the strong ethical stance that underscores his depiction of social reality (164).[7]

Following the conventions of the postwar image or the Deleuzian time-image, Reygadas's *Stellet licht* is structured paratactically as a juxtaposition of scenes linked by the presence of Johan, the male protagonist. The movie loosely follows his daily life, family, and farm, with his occasional forays to the body shop and into his lover's arms. Though the camera shows the different scenarios and sutures the man into them, it offers his point of view when Esther begs him to stop, since he follows her shape in the storm. After staring for some time at the dashboard he decides to look for her. The interval appears in the blackout suggested by Esther's catatonic state. It reappears at the site of the wake when the camera, located outside, focuses on the windowpane and shows the events taking place inside—Esther's dead body being moved into the coffin—and the reflection of the farm, symbolizing the ongoing nature of life, and perhaps more poignantly, her catatonic state, suspended as she is between life and death. To the extent the shot becomes an allusion to the French sublime school, the interval enters into relationships with the other shots, underscoring the limits of the imagination to conceive of death and/or a catatonic state.

Ironically, the question of Esther's awakening brings the question of undecidability to the fore. Her daughters are not surprised because they were told their mother was sleeping; her husband and relatives, however, will have to decide whether she was catatonic or her awakening is the result of a miracle. In these secular days, the ending allows for an allegorical reading of the film to the extent that Reygadas chooses not to delve into the psychological state of his characters and searches instead for opacity regarding their motives.

The postwar image defined in terms of the voyage, the dispersive situation, the deliberately weak links, and the condemnation of plot that the directors of the New Latin American Cinema adopted through the influence of neorealism also appears in *Stellet licht*. Though Johan and Esther's voyage is psychically limited, the nature of the affair leads Esther to the unplumbed depth of death and back. Reygadas's insistence on withholding character motivation results in the condemnation of plot as the audience attempts to interpret the psychological impact of the affair through study of the character's actions. The deliberately weak links between scenes emphasize the dispersive situation. Shots like those of the family being mirrored in the pendulum of the clock or the initial and final shots suggesting the eternal cycle of nature suggest consciousness of clichés, as Reygadas meets certain criteria in film after film, enhancing his stature as an auteur with a recognizable style.

The captivating effect of the film at least partly results from the por-

trayal of ritual time. Depicting a cycle of life through marriage, reproduction, and gender-specific daily activities closely connected to the
domestication of the land by way of agriculture reinforces the aptness
of filming within the Mennonite community. Ritual time perpetuates itself
despite the ephemeral nature of human life: social relations retain a relative stability although the members of each specific society change constantly due to the cycle of life and to exchanges between groups through
marriage. While agrarian societies are structured in terms of time, theirs is
not a sense of historical time comparable to our own but of a time made
up of interconnected cycles (Lefebvre, 317, 319). Reygadas's films are attuned to the cycle of life: *Japón* illustrates the urbanite's discovery of a
traditional rural lifestyle, and *Batalla* resorts to an urban setting to focus on
the intertwined cycles of life among people from different social classes
who cannot meet as equals despite sharing certain spaces. By focusing
on a community that shares a traditional religious and agricultural lifestyle,
Reygadas sets up the characters of *Stellet licht* as equals. The nature of
their predicament undermines their uniqueness, however, by turning them
into ciphers, mere players in one of the most ancient plots. Nonetheless,
since a love affair is such a private matter, time becomes a significant factor in measuring the development of emotions.

The Deleuzian crystal-image, the most fundamental operation of time,
splits the present into the future to make the present pass on, while the
other part falls into the past to preserve it all (*Cinema 2*, 81). Such aspects
of time and image apply to every action, as Marianne's status as the mistress and not the wife taints her love with sadness and deepens Johan's
sense of guilt. Neither of them shows regret, yet these feelings appear to
be played out at each meeting with a cumulative effect; despite the ambiguity that pervades the relationship, on different occasions both attempt
to put an end to the affair.

Regarding the notion of sheets of time, Deleuze notes that the past appears as the coexistence of circles, constituting strata, and sheets, each of
which contains everything at the same time and the present of which it is
the extreme limit (*Cinema 2*, 98–99). While the Mennonite customs suggest timelessness, such sheets of time are particularly evident in the farm.
The design of the house is typical of the community; the weather-beaten
adobe walls attest to the passing of time and assimilation to Mexican
customs. The ritual nature of the wake harks back at the notion of actions
sculpted in time. Lastly, defining peaks of time, Deleuze adds that the

present is the presence of something, which precisely stops being present when it is replaced by something else. The possibility of treating an episode as a single event provides the basis for the implication of presents (*Cinema 2*, 100). When Johan drives Esther to the doctor she recalls the times they have gone down the road in the past. Habitual actions relished in the past, such as singing on the way or Esther's falling asleep, spoke of their love. Moreover, Esther shows dependency by admitting that she feels alive and aware of life through Johan. Therefore, when Esther, who has known about the affair from the beginning, learns that Johan has been with Marianne once again, she feels utterly cut off from life: the ensuing overwhelming grief appears to trigger her heart attack.

To conclude, as homage to Dreyer's *Ordet* (1954), Reygadas's *Stellet licht* is the latest transmutation of Munk's play and a testimony to the Mexican director's intellectual development. The admixture of features of the documentary and neorealism—the involvement of nonprofessional actors and the use of real locations (place, architecture, dress, language), for example—stress the symbiosis in a film that sets out to present a timeless, placeless archetype. As Reygadas's film showcases the categories of time that Deleuze has identified in film, namely, the crystal-image, peaks of present, and sheets of the past, *Stellet licht* demonstrates the rich and experimental nature of the Mexican director's aesthetics. The inclusion of the five characteristics that Deleuze attributes to the postwar new image—the voyage, the dispersive situation, the deliberately weak links, the intentional condemnation of plot, and the consciousness of clichés—all link Reygadas's 2008 film to his earlier ones, to neorealism, and to the New Latin American Cinema.

By focusing on the plight of a Mennonite couple in northern Mexico, Reygadas stretches the Mexican imaginary, shedding light on sameness and alterity while examining timeless questions of love and betrayal. Where his first film, *Japón*, depicts a single unnamed protagonist as alienated and engaged in death and *Batalla* opens up that auteur consciousness to multiple conflicting points of view, within Reygadas's trademark for setting and landscape, *Stellet licht* presents the most ambitious and complex of the director's work to date in its engagement with the themes of representation and taboo, multiple temporalities, and neorealist features, among them the Mennonite dialect of Chihuahua.

CHAPTER TWELVE
CYCLICAL SCAPEGOATING

Inés de Oliveira Cézar's *Extranjera*

As introduced in *Como pasan las horas*, Oliveira Cézar's directorial signature lies in sculpting actions in time; however, the director goes beyond
Tarkovsky's notion of inscribing time in actions by tracing similarities
between civilizations in different geographical locations and periods. Thus,
in *Como pasan las horas*, Virginia's pouring wine for the dead reenacts
a libation ritual that she attributes to Persian poets. In *Extranjera* and *El
recuento de los daños*, the gesture of cultural crossover is set against
ancient Greek myths rehearsed repeatedly through the cycle of tragedies.

Oliveira Cézar's second film, *Extranjera* (2007), presents a free
version of Euripides's *Iphigenia in Aulis* (408–406 BCE), suggesting
similarities in three archaic societies to underscore the notion of actions
produced (sculpted in time) under certain conditions despite considerable geographic and temporal distance. *Extranjera* sets motifs of the
Greek tragedy to an isolated community in a semidesert region. A severe
drought decimates the livestock (goats and sheep) and announces the
community's own demise; its leader offers a human sacrifice to forestall
the dire predicament.

The father, who parallels Agamemnon (Carlos Portaluppi), is portrayed as a failing medicine man who raped the mother (Clytemnestra/
Eva Bianco) only to take their daughter (Iphigenia/Agustina Muñoz) away.

Clytemnestra reproaches him: "Me la sacaste, ¿te acordás? Me la hiciste y me la quitaste" (You took her away from me, remember? You forced me and you took her away from me). It is not clear whether the mother, the father's young lover (Cassandra/Aymará Rovera), or even his sister gave birth to the boy (Orestes/Agustín Ponce). The poignant question posed by the foreign mining prospector (Achilles/Maciej Robakiewicz) about whether they are siblings remains unanswered. Iphigenia refers to Orestes as her brother, and Cassandra caresses the child as she goes by. There is, however, a discrepancy regarding Orestes's age. Rather than a babe, the denouement requires a four- or five-year-old boy, despite his being carried during most of the action presumably because his feet have been blistered.

Figure 12.1
Iphigenia's devotion to Orestes.
Courtesy Inés de Oliveira Cézar.

Figure 12.2
As sister or slave, Iphigenia constantly carries Orestes. Courtesy Inés de Oliveira Cézar.

Figure 12.3
The prospector's garbled warning. Courtesy Inés de Oliveira Cézar.

Achilles fails to save Iphigenia: spouting terms in French, Polish, and different dialectic variations of Spanish, he warns her about Agamemnon's criminal intentions and suggests that she flee toward the sea beyond the mountains.

As the denouement suggests, his effort is not in vain. Achilles's discovery of Agamemnon's brother's corpse underscores the futility of Iphigenia's sacrifice and Agamemnon's deviousness, since the root he gave his ailing brother to chew on may have been poisonous. Finally, a group of women (chorus) allows for establishing the protagonist's predicament: "Está maldita" (She is cursed). Ironically, the two girls playing a game with stones provide an explanation, "Tá maldita. Por eso no hay agua" (She's cursed. That's why there is no water), and share the news with the protagonist, "Tu padre te va a matar" (Your father is going to kill you). Though she spits at them, she does not seem surprised. Yet, she distances herself, sitting down on the top of a windswept mesa to ponder their words.

The frenzied, circular movement of Agamemnon's horse suggests his confusion when Clytemnestra confronts him about taking their daughter's life. After begging the father to spare Iphigenia, she suggests sacrificing an animal or even his dying brother. Clytemnestra also attempts to speak to the protagonist, who has just learned about her father's plans. Despite giving away her identity by mentioning that she could in fact be her mother and addressing her as "chiquita," the woman is rebuffed, perhaps because growing up motherless turned Iphigenia into a "huacha" (orphan), a foreigner. Clytemnestra fails to entice the daughter into poisoning Agamemnon before he kills her. However, Clytemnestra's plan appears to succeed after her daughter's sacrifice, since the outraged Orestes places the poisonous mushrooms in a visible place for his father to consume. Agamemnon's impending demise suggests a new beginning, as his being deceived by the gift signals that the mother's power or knowledge has finally surpassed his.[1]

Later, when Agamemnon seems to hesitate, Iphigenia belittles him, telling him that he has always been a coward. She walks to the site of the sacrifice and bids farewell to her brother, Orestes, telling him she has to go, hopefully for the best: "Que sea para bien" (May it be for the common good).

Iphigenia shows the decorum and bravery expected of a woman in a Greek sacrifice; she places the noose around her neck and awaits the end that comes when Agamemnon kicks away the chair on which she is standing. As in the Greek drama Iphigenia's death is elided yet suggested by the camera's focus on the torn rope.[2] The movie's closing shot shows Clytemnestra carrying Iphigenia's body on the mule and pans from there to the little brother, who, having watched her demise walks away along the winding road; he has become the classic Orestes of the myth.

As implied in the line from English literary critic William Empson that closes the movie, "We choose to live in the present as a question of habit," *Extranjera* focuses on the notion of actions sculpted in time. The shots of spiders and snakes reinforce recurrent cycles of life common to many places of the planet, as Oliveira Cézar's film emphasizes the similarities in communities of the Greek Bronze Age, the Comechingones, and other archaic societies like the isolated community portrayed in the film. The similarities emerge from a summary of the societies' main traits, beginning with the archaic Greece during the Trojan Cycle, rooted in the real world of the Mediterranean Bronze Age of the third and second millennia BCE, and the Trojan War, set at the end of the Mycenaean Bronze Age, from the fifteenth through thirteenth centuries BCE. Though the palace state of Mycenae dominated Greece, warfare was frequent. Palaces were production and trading centers, and writing was used to keep track of every item, including slaves (Thompson, 16). References to agriculture—barley, figs, olive oil, flour, and wine—appear in surviving tablets. The livestock included horses, sheep, goats, and oxen. Tablets record explicit references to human sacrifices, which also appear in Homer and shape the plots of

Figure 12.4
Communal condoning of the sacrifice.
Courtesy Inés de Oliveira Cézar.

Figure 12.5
Orestes's isolation and rebirth.
Courtesy Inés de Oliveira Cézar.

many tragedies.[3] Whether through war, pestilence, or famine, the Bronze Age culture abruptly ended by the thirteenth century BCE (Chadwick, 14).[4]

Sixteenth-century Spanish explorers first encountered the Comechingones in the mountainous region that now spans the Argentine provinces of Córdoba and San Luis. In contrast to other natives, they were described as tall, brown people and the men bearded. They settled near springs and streams and planted maize, beans, and quinoa (Aparicio, 676–677). Their diet was complemented by wild vegetable foods such as the algarroba, *chañar*, and *mistol*. Comechingones lived in cave dwellings and underground houses that blended with their surroundings; however, their plantations would allow for detection (Canals Frau, 45). As documented in their pictographs, the Comechingones were herdsmen with large flocks of llamas and many fowls. They hunted guanacos, rabbits, deer, and other game (Michieli, 2, 21). Comechingones dressed with wool or highly crafted skins. They wore long capes of coarse wool in winter and short woolen tunics in summer that were woven with beads in a technique of small meshes of delicate work around the openings and the bottom edges. They lived in groups of ten to forty dwellings under chiefs who did not recognize any central authority (Aparicio, 680–683). In the course of one century, during which they lost their culture and dignity, the Comechingones were exterminated by illnesses and forced labor (*encomiendas*) (F. Torres, 26).[5]

The similarities between the Greek Bronze Age and other archaic societies such as the Comechingones are embodied in the isolated community portrayed in the film. The drought hampers agriculture and echoes one of the reasons for the demise of the palace states, given its devastating effect on livestock in the movie (sheep, goats, horses). The drought is omnipresent and almost a character in *Extranjera*. The inhabitants seem to chew roots to ensure the production of saliva. While the protagonist carries her brother to the faint trickle of a spring, their uncle lies dying beside the remnants of another spring that is festering with larvae. The dwellings offer the most vivid recollection of the Comechingones, not only because they are partly caves and partly constructed with rock but more importantly because the director scouted locations to shoot authentic dwellings.

Likewise, Oliveira Cézar recreated Comechingón clothing: Clytemnestra wears a typical leather tunic, and Iphigenia's blouse is reminiscent of their elaborate embroideries. The simplicity of Iphigenia's trousers, which billow in the breeze as we would expect of Greek clothing, emphasizes the connection with ancient times. On the other hand, the prospector's clothing and the son's boots would seem to date the movie to the turn of the nineteenth century. Even the obviously contemporary plastic bottles acquire the splendor of amphorae as they fulfill the ancient function of water vessels. By paring down the costumes Oliveira Cézar suggests the feeling of immersion in mythical time outside of history, as is typical of tragedy. All of this is reinforced on the occasion of the sacrifice, when the mere outlines of the women standing on the hilltop are set like a frieze against the sky. Rather than romanticizing a Comechingón lifeway, Oliveira Cézar underscores the similarities and the continued survival of their social constructs, as evidenced in the strongly inflected accent of the Cordobés Spanish dialect.[6]

Oliveira Cézar's penchant for actions sculpted in time is grounded in the Marxian concept of simple reproduction as inherent in precapitalist societies, complemented by the notion that social relations transcend individual existence.[7] That social practices survive us is subtended by Pierre Bourdieu's notion of habitus, defined as the systemic organization of perception, appreciation, and action of a social body (in Bourdieu and Wacquant, 126—127).[8] The archaic social matrix portrayed in Oliveira Cézar's *Extranjera* resembles the Greece that gave birth to the myth of Iphigenia as well as the Comechingones who inhabited the area where the movie was shot. Minimal convergences characterize these archaic civilizations, which are set apart by time and place—Euripides wrote in 400 BCE, and the Comechingón sixteenth-century culture does not appear to have involved human sacrifices. Rather, the plausibility of the plot arises from the alienated, almost enslaved status of the protagonist and the possibility of sacrificing her given the community's predicament.

Following the neorealist dictum, Oliveira Cézar offers a mix of professional and nonprofessional actors. Among the latter, the indigenous and mestizo phenotypes of the neighbors strengthen the link to the Comechingones. Oliveira Cézar also follows the neorealist tenet of natural settings, another hallmark of the New Argentine Cinema (Bernardes, Lerer, and Wolf, "Introduction," 10). By portraying Comechingón cave dwellings in the arid panorama of the Sierras de Córdoba, the camera suggests the survival of social morés through the generations. Finally, the prospector's allusion to the sea beyond the hills toward which he entices Iphigenia to escape and that appears to become Orestes's destination, is realized for Argentine audiences who are aware of the huge salty lake (Mar Chiquita) in the northeastern region of the province.

As an experimental auteur, Oliveira Cézar's *Extranjera* demonstrates the five characteristics of the postwar new image. Repudiation of plot, the concomitant dispersive situation, and deliberately weak links are evident insofar as the protagonist is placed in an ongoing situation yet remains unaware of the causes that led to it. Oliveira Cézar's characteristic stress on the interval results in a paratactical structure and increases suspense. The neorealist emphasis on the seer and no longer the agent appears in the protagonist's role of witness. *Extranjera* is structured in terms of a truncated voyage, as Iphigenia's habitual actions are cut short by her being sacrificed. A judicious use of location and costumes likewise precludes clichés.

Aesthetically, Oliveira Cézar stresses the treatment of time. In *Extranjera* the very nature of the plot lends credence to the assertion that for Orestes the link between past and present will forever define the last day spent with his sister. While the rugged rock landscape suggests timelessness, time is inscribed in the film, following Tarkovsky, when the camera registers a snake sliding between the rocks. Sheets of time are particularly evident in the stone homes dug in caves, for the community depicted in the film appears to live in dwellings made by the Comechingones. From Iphigenia's perspective, awareness of the repetition of certain actions such as carrying her little brother around or rocking him to sleep would probably remind her of happier times, especially knowing her life is running out. Though it is hard to speculate because *Extranjera* focuses on one day, following the Aristotelian unit of time, Iphigenia seems to have been cut off from all community members other than her brother, Orestes.[9] Perhaps she did not become a scapegoat all of a sudden. Therefore, every time she is rejected by community members would be experienced as a peak of the present.

Extranjera elicits a strong affective reaction based on the diegetic references to the drought, such as Agamemnon's willingness to sacrifice a sheep to drink its blood, Cassandra's request to have intercourse because she can no longer bear the thirst, and the constant sucking of all characters in the hope that the production of saliva will alleviate their thirst. Iphigenia finds solace in a partial towel bath and provides it by distributing an ointment to relieve the chapped lips and her brother's blisters. These actions are reinforced by the use of close-ups to compound the effects of the heat and the thirst. In this cinema of the senses it becomes difficult to continue to witness the collective suffering. In addition to the affective pull of the close-ups, there is an intertextual link to Euripides's tragedy that underscores the slippage typical of affective films: the event appears to ricochet beyond its own causes and refer to other effects. Very much like Reygadas's films, Oliveira Cézar's flattening out the third dimension connects the second dimension with the affect and the fourth dimension of time along with the fifth dimension of the spirit, lending authority to the allegorical reading (Deleuze, *Cinema 1*, 17).

Oliveira Cézar's *Extranjera* engages in social critique, following Euripides's opposition to the Peloponnesian war to which Athenians sacrificed their youth for the last twenty-five years of the Greek playwright's career (Dimock, 4). Though it may not be broadly known, theaters across the globe staged *Iphigenia* to protest the American invasion of Iraq. Oliveira Cézar's film offers a lasting protest in response to the carnage of war. *Extranjera* is also very much like Euripides's play in showing the passing of a patriarchal to a matriarchal order. Thus, Agamemnon's sacrifice of the modern Iphigenia is but a vain attempt to remain in power that only speeds his impending death. Despite the haunting representation of the drought, the protagonist's acquiescence to her immolation is hard to accept for an audience accustomed to the generic conventions of Hollywood movies. In other words, at home and abroad a contemporary audience expects the protagonist to resist. Yet, rather than endorsing the goals of commercial cinema, Oliveira Cézar adheres to the Greek preference for the way events are presented rather than their originality. This choice, coupled with her experimental aesthetics focused on sculpting actions in time, defines Oliveira Cézar as an auteur.

CHAPTER THIRTEEN
THE IRREVOCABLE
NATURE OF CURSES

Inés de Oliveira Cézar's *El recuento de los daños*

By establishing connections across temporal and geographical variations, the focus on time broadens the scope of events, allowing for a certain sliding of the signifier between the texts and suggesting other implicit possibilities. In addition to the interval that results from the paratactical articulation of the film, intertextuality generates an interval, which is amplified as it ricochets between the texts; furthermore, awareness of one of the terms of the comparison, as in the case of Oliveira Cézar's tragedies, elicits not only an active but also an affective response from the audience. Oliveira Cézar continues her exploration of actions sculpted in time in *El recuento de los daños*. This work by the Argentine director draws from *Oedipus Rex* (c. 429 BCE), yet Oliveira Cézar need not reproduce the names of Sophocles's characters, which are here contextualized among the after-effects of Argentine state terrorism during what the government called the Proceso de Reorganización Nacional (Process of National Reorganization, 1976–1982), widely known as the Dirty War.

Overt intertextual references to *Oedipus Rex* occur from the film's very outset. As an unidentified foreigner drives, he listens to different radio stations, beginning with a religious program that alludes to a mysterious curse, "¿Quieres que te hable de todos los pecados cometidos por todo el mundo? Yo quiero hablarte de tus pecados" (You want me to speak about the sins committed by whole world? I want to speak to you about your sins). The young man turns the dial, and the announcer on another station mentions the possibility of reduced prison terms for the appropriators of babies as long as they collaborate in returning the children to their rightful families. A random reference to the riddle of the Sphinx prepares us squarely for the action.

Consistent with the myth's action, the film opens by focusing on the right side of a moving car that is forced off the road because the highway is flooded. Hours later, back on the highway, the foreigner (Oedipus/Santiago Gobernori) has a flat tire. The careless driver leaves the car on the road and neglects to turn the lights on as he goes off on foot to search for assistance. Another driver then attempts to avoid slamming into the car by swerving to the left, but an oncoming vehicle forces the second driver into a brusque maneuver that results in a rollover, as is suggested by the noise, dust, and flames reflected in the driver's mirror. Darkness keeps the foreigner and the mechanic who changes the tire from noticing the accident. However, the foreigner's reference to smoke leads the audience to infer that the accident was fatal. The pacing of the diegesis is extremely effective, since the crash that claims Oedipus's (step)father's life takes place as the credits roll. The nine remaining sections, all of which are explicitly numbered, reinforce the allusions to Sophocles's play.

Section 1 of the film introduces the characters. Echoing the initial scene of *Como pasan las horas*, the younger daughter (Ismene/Dalila Cebrián) plays the piano. The mother (Jokasta/Eva Bianco, who plays the same role in *Extranjera*) enters and lounges on the sofa, lighting a cigarette. The unstated crisis is played out when the elder daughter (Antigone/Agustina Muñoz, who plays Iphigenia in *Extranjera*), brings tea, since the uncle (Kreon/Marcelo D'Andrea) urges everyone to partake before it gets cold, but the youngest daughter and the mother leave. The section ends with the uncle embracing his niece. Section 2 begins with smoke dissolving into the image of an industrial site, and the foreigner from the opening scenes returns. We learn that he represents the French company that holds most of the shares of the family's factory. When he meets the uncle, who seems to be in the midst of a traumatic event, the latter admits, "Nosotros estamos en una situación que hay que resolver . . . que está resuelta" (We have this . . . situation that needs to be solved, well . . . it is solved). After the young foreigner discovers that the general manager has recently passed away (in section 3), the youth then volunteers critical information: he was raised in France by elderly parents who could not have children, and his mother, who is Argentine, taught him Spanish. The uncle, an astrologer, reciprocates by mentioning that his brother-in-law recently died in a highway accident.

Unbeknownst to the audience, the uncle, who also takes on the role of Sophocles's Tiresias, senses the foreigner's identity. As he asks his sister how old he would have been, her initial reply, sixty-five, shows that she refers to her disappeared husband, thus suggesting the effect of trauma. In section 4 the uncle tells the elder niece about the curse that Apollo

Figure 13.1
Jokasta upset about the foreigner's suggestions. Courtesy Inés de Oliveira Cézar and Alejandro Israel.

Figure 13.2
Tiresias confronts Oedipus about manslaughter. Courtesy Inés de Oliveira Cézar and Alejandro Israel.

cast on Cassandra, that she would have the gift of clairvoyance, but her prophecies would not be believed. In the meantime, the mother lashes out at the foreigner's suggestion about the management of the factory: she is dead-set against lowering wages or reducing personnel.

That evening she drops by his apartment to apologize, and their sexual attraction plays out. In section 5 the foreigner learns that the mother has lost her partner and a baby boy during the Dirty War. By section 6 the mother supports the foreigner's suggestion of instituting double shifts to increase the factory's production while overriding the uncle's concerns that it is "muy peligroso trabajar con las máquinas cansadas" (very dangerous to work with tired machines). Yet, in section 7 a machine catches fire, lending credence to the uncle's preoccupations. After an interview with a policeman, the uncle blames the foreigner for his brother-in-law's death.

In section 8 the uncle tells the foreigner that his sister bore a child in a clandestine detention center. He adds that the baby was taken away immediately and begs him to leave. While the mother reassures the foreigner that her husband's accident could have happened anyway, he seems more peeved about her apparent lack of concern for the abducted son. In the following scene, the uncle blames the foreigner for the workers' strike and warns him, "Estás jugando con fuego" (You're playing with fire). Later, the elder daughter asks the foreigner to take a DNA test. By evening, he seems overwhelmed.

Finally, in section 9 the audience overhears the foreigner's exchanges over the phone: "Se me ocurrió preguntar" (I'm just asking). We learn that his mother is upset when he asks her to let his father know that he intends to spend time in Argentina. His closing remark, "¿Por qué siempre peleamos?" (Why do we always fight?), suggests he was appropriated by his parents, thus echoing Alejandro Agresti's *Buenos Aires viceversa* (1996). In the meantime, his biological mother tells her younger daughter, "Estoy preocupada porque tu padre no llegó" (I'm worried because your father isn't back yet). While the younger registers surprise, the elder daughter realizes that the mother has lost her mind. Back at the empty factory, the uncle asks the foreigner, "¿Ya sabés quién sos?" (Now do you know who you are?). Though the foreigner wishes to break the news to his mother, the uncle replies that she will be unable to comprehend it, as proven by the younger daughter's vain attempt to bid farewell to the unresponsive woman.

Figure 13.3
Oedipus's final awareness. Courtesy Inés de Oliveira Cézar and Alejandro Israel.

Oliveira Cézar selectively uses the most relevant aspects of the Greek tragedy. The mother and the foreigner sculpt time by repeating Jokasta's and Oedipus's actions, which break a foundational taboo of Western civilization, the interdiction on sexual relations between mother and son. The uncle stands as both Kreon and Tiresias, given the heavy-handed comment about his being an astrologer. The reference to Cassandra's curse and the pointed question about the current age of the son his sister bore suggest his early awareness of the possibility of kinship between the couple. Like Sílvia in *O homem que copiava*, the uncle is self-conscious about playing a role. In Sophocles's play the identity of Laius's murderer hinges on whether the king was accompanied, but Oliveira Cézar updates the Greek play by leaving the burden of proof to DNA analysis. This has the effect of making Oedipus less of a detective, a searcher after his own identity, than the one in the myth. Where the tragedy requires Jokasta's suicide as expiation of her family's ruined honor, Oliveira Cézar has Antigone take care of her insane mother. Antigone accompanies blind Oedipus into exile in the Greek tragedy, while Oliveira Cézar redeems him by helping his sister Ismene succeed as a concert pianist.

Oliveira Cézar elides the problematic aspect of female complicity in the appropriation of the baby. The Argentine woman who raised the boy may have been unaware of the circumstances surrounding his origin, as is initially the case in the Oscar-winning film *La historia oficial* (1986). On the other hand, the huge investment made by the Argentine military juntas and specifically by the late Admiral Emilio Massera to create a venue to disseminate state propaganda in France would lead us to question the woman's innocence.[1] Ambiguity also surrounds the foreigner's future. He tells the woman who raised him that he will remain in Argentina for some time. To the extent that the child was appropriated, he was raised in exile. To the extent that he was unaware of his birthplace, exile means remaining in Argentina. Considering the phone exchange with his mother in France and Ismene's luggage, he may be moving elsewhere (Buenos Aires, for example) or returning to France. This offers a variation on the theme of Oedipus's condemnation to a life of wandering following the full revelation of his crimes.

As an auteur, Oliveira Cézar shares the neorealist penchant for shooting on location. Her choices echo and reverberate with the setting of the tragedy. *El recuento de los daños* is set in the industrial port city of Rosario, with its flowing waters and the broad fluvial expanse. The size of the passing ships allows for indirect reference to the Greek archipelago.

As we have seen, the five characteristics of the postwar image appear in all of Oliveira Cézar's movies. The repudiation of plot, concomitant dispersive situation, and deliberately weak links evident in *El recuento de los daños* set up the protagonists in an ongoing situation whose causes they do not know. As in her other films, Oliveira Cézar stresses the interval; all of the scenes are structured paratactically. To that extent, the lack of transitions increases suspense. For instance, in section 1 of *El recuento de*

Figure 13.4
Antigone and Ismene embrace, symbolic contrast of their bleak and bright futures, respectively. Courtesy Inés de Oliveira Cézar and Alejandro Israel.

los daños, the characters' self-absorption and the uncle's final embrace remain ambiguous. The accident takes place in the opening scenes, but the victim's identity isn't revealed until section 3. Though we learn that the mother has suffered many losses, her final bout of insanity in section 9 is unexpected.

The process of revealing the circumstances that led to the baby's appearance in France is similarly obscure. As in *Oedipus Rex*, destiny plays a major role in the fates of the characters. Our contemporary Oedipus, like the ancient one, is unaware of the outcome of his actions and more importantly of his own identity. Once again, the movie is structured as a truncated, neorealist voyage as the foreigner's purported goal of writing a report for the French company that owns most of the factory's shares is cut short by the unexpected death of the general manager and an unforeseen strike. The foreigner's journey plays out a destiny of return to his birthplace, where he ultimately discovers his identity. Lastly, the consciousness of clichés appears in the avoidance of stock images, replaced by dissipating smoke, flowing water, and ships, all of which suggest the co-presence of myth in *El recuento de los daños*. Oliveira Cézar's penchant for myth stems from or reflects her background in theater direction and an interest in psychology, both of which are intertwined in the classical Greek myths. The filmmaker's proclivity is shared by a significant sector of the population, since engagement in psychoanalysis is a defining feature of urban Argentine ethos. By rewriting Sophocles's *Oedipus Rex*, Oliveira Cézar harks back to Freud's search for a universal pattern of sexual development. Oliveira Cézar's film inscribes the standard reading of Freud, yet *El recuento de los daños* does not endorse that standard reading's obsession with guilt and punishment. The words mad Jokasta offers as consolation are never acknowledged as Oedipus's desire: "This marriage with your mother—don't fear it. / In their very dreams, too, many men / have slept with their mothers. / Those who believe such things mean nothing / will have an easier time in life" (Bagg's translation, lines 1120–1126). Instead, Oedipus replies, "A brave speech! I would like to believe it. / But how can I if my mother is still living? / While she lives, I will live in fear, / no matter how persuasive you are" (lines 1127–1130).

In "The Development of the Libido and the Sexual Organizations" (*Introductory Lectures*), Freud draws a parallel between Sophocles's play and psychoanalysis, insofar as the tragedy showcases the process whereby an action buried in the past is retrieved and analyzed through the recovery of recent evidence. However, Freud argues that Sophocles's rendition is amoral in that men's moral responsibility is deflected to the gods; it also belittles the moral struggle against crime. Yet, the issue of moral responsibility relates to the Argentine context of state terrorism during the Dirty War. Freud's critique of Sophocles's version is twofold, since he argues that it appears that he had recognized the Oedipus complex through self-analysis as he simultaneously became aware of how the role of the gods disguised his own unconscious. Freud concludes that Oedipus seems forced to remember the two wishes—to dispatch his father and take his mother as wife—and to be horrified by these deeds (410–411). The double-pronged strategy Freud attributes to Oedipus is a leap of faith that mirrors the relationship between the Greek myth and the universal nature of the Oedipus complex. Freud's argument is based on the following propositions: Greek culture has universal and timeless validity; Freud's theory fits a Greek story; hence, Freud's theory is universally and timelessly valid (Marcel, 117). Argentines have consistently claimed their Judeo-Christian Western heritage as key to their interest in myth and psychoanalysis.[2]

Conversely, Oliveira Cézar offers a critique of Freud's usage of the term "Oedipal complex" in her remake of Sophocles's play. Critics wonder why Freud opted for Sophocles instead of Aeschylus, who authored *Laius*, *Oedipus*, *Seven against Thebes*, and *Sphinx*. This is particularly relevant because Sophocles does not dwell on Oedipus's fate as a consequence of the curse cast upon Laius and his descendants for abducting Pelops's son Chrysippus. Thus, by breaching the laws governing homoerotic rituals Laius brings about "the plague on Thebes and the curse on his family" (Marcel, 138).[3]

Oliveira Cézar's rendition is remarkable in drawing a similarity between homoerotic readings of Freud and the tight bond between members of the Argentine army as a homosocial body that has largely kept to the conspiracy of silence in terms of planning, devising, and disappearing dissenters as well as appropriating their children. This conspiracy unleashed a curse that engulfs the survivors of the camps, the children who were robbed of their identities, with ongoing implications for the society at large.

Given that both of these films by Oliveira Cézar represent traumatic events recounted in terms of ancient myth and drama, a metaphoric approach might do them more justice. In *Poetics of Relation* Edouárd Glissant employs the symbol of the abyss to refer to the trauma of slavery. The figure is so effective because the millions of slaves who survived

being displaced from their everyday lives were locked in the belly of the
boat, in turn navigating the abyss of the depths of the sea; the abyss thus
becomes a reverse image of what was left behind. As this shared experience profoundly marked their descendants, the abyss is projected into
the future as the unknown (5–8). So does the abyss help us to imagine
the desperation of an isolated community experiencing a prolonged and
devastating drought as depicted in *Extranjera*. In *El recuento de los daños*,
the unfathomable terror of the abyss sheds light on the desperation of
those detained in clandestine centers during the period of state terrorism
officially called "national reorganization" and the subsequent difficulties
of constructing a future. To this extent, it suggests the mother's traumatic
loss of her son and her partner as well as possible survivor's guilt. Though
trauma would preclude the mother's awareness of repetition, the lovemak-
ing scenes with the foreigner would mirror those with her partner thirty
years before.

Oliveira Cézar's work is deeply engaged in the cultivation of undecidability. In *Como pasan las horas* the lack of information on the backgrounds and thoughts of the characters enhances identification on the
basis of subject positions, as viewers draw similarities with their own real-
life experiences. Juxtaposing lifelong habitual actions with the recurrent
cycles of nature shores up a quasi-allegorical reading of the film *Como
pasan las horas* underscored by Heraclitus's paradox of constancy and
change. Taking Tarkovsky's notion of sculpting time to the limit, Oliveira
Cézar's films stress the repetition of actions throughout cultures and
periods. They inscribe and subvert gendered constructions of time and
space, and they coincide in reinscribing fatherhood by means of gentle
and caring male characters such as Juan in *Como pasan las horas* and the
uncle in *El recuento de los daños*.

On the other hand, despite timeless conflict, apparent neorealist local
color, and the mix of professional and nonprofessional actors, the experimental nature of *Extranjera* gives another twist to the engagé tradition
of the New Latin American Cinema, following well-established neorealist
tenets of the New Argentine Cinema. Although most of the action takes
place outdoors, the film also inscribes a traditional complementary divi-
sion of chores and spaces, of women sitting together spinning and cook-
ing, adolescent girls playing together, and boys working together alongside
their elders in mending a stone fence. At the same time, however, Oliveira
Cézar suggests the end of patriarchal rule in the portrayal of the medicine

man (Agamemnon) whose power failed to save his brother and whose un-
necessary sacrifice of his daughter (Iphigenia) alienates his son (Orestes),
who presumably leaves the community. To the extent that his son leaves
the poisonous mushrooms in a visible place as an offering to his father, the
latter's victim Clytemnestra, the woman Agamemnon raped repeatedly,
appears to gain the upper hand.

The abyss of the past stretching into the future is most poignantly revealed in *Como pasan las horas* and *Extranjera*, which leave open a set of
questions about the fates of these fatherless and/or orphaned boys: they
may allude to the futility of war or symbolize the nation in an era of ruthless
globalization. In her postmodern inscription and subversion of Sophocles's
Oedipus Rex, Oliveira Cézar fleshes out an instance of the ongoing national trauma that afflicts Argentines nearly three decades after the demise
of the military juntas that instituted state terror through the Proceso de
Reorganización Nacional. During that abysmal period 30,000 people were
disappeared, and about 500 babies born to mothers in captivity were appropriated.[4] As with other films in this book, the diegesis of *El recuento de
los daños* elicits an affective response due to influence of the interval and
ultimately from the sliding of the signifier due to the intertextual relations
between the film and the ancient, profound, pervasive myth of Oedipus.

Within the considerable corpus of cultural production on the issue
of state terrorism in Argentina, Oliveira Cézar's approach is one of the
most original. She has contributed to the development of an experimental
cinema that is effective, given the intertextual echoes of such well-known
cultural icons. Oliveira Cézar's position as an experimental filmmaker is
clear when we factor in her rejection of the Hollywood formula. In conclusion, the extreme situation presented in every one of Oliveira Cézar's films
draws the audience into a tragic event that is painful to watch and that,
following the Aristotelian requirement, results in catharsis.

CHAPTER FOURTEEN

SPLINTERED MIRRORS, ECHOES, AND REVERBERATIONS

Fernando Pérez Valdés's *Madrigal*

Fernando Pérez Valdés is a transitional figure whose cinematic production presents an alternative, as it is closely tied to the history of ICAIC and thus allows us to trace the movement from overtly politicized films to more subtle, experimental, ambiguous productions that aim for allegorical readings that allow for a critique and a celebration of the revolution. Pérez, born in Havana in 1944, is part of a generation of Cuban filmmakers who learned the trade as apprentices at the ICAIC.[1] Pérez has directed three documentaries that are each twenty-four minutes long: *Cascos blancos* (1975), *Siembro viento en mi ciudad* (1978), and *Camilo* (1982). His *Omara* (1983) is barely two minutes longer. In the late 1980s Pérez directed two feature films that offered fictional accounts of the prerevolutionary era. *Clandestinos* (1987) is an action-packed account of the underground guerrilla struggle against Batista. Pérez's *Madrigal* (2006) uncannily recycles earlier images of Havana rooftops and the main sewer system, which in the film are vital for the insurrection as well as for escaping from the corrupt police force.

Hello Hemingway (1990) revolves around how hopes and aspirations of a bright and ambitious high school girl are dashed by the restrictions imposed by social class. The bittersweet story is counterpointed with references to the plight of the old fisherman in Hemingway's *Old Man and the Sea*. The defeat and despair with which both of these texts end are tempered, for the audience, by the knowledge that the film's events occur very close to the beginning of the revolution. Therefore, these films by Pérez can be interpreted as denunciation of the oppressive conditions facing the have-nots during the Batista regime as well as of the violence of its repressive apparatus. Despite the collaborative nature of much of the New Latin American Cinema of the 1960s, Pérez gradually acquired a distinct, lyrical style that counters or complements plots anchored in the experiences of everyday life. Pérez's movies offer different approaches to a quest that, contrary to the discourse of the revolution, would appear to be individual and yet is reflected by members of the broader community.

Madagascar (1994) contrasts the attitudes of three generations of women who face uncertain times. By dwelling on the generational divide, especially the gap between the teenage daughter and her middle-age mother, Pérez focuses on the quest for meaning in life. However, Pérez underscores the generational nature of the quest by showing many other youths chanting "Madagascar" as they face the setting sun from Havana rooftops. As the girl and her mother and grandmother move repeatedly from dwelling to dwelling, the middle-age mother is forced to reckon with the past, come to terms with the unfulfilled promises of her career, and embrace change. Despite the apparent light-heartedness of *La vida es silbar* (1998), Pérez explores the need to humanize bureaucracy in order to accept difference, as well as the need for self-awareness so as to strike a balance between personal choices and parental wishes. Surprisingly, Pérez's comedy deploys the discourse of psychoanalysis to allow the characters to come to terms with their pasts and as a prerequisite for moving ahead.

A madrigal is a vocal piece with a complex polyphonic structure based on a secular text. Though the form emerges in the sixteenth century, within the context of Pérez's film the madrigal is an actual song and a structuring device. Pérez took the associative rhythm of a montage of suggested similarities in the lives of the protagonists of *Suite Habana* and transmuted it into the echoes, inversions, and blurry mirror images of *Madrigal*.

Madrigal opens with a theater director wondering whether to offer a performance when there is no audience. Upon the arrival of a single spectator, Luisita (Liety Chaviano), the play begins. Twenty-four male actors march in lines of six, cross-dressed in the habit of the Sisters of Charity, sporting their significant cornettes. The actors accompany a female lead,

Figure 14.1
Polyphonic structure of a madrigal: Ángel's chants are echoed by the ersatz nuns below. Courtesy Wandavisión.

Figure 14.2
Javier and Eva concoct Javier's seduction and disposal of Luisita. Courtesy Wandavisión.

Eva (Carla Sánchez), who wears a bra and trousers. The pseudo-nuns interact with Ángel (Luis Alberto García), the male lead, whose role demands that he be suspended in mid-air during much of the performance.

Dressed up as a young nun, Javier (Carlos Enrique Almirante) advances toward the only member of the audience, all the while singing a bonafide madrigal: "El tiempo descansa en mi pecho / si estás a mi lado / heridas pasadas se cierran / me lleno de amor / contigo presiento / que el mundo me canta en silencio / sus tiernas canciones me arrullan / como un madrigal" (Time stands still in my chest / If you are by my side / Old wounds heal / I am filled with love / With you, I sense that the world / Sings to me in silence / Its tender songs lull me / Like a madrigal). At this Luisita stands up and leaves. While the reaction of the other actors is withheld, the camera follows Javier, who wants to know why she left. Once at the front doors of the theater, the camera pans to the street. Javier sees some workers emerging from a manhole, a Sister of Charity walking by, and Luisita disappearing into the foglike smoke spewed by a fumigating truck.

In subsequent scenes we learn that Javier lives on the terrace of his cousin's apartment and is romantically involved with Eva, who, however, feels shunned because Javier seems equally, or more, interested in writing a short story. Javier now also wants to solve the mystery posed by Luisita's exit. While Eva taunts Javier by saying that Luisita is fat, she acknowledges that Luisita is wealthy and suggests that Javier win Luisita's love only to poison her. With Javier in possession of Luisita's wealth, Eva would move

Figure 14.3 Javier is unaware of the upcoming end of his affair with Eva. Courtesy Wandavisión.

Figure 14.4
Repetition with variation: Luisita and Javier in the ubiquitous rain. Courtesy ICAIC and Fernando Pérez Valdés.

Figure 14.5
Repetition with variation: Javier's affair with Luisita. Courtesy Wandavisión.

in. Javier then becomes embroiled in a tragic love story: as he attempts to seduce Luisita, Eva leaves him for Ángel, who proposes marriage.

Cut to the quick by jealousy at the proposal and furious at Ángel for taunting him as a bad actor and worse prop man, Javier seems to engineer Ángel's death. Since the theater company has secured a contract to play in Barcelona, Javier is offered the main role, but Luisita is unable to watch the performance because Elvira (Yailene Sierra), Javier's cousin's wife and landlady, who appears to feel jealous of his success, tells Luisita that Javier is merely manipulating her. At the morgue, Javier steals Ángel's wedding ring, purportedly to purchase the harp for which Luisita longs. As Luisita is in charge of the morgue, her reputation is tarnished. Distraught at his deceit, Luisita commits suicide. Upon the theater company's return from Barcelona, Javier delivers the harp to Luisita's bedroom. As he weeps, he wraps his short story among the harp's strings.

Because the ill-starred love stories take much of the diegesis, the audience only sees parts of the play performed by the protagonists: the main love interests absorb seven of the film's eight chapters. The last chapter represents a dystopia whose main characters are Ángel and Eva, in a cinematic rendition of Javier's short story. Set in the year 2020, under the aegis of the Empire of Eros, Ángel, no longer dead, arrives at a hazy place where people are having sex in the street amid the eroticizing, aphrodisiacal fog; freedom is defined as the right to have intercourse with whomever one wishes. Ángel meets a teenage sex worker but declines her services.

As he leaves, he meets Eva, now a cab driver, who offers to take him to his hotel. There, over a glass of wine, she finds out that Ángel is trying to locate his daughter, whom he has not seen for years. Since Ángel is dissatisfied with the regime, Eva leads him down a manhole to a place where nuns are running a lottery in which those who win have the right to escape. Eva pawns her engagement ring for two lottery numbers, and they

Figure 14.6
Ángel meets his estranged daughter in the Empire of Eros. Courtesy Wandavisión.

are called. Despite being smitten by Eva, Ángel offers the teenager whom he identifies as his daughter the opportunity to escape. Awaiting Ángel near the ship that will carry them far from the Empire of Eros, Eva meets the teenager, who carries a harp. Ángel watches them from behind some barrels. The three-dimensional image is promptly flattened out into a huge blown-up picture that fills the back of the stage at the very beginning of the performance of the play. Surprisingly, Luisita, no longer dead, claps frantically among others in the audience.

Thus, the viewer cannot but wonder about the interconnections of the stories, especially since their endings seem to be mutually exclusive. While the short story incorporates many details of the personal lives of the members of the theater company, its denouement offers a third reading. Since the cinematic rendition of the last scene of the story is foreshadowed by the backdrop of the stage in the initial scenes of the performance of the play, we may wonder whether the play includes the sci-fi story, which becomes a shadowy reflection of the relationships among the actors, and the play they stage. Despite vexed questions about a verisimilitude that allows for the paradoxical inscription and subversion of these possibilities, the final frames of Luisita alive and clapping support the idea that the play includes the initial scenes as well as the sci-fi story. In sum, *Madrigal*'s polyphonic nature is mirrored in the interconnections among the film's multiple elements, from the scene of the purported play to the depiction of the ill-starred love stories to the cinematic representa-

Figure 14.7
Reborn Luisita returns.
Courtesy ICAIC and Fernando Pérez Valdés.

tion of the sci-fi short story to the coda that arises from its destabilizing denouement.

Support for the above interconnections arises from tracing the echoes and reverberations within the performance of the play. The series of opening scenes showcases a dialogic relation between the male lead suspended in mid-air and the group of male artists whose chanting and simultaneous movements stress the polyphonic nature of the work. Critical repetition with variation underscores sound and structure, generating dialogic exchanges. Repetition with variation appears in the dialogue within the so-called play when Ángel delivers a disquisition on the nature of good and evil's interconnection in everyday life: "Qué soy, Dios mío, ¿qué soy? ¿ángel o bestia? ¿ángel y bestia? ¿bestia y ángel a la vez?" (What am I, God? What am I? angel or beast? angel and beast? a beast and an angel at the same time?). After the wires that prop him up break—presumably due to Javier's interference—and Javier takes over Ángel's role in the play, these lines acquire different connotations or become altogether meaningless.

Repetition with variation also interconnects the exchanges and costumes of the play performed with the dialogues between actors and/or other characters such as Luisita. For instance, Luisita asks Javier to meet her at the morgue dressed as a nun. Later, still in costume, Javier stares at Ángel's corpse and asks for forgiveness. The links between the script of the play performed by Ángel and the behavior of the actors in real life include the words that Javier hears upon stealing Ángel's ring. Ángel's disquisition about being an angel, a beast, or both simultaneously acquires new meaning since it suggests Javier's guilt and from a Christian point of view represents the voice of his conscience.

Other instances of repetition with variation subtend performativity in the purported real-life scenes. For instance, when Javier visits Luisita, she offers, "café, té, o algo en especial?" (coffee, tea, or anything in particular?). Javier repeats the question verbatim when Luisa visits his cousin's house, which Javier pretends to own. Similarly, while Javier is wily, Luisita stresses the value of honesty; nonetheless, thinking him asleep she confesses, "Este es mi único secreto, yo te elegí . . . Y te voy a cuidar todas las noches, y todas las noches voy a velar por ti" (This is my only secret. I chose you . . . I'll take care of you every night. I'll watch over you every night). Ironically, Eva justifies leaving Javier on the same grounds: "Ángel . . . me cuida, vela por mí" (Ángel . . . takes care of me, watches over me). Lastly, repetition with variation interconnects Luisita and the actors with the script of the play when Javier arrives at her apartment and Luisita tells him, "Todos los hombres que se me acercan quieren una sola cosa, mi casa" (All the men who come to me want only one thing, my house). When she invites him to go for a walk she states, "Mírame. Soy invisible y ustedes los hombres son transparentes" (Look at me. I'm invisible and you men are transparent). Luisita's exchanges echo Eva's lines in the play: "Todos los hombres que se me acercan quieren una sola cosa. Son transparentes" (The men who come to me want only one thing. They're all transparent).

The hallucinatory effect of dialogic exchanges echoed by repetition and intertextual allusions is enhanced by ambiguity and introduced by the counterpoint of the initial close-up of a nun's cornette and a shot of streaming urine. Moreover, Javier's boyish, almost adolescent features suggest indeterminacy, and Eva begs him, "Madre, esta noche póngame el diablo en el cuerpo" (Mother, make the Devil enter my flesh tonight). Ironically, Luisita, who symbolizes innocence, explicitly refers to the topic of ambiguity: "No todo lo que parece es" (Not everything is as it seems to be), a popular saying that becomes a leitmotif as well as an epigraph of the movie.

The cinematic representation of Javier's futuristic sci-fi story allows for further echoes and reverberations. A reborn Ángel is once again in the lead, and Eva plays the love interest in a rather chaste affair. Javier's voice-over sets the tone of dystopia: "Escapar parecía tan inútil como rebelarse" (Escape seemed as futile as rebellion). The two are trapped in a society ruled by "the right of each individual to possess the other" (el derecho de cada individuo de poseer al otro).[2] Their senses altered by the eroticizing power of the smoke, blurred groups of nude bodies engage in multiple types of sexual acts. Though some of the group members look far from happy, the few loners appear dejected and utterly drugged. Within Javier's sci-fi story, abstention is a crime to be punished by rape. The concierge dismisses the complaints about Ángel's and Eva's celibacy and then proceeds to punish them by sexually assaulting the couple aided by two women who play other roles in the so-called reality of the main plot— Luisita's neighbor and the receptionist at the morgue where Luisita works.

The oneiric atmosphere suggested by the ubiquitous smoke is buttressed by the displacement typical of dream work. According to the main plot of the film, Luisita leaves the theater as soon as Javier finishes chanting the madrigal. Piqued, Javier follows her into the street, where he is surprised first by a nun and then by a worker emerging from a manhole. Smoke from a passing car slowly envelops the scene. Javier's story begins

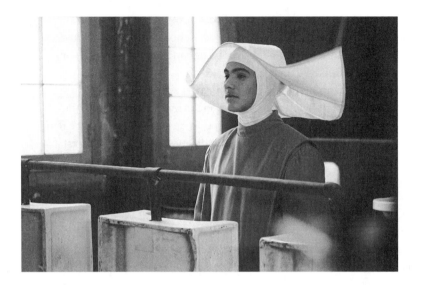

Figure 14.8
Ambiguity: Urinating nun.
Courtesy Wandavisión.

at the same place; however, the theater's sign reads "sex," the nun is help-ing two men escape through a manhole, and an eroticizing smoke affects the senses.[3] The link between the smoke and its eroticizing effect can be traced back to Luisita's apartment on the day of Javier's first visit when he notices a commotion: smoke billows out of one of the units, and its owner is frantic about her dog. Drama turns into comic relief when those around her notice that the dog is frolicking nearby, intent on mating. The smoke was not a result of fire but of fumigation. Further elements in the eroticism of the story are the orgasmic sounds that Javier hears as he climbs the stairs to Luisita's apartment. On another occasion, Javier passes a couple copulating on the stairway.

The settings in the adaptation of the short story are essentially the same—the theater, Javier's room on the terrace, Luisita's bedroom, the brewery where Luisita's mother works, and the morgue—and most of the action occurs at night among a proliferation of neon signs with sexual allusions. Thus, "Fast Pleasure," the name and logo of the pornographic magazine in which Luisita's mother models, appears as a neon sign above Javier's old bedroom. Other elements that underscore the continuity between the diegesis and the short story are the costumes, the persistent rain, and the ubiquitous nuns. Male actors wear habits in many scenes of the play, and female nuns reappear in the cinematic adaptation of the short story, since they run a lottery that raffles a few chances to escape from the Empire of Eros. Their cornettes allow for an intertextual allusion to the first section of Humberto Solás's *Lucía* (1968), in which the mad-woman Fernandina was a Sister of Charity who took care of the wounded on the battlefield and lost her mind after being raped by Spanish soldiers hiding among the dead and dying.

There is, however, another similarity in Javier's short story and the relationships among the actors of the play in the main plot: Eva and Án-gel's love story is played anew. As an Ibermedia co-production, Pérez's film has a Spanish actress as the female lead in the play, Luisita's antagonist in the love story and a cabdriver in the sci-fi story. Eva offers Ángel a ride first because she notices he is foreign, "Usted huele a virgen" (You smell like a virgin), echoing Javier's comment when he makes love to Luisita. The old brewery where Luisita's mother worked in the love story is Ángel's hotel in the adaptation of the short story. Its sign reads "Rioja 86," the wine that Javier asks Luisita for in his first visit. Furthermore, the hotel bedroom is Luisita's bedroom. As a self-reflexive echo, Ángel carries a short story titled "Madrigal," dedicated to "Ángel, que vela por mí" (who watches over me), a phrase that echoes Eva's rationale for leaving Javier. Moreover, as Luisita assures her lover in the main plot, Eva tells Ángel, "Te elegí" (I chose you). And like Luisita, Eva asks Ángel to meet her when it rains. Finally, Eva wears the same diamond ring that in the short-story adaptation she gives up (to the same pawnbroker) for a chance at a new beginning.

In the adaptation of the short story, Ángel is a tormented man on a quest for his wife and the four-year-old daughter he lost some twelve

Figure 14.9
Ubiquitous cornettes.
Courtesy ICAIC and Fernando Pérez Valdés.

years earlier. His search is rekindled when someone leaves him a short
story attributed to his daughter. As the adaptation of the short story un-
ravels, we notice that many elements undergo a process of displacement
similar to dream work. For instance, Ángel's alleged daughter (Ana Celia
de Armas) works at Javier's old dwelling. When Ángel refuses her sexual
services, she withdraws behind Javier's old light-blue bead curtain only to
emerge wearing the pendant left by Luisita's mother.

Other features include repeated maternal abandonments. Unlike
Luisita's mother, who was a sex worker, the girl's mother became a nun—
what Luisita longed to be. Moreover, the leitmotif of the harp reappears.
Luisita could not purchase a harp because the pendant with which she
wanted to pay for it proved to be of no value. Javier's attempt to buy the
harp with the stolen ring fails because the old man, who happened to
be Ángel's grandfather, had already sold it to a European tourist called
Stella Maris—the name of Ángel's alleged daughter. The shots of Javier
delivering the harp bought in Barcelona are mirrored by the shots of Ángel,
his daughter, and her harp on the way to the ship named *Barcelona*. To
conclude, though utopia is at hand, Ángel's words "Es como mucho correr
para estar en siempre en lo mismo" (It's like running and running and going
nowhere), which should have given Eva pause, echo an earlier complaint
by Elvira (Yailene Sierra), Javier's cousin's wife and landlady, about her
predicament. The ending of the sci-fi chapter is open, as the teenage girl's
arrival at the port forces Eva to decide whether to stay with Ángel despite
the rule of Eros or choose an unknown utopia.

Pérez is known for his exploration of subjectivity during the Special
Period. Diverging markedly from the leftist discourse of the revolution,
Pérez resorts to the discourse of psychoanalysis in *La vida es silbar* and to
the dialogic relation in different types of love, including Christian doctrine,
in *Madrigal*. In these films, ethics are articulated through Emmanuel Levinas's notion of "anarchic obligation," that is, "a nonappropriative relation to
the other" (2). Thus, freedom becomes an engagement in a transformative
practice motivated by an obligation for the other. The contrast between
the love stories in the plot and in the sci-fi story points to the shimmer-
ing variations of intertextuality. The structure of repetition with variation
sheds light on Pérez's dedication to René Clair (1898–1981). But rather
than working with surreal superimposed images—as in the French director's *Entre'acte* (1924)—*Madrigal* deploys intertextuality as a relation of
co-presence of two texts. The audience's recognition of the recurring
elements and their interrelation sets up (in their brains as on the screen) a

process similar to Clair's montage of superimposed images. This process of recurring elements is underscored by the appeal of mutually exclusive endings, drawing from breaches in verisimilitude regarding characters (the dead—Luisita and Ángel—return) and chronology (the futuristic sci-fi story).

The last section of the film transmutes and displaces the others in a slippage that may be compared to that of affective films, where the event goes beyond its own causes, referring to other effects whose causes in turn fall aside. Following the movement of intertextuality, the final section of *Madrigal* allows for the constant intersection of the two presents, articulated as the endless arrival of the one while the other is already established (Deleuze, *Cinema 1*, 106). The affective appeal is further underscored by the theatrical connotations of the topos of life as a dream—epitomized by Pedro Calderón de la Barca's *La vida es sueño* (1635), in which theater stands for the multiple experiences of life. It is as location that the theater best represents the notion of any space whatever, that is, interchangeable place, a singular place that has lost its homogeneity, thus allowing for an infinite number of linkages to be made in an infinite number of ways, a prospect that ultimately underscores its affective appeal (ibid., 111).

Despite the profound, ongoing impact of the Padilla affair (1971) in discouraging overt dissent, Pérez has consistently developed a highly metaphoric cinematic language that celebrates Cuban resilience despite the revolution's many failures. The film chronicles survival despite the daily lacks that are only met upon leaving the island. The nightmarish dystopia suggests that the echoes, repetitions, and displacements of *Madrigal* recall both dream work and trauma. Like Sysiphus, Eva and Ángel evidence the Cuban predicament, "running to get nowhere," in the despair of daily defeat. Their experience of continued drudgery spirals into the short story's chronicle of loss of bodily control. The present, inexpressible trauma is projected into the future, occluded by its connection with the oppression of a sexuality currently subjected to capitalism. Hope, or the lack thereof, is underscored by the scant chances afforded to the very few by the lottery.[4] The echoes and repetitions of the play, the diegesis, and the cinematic representation of the sci-fi short story all underscore the performative nature of contemporary trauma, inexpressible as it is. Indeed, as the film is structured like a chorale, H. Tomlinson's words in the epigraph—"We see things not as they are, but as we are"—cannot be more accurate.

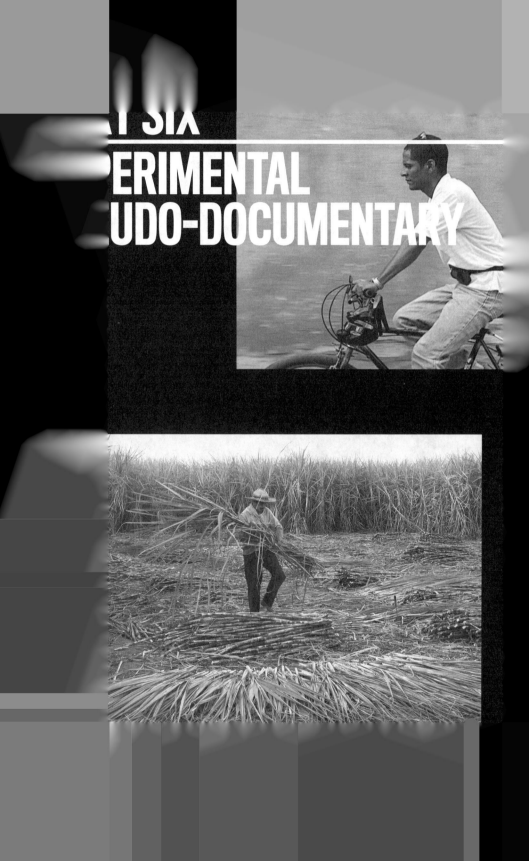

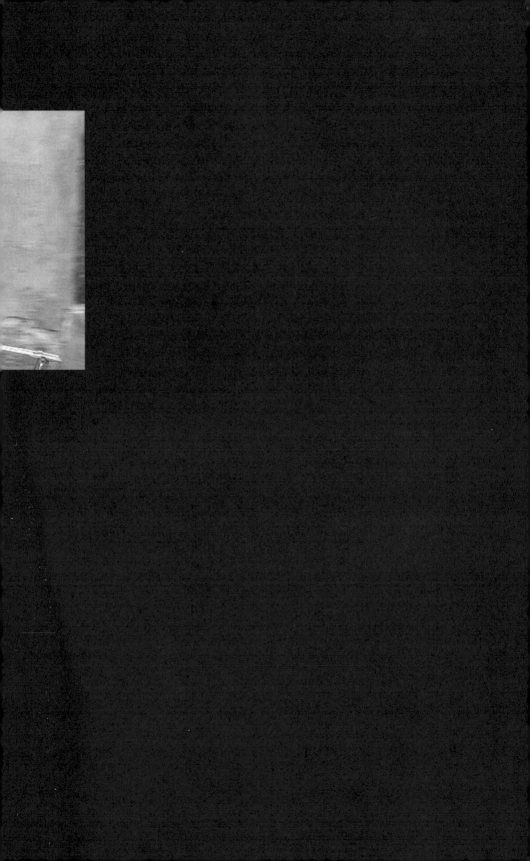

CHAPTER FIFTEEN
ROOM WITH A VIEW

Fernando Pérez Valdés's
Suite Habana

The amazing use of montage turns Fernando Pérez Valdés's documentary *Suite Habana* (2003) into one of the most experimental Latin American films of recent times. The reinscription and subversion of Bill Nichols's observational documentary mode allows for teasing out the synergy between drama and different types of documentary approaches present in most contemporary Latin American cinema. From the perspective of auteur cinema, Gilles Deleuze's writings shed light on the affective impact of the close-up, complementary to his views on the effect of the extreme close-up, whose paradoxical proximity results in a distancing effect that resists representation and might allude to a (self-) censorship that is significant to the situation of Cuba in the twentieth and twenty-first centuries. I conclude this chapter by thinking through the metonymical reinforcement of shared realities, since *Suite Habana*'s focus on ordinary people connects it to the radical Cuban cinema of the 1960s and 1970s (Tierney, 50).

Genealogically, *Suite Habana* develops from foundational movies like Walter Ruttmann's *Berlin: Die symphonie der Großstadt* (1927) and Dziga Vertov's *Chelovek s kino-apparatom* (1929) that did away with sets and professional actors to focus on montage. Yet Pérez's *Suite Habana*, a transnational venture that originated as a fifty-five-minute documentary on video for European television (Stock, 73), seems far from Ruttmann's depersonalized functionalism. Where Ruttmann purportedly emphasized the organic life of the city,[1] Pérez focuses on the daily life of thirteen of its inhabitants who are clustered into three interconnected groups. The first includes Francisquito Cardet, a ten-year-old autistic boy, and his father Francisco Cardet, a fifty-five-year-old architect who began working on his own seven years after the death of his wife. Also in Francisquito's circle are his grandmother, Norma Pérez, a seventy-year-old retired art instructor, and her husband, Waldo Morales, a seventy-one-year-old retired professor of Marxism. In the evening, Francisquito buys peanuts from Amanda Gautier, a seventy-nine-year-old retired textile worker. Francisco's current work allows for linking him to Ernesto Díaz, a twenty-year-old ballet dancer who supports his widowed mother.

A second group, and the order is arbitrary, consists of Iván Carbonell, a thirty-year-old who does the laundry at the Salvador Allende Hospital, and Raquel Nodal, his forty-three-year-old partner, who works at a cosmetics factory. The high heels that Iván takes to be fixed link him to Julio Castro, the sixty-nine-year-old shoe mender who frequents the Benny Moré dance hall.

Heriberto Boroto, a divorced, forty-year-old repairman of railway lines, lives with his mother and his grandmother. Boroto moonlights playing the trumpet at the Benny Moré.

Figure 15.1 Ernesto Díaz hopes to be a successful ballet dancer. Courtesy Wandavisión.

Figure 15.2
Iván Carbonell works at a hospital.
Courtesy Fernando Pérez Valdés and ICAIC.

Figure 15.3
Heriberto Boroto moonlights playing
the trumpet. Courtesy Wandavisión.

A third group is isolated by the pain of exile. This final group revolves around Jorge Luis Roque, a forty-two-year-old engineer who is planning a departure to Miami, where he is to live with Aidy, a Cuban American. Other members of this group include his brother, Juan Carlos Roque, a thirty-seven-year-old medical doctor, and their seventy-year-old mother, Caridad. Though not strident, the structure of the groups relates Pérez's interest in organizing by way of a "suite."

The intertitles only mention the names and ages of the protagonists, so that the information in the interconnected suite provided by the epilogue reinforces a mode of characterization that pushes viewers to reexamine their inferences. Francisquito's desire is to climb the heights, hence every night father and son climb up to the roof to stare at the stars. While Francisco wishes to be there for his son, Norma hopes that Francisquito can become independent, and his grandfather only wishes to be healthy. In the second group, Heriberto aspires to be a musician, Iván dreams of being recognized as a performer, and his partner, Raquel, is eager to travel. Juan Carlos Roque would like to be an actor, but his sibling, Jorge Luis, dreams about reuniting the family. Julio Castro's desire is to don a different suit every night, and Ernesto Díaz wants both to repair his home and to be a great dancer. Conversely, Amanda Gautier no longer has any dreams.

As in *Berlin: Die symphonie der Großstadt*, *Suite Habana* explores variations in a city's rhythms. The initial shots of the lighthouse in *Suite Habana* are ambiguous, as they lead into the port and suggest a Panopticon, an around-the-clock surveillance machine. The civilians who sit by the statue of John Lennon to prevent the theft of its eyeglasses take turns braving the elements day and night.[2] For others, time is marked by everyday routines such as having breakfast, going to school or to work, stopping for lunch, and returning home. Time crawls for Walter, who watches television from his rocking chair, and it seems to stand still for Heriberto's ninety-seven-year-old grandmother, who sits hieratically in front of the TV set. For Amanda's husband, immobile and anchored in his chair, time similarly becomes an aporia of motionlessness.[3] An allegorical approach might treat this as symbolizing the predicament of the island.

In a postmodern gesture, Pérez inscribes and subverts the conventions of the documentary's observational mode, in which speech is overheard among social actors who engage with one another rather than speak to the camera. Synchronous sound and relatively long takes anchor speech to images of observation that locate sound and dialogue in specific moments and historical places (Nichols, 39). While Pérez includes relatively long shots, sound synchronization is kept in abeyance by precluding dialogue. Words are absent, with the exception of the teacher's instructions, the clown's clichés, and the fortune-teller's advice.[4] However, actions are set against the sounds of traffic, airplanes, jackhammers, the loading and unloading of large garbage containers, as well as of music such as Edesio Alejandro's, like a voice over the characters' silence (Patterson, 186–189). The lack of dialogue creates a feeling of *oestranone*, estrangement, or defamiliarization, according to Salazar Navarro (282), and the audience's feelings, ideas, and points of view fill the void of the absent words. Interpretation mediated by the public shows the strong impact of ideological variations. In Miami the film was presented as a critique of the socialist system. In Cuba it was interpreted as a celebration of the stamina of Cubans, who overcome adversity and become energized by the most intimate everyday activities.

Despite the absence of dialogue among the characters, *Suite Habana* feels like a feature film. As in classic narrative fiction, the observer's location is readily determined in each scene, which gives every indication of belonging to a real historical world rather than to a fabricated mise-en-scène (Nichols, 39). This attention to verisimilitude grounds identification, as the run-down condition of the buildings and the abject poverty of the protagonists lead the audience to acknowledge the heroic nature of their everyday struggle for survival. In terms of the subversion of the norms of

Figure 15.4
Amanda Gautier no longer has any dreams.
Courtesy Wandavisión.

the observational mode, crucial to postmodern documentary, the shots supposedly anchor the events in space, while the sound refers the dialogue back to a specific historical moment. Even as Pérez's movie focuses on a day in the lives of the protagonists, the absence of any reference to a specific date lends the movie an aura of timelessness. The deterioration of the buildings may remind us of the many direct and indirect catastrophic effects of the U.S.-imposed embargo.[5] Details like Juan Carlos Roque's performance as a clown and Iván Carbonell's impersonation of Celia Cruz indicate the presence of a parallel dollarized market that at once seeks and refuses the face-to-face encounter of live theater and musical spectacle. The paradox resulting from the depiction of daily life in a seemingly continuous present is reinforced by the film's adherence to the conventions of the observational documentary, as protagonists are social actors expected to portray their daily lives in their recognizable historical contexts. Ironically, in observational documentaries, the audience is not expected to identify with the characters but rather to behave as observers of the historical context they witness (Nichols, 42–43).

Pérez resorts to Eisenstein-inspired montage for visually based characterization. In terms of montage, Eisenstein is known for the dialectical method, which posits that a new concept will arise from the juxtaposition of two film pieces of any kind (*Film Sense*, 4). Accordingly, in 1929 Eisenstein compared montage to the *huei-i*, the second category of Japanese hieroglyphs, in which the combination of two hieroglyphs is regarded not as their sum total but as their product, that is, the creation of a value of another degree. In other words, taken separately each corresponds to an object, yet combined they correspond to a concept. Thus, the representation of a mouth and a bird implies "to sing," a knife and a heart define "sorrow," and so on ("Beyond the Shot," *Selected Works*, 139).

Such use of montage and symbol appears in the juxtaposition of the close-up of Iván's visage and the high-heel sandals hanging from the handlebar of his bike. The combination foreshadows his cross-over from a hospital laundry employee to a Celia Cruz impersonator.

Despite a hegemonic normative heterosexuality that allows viewers to disregard these signs until we actually see Ivan impersonating Celia Cruz, Raquel consulting a fortune-teller and carrying Iván's costume suggest that the *transformista*'s performance may be tolerated but is not quite the norm.[6] Similarly, as Francisco purchases a bouquet of flowers and spends time in the cemetery, we surmise that he is a widower. Along these lines, the letter that Jorge Luis Roque reads and the picture he stares at while he prepares his luggage foreshadow his departure into exile. The paintbrush-es point at Norma Pérez's artistic bent, and the high-frequency radio sig-nals her husband's nagging political interest. Juan Carlos Roque's donning a clown suit at once suggests his interest in acting and alludes to the cliché of a smile masking pain. The battle Francisquito wages with his clothes as he gets dressed connotes his condition, and the peanuts Amanda sells speak to her minimal survival. While the close-ups discussed in earlier chapters of this study focus on series of faces, Pérez provides information

Figure 15.5
Iván Carbonell's shoes suggest his impersonation of Celia Cruz.
Courtesy Fernando Pérez Valdés and ICAIC.

Figure 15.6
Another view of Iván Carbonell's high-heeled shoes.

on the different protagonists by establishing counterpoints between them and objects that indexically point at their identities.

Eisenstein's work on montage identifies the visual counterpoint within the shot that could be defined in terms of graphic or spatial conflict, conflict between planes or volumes, or conflict in lighting or tempo ("Dramaturgy of Film Form," *Selected Works*, 166–172). Spatial conflict is apparent in the counterpoint between a subjective shot from Francisquito and his grandmother's point of view as they walk toward and under their building's dilapidated staircase; the shot ends with setting their bodies against the light as they walk out into the street. The initial upward shot is set against another in the opposite direction when they arrive at school: because the camera is positioned on the staircase of the first floor, they look rather squashed. Despite the differing camera angles, the cumulative ideological effect of the shots is to reinforce the idea of deprivation within the meager opportunities awaiting the child.

Eisenstein defined in 1929 other types of montage, among them metric, rhythmic, tonal, overtonal, and intellectual. *Suite Habana* evidences rhythmic montage, in which content determines the actual lengths of the shots ("Fourth Dimension," *Selected Works*, 186–194). This is particularly obvious with the acceleration of activity at midday. The dancing of the valves of pressure cookers is thus juxtaposed against a close-up of the face of a black woman whose bouncy walk is mirrored by that of another woman, whose buttocks are barely covered by an extremely short Lycra dress, as well as by a shot of a third woman, who wears glove-tight jeans. Therefore, well beyond the shared rhythm (valves and gait), these shots suggest the broiling, unfettered passion stereotypically attributed to black women.[7]

Faithful to its title, *Suite Habana* presents different musical tones, and these are reflected in montage and in the presumed effects on the audience's affective responses. Tonal montage is defined by the emotional tonality of the shot (*Selected Works*, 188). Though the rhythm changes, midday is marked by a rallentando connoting an after-lunch lethargy and sorrows that Francisco feels at the cemetery and that Jorge Luis's family evidences at the airport. As the sky becomes overcast, pathetic fallacy takes over, since the storm reflects the sadness felt by some of the protagonists. The tone is maintained as they return home, although Francisquito happily enjoys the ride.

The introspective tone is superseded by the cheerful music broadcast by the radio while Raquel bathes. The transition to instrumental music is made by a TV broadcast as Iván, Heriberto, and Julio shave, Amanda roasts peanuts, Heriberto's mother touches up his suit, and Francisco teaches Francisquito to prepare dinner. The cadence is maintained while Francisquito bathes and Amanda pours peanuts into paper cones. The transition to the trova is marked by Silvio Rodríguez singing "Mariposas" on TV. Thus, the bolero "La tarde" allows for an accelerando marked by the allegro molto of the code of the "Pas de six" of Tchaikovsky's "Swan Lake." The crescendo marked by applause leads to a change in location as Julio enters the Benny Moré dance hall.[8]

The dancing multitude sways like waves, and Heriberto begins to play the trumpet. A montage of hands waving fans from opposing angles allows for a transition to the cabaret, and the rhythm accelerates with Iván's singing of the rumba "Ya no hace falta." Then there is a rallentando, since the slow piano notes are set against relatively long takes of Ernesto, Heriberto, Iván, and Raquel walking back to their respective homes. Francisco and Amanda sit by their sleeping charges, Juan Carlos leafs through a magazine to distract his angst, and his mother smokes furiously. The rain pours, again, accompanied by the bolero "Quiéreme mucho." The image of the surge pounding the coast closes the circle. In other words, the rhythms change just as in a suite, reflecting the feelings of the protagonists and presumably influencing the audience's affective response. Pérez's work shows just such an awareness of the correspondence of sound, image, and movement.[9]

Employing such tonal, rhythmic, and associative montage stresses the shared nature of everyday actions, establishing and deepening the interrelationships of the characters.[10] Despite the variations in the lengths of the shots—some are almost imperceptible—the associative montage builds the illusion of the simultaneity of the story lines, which evidences Pérez's attention to detail and attempt to chronicle everyday life by underscoring shared experiences.[11]

By making a norm of fragmentation and hybridity the film advances through accumulation (Aubert, 258). Pérez fits his film into the mode of an observational documentary. The viewer, who observes parts of the lived experience of others, becomes aware of the rhythms of everyday life, in which the senses register colors, shapes, and spatial relationships (Nichols, 42). Pérez subverts some of these generic conventions by eliminating dialogue so that the characters of *Suite Habana* appear more introspective and almost mechanically engaged in their daily activities. Audience identification is enhanced by the constant use of the close-up. Therefore, the deep wrinkles on Caridad's gaunt face connote visceral pain, and Amanda's detached expression denotes skepticism. Perhaps those who escape their dreary daily activities by resorting to art evidence ambition, epitomized by Enrique's smile at the end of the ballet. In other words, given the alternating expressions of those who struggle to survive and those who strive for artistic expression, the audience cannot but admire the protagonists and recognize the poignancy of their plight.

Within the serial aspect of the film, the subject of a close-up is not necessarily restricted to a face, as is evident in the shots of the alarm clock that startles Francisquito and the coffee maker that announces breakfast.[12] Deleuze notes that directors transfer their penchant for the close-up as a reflective or intensive surface to things, which tears the objects away from their spatiotemporal coordinates and/or converts them into icons (*Cinema 1*, 96–97). This process is heightened in the cruder and more direct images of digital video, whose strange hyperreal quality alludes to the fragility and resilience of the postsocialist civil order (Tierney, 53). Focusing on dilapidated buildings and the modest objects that allow the characters to transcend their plights makes Pérez's *Suite Habana* a testament to the heroic resistance of Cuban people.

The extreme close-up allows for focusing on a highly significant detail; however, the lack of dialogue that underscores the introspective nature of the representation results in a certain verfremdungs-effekt, since the paradoxical proximity does not allow the audience to learn anything more about the characters. Yet, once again, by allowing for audience identification, reactions vary greatly. Young argues that the film sheds light on the gap between the ideals of the revolution and reality (39); Chanan conversely argues that Pérez's juxtapositions articulate the lack of public interest in "the collapse of the established order" (487). In either interpretation, the protagonists' performance of everyday life breaks the silence (self-censorship) and points at the contradictions in their apparent living conditions. The documentary feel of this film echoes Cuban experimentation with photorealism in the 1970s, yet Pérez also reinscribes *cine imperfecto*, calling attention to the medium without transforming it into a mouthpiece for a didactic political message (Young, 36).

The conventions of the observational documentary illuminate Pérez's subversive approach as well as his inscription of the early avant-garde cinema by way of *Suite Habana*'s extraordinary deployment of montage. Bracketing language increases the affective impact of montage, be it within the shot, tonal, or rhythmic. Associative montage is particularly effective by suggesting parallel actions and allowing for a catachrestic approach to Cuban reality. The documentary approach to historical reality matters, especially for the observer. This is reinforced by the apparent absence of the director, who thereby conveys the feeling of an unmediated access (Nichols, 43). Historical reality also appears in how the affective impact of the close-up increases the spectator's admiration for the protagonists' daily struggles, especially given that their lack does not overcome the desire to escape that reality through art.[13] In effect, Francisquito's predicament symbolizes that of the island, and his disability the blunders of history in which mere survival constitutes a form of rebellion. Yet, the rich interaction of the multiple layers of visual representation noted by Macrae (258) constitutes a guarded critique of current conditions and a reaffirmation of the resilience of Cuban people given their dire predicament. At the close of the 1990s Pérez was named filmmaker of the decade. The Cuban director's style continues to evolve, as the light-hearted tone of *La vida es silbar* (1998) turns into the implied denunciation of *Suite Habana*.

CHAPTER SIXTEEN
LIFE IS AND IS NOT

Paz Encina's *Hamaca paraguaya*

An accurate representation of the Paraguayan ethos appears throughout the unabashedly experimental film *Hamaca paraguaya* (2008). Yet the film's director, Paz Encina, somewhat paradoxically counters these arguments by stating that the film offers an accurate representation of the Paraguayan ethos: "Paraguayans have a slower rhythm than the rest of Latin Americans. Why would I move the camera if my intention was to express it?" (interview by Jemio).[1] Encina's opera prima inscribes and subverts the conventions of the observational documentary. The minimalist aesthetics hinges on the use of a fixed camera, harking back to the origins of film. Montage depends on the distance of the shots. Having shot on location in Guaraní, Encina undermines realistic assumptions by breaking lip synchronization and thus unhinging the voice, which acquires an ambiguous status since the exchanges allude to the present as much as to recollections of the past. If the voice refers to the recurring memories of trauma, the linear exposition based on causality and temporality is no longer viable.

The action of *Hamaca paraguaya* begins in early morning as an elderly couple of peasants, Ramón (Ramón del Río) and Cándida (Georgina Genes), whose only son is at the front, look for a shady spot to hang the hammock. While the overcast sky announces rain, the unbearable heat foregrounds the drought. Their irritation with a barking dog subsides into concern as they remember that their son left it in their care. As Ramón works in the cane field, he remembers his son's farewell.

Meanwhile, as Cándida washes clothes at a spring, she also remembers her son's farewell and the way she begged him to go AWOL. Ramón's ruminations about the wear and tear on the hammock and the surprising silence of the dog turn into a dialogue with Cándida, who appears shortly

Figure 16.1
Ramón remembers his son's farewell.
Courtesy Wandavisión.

Figure 16.2
Ramón learns that the war is over.
Courtesy Wandavisión.

after. Their exchanges counterpoint Ramón's hope against Cándida's skepticism. Cándida infers that the dog is quiet because it is sick, so Ramón takes it to Don Jacinto. While the veterinarian saves the dog from dehydration, he tells Ramón that the war is over.

In the meantime, a messenger runs into Cándida, who tends to the embers in a *tatakuá* (outdoor bread oven). The messenger tells her that Máximo Caballero died at the front and offers his bullet-ridden shirt as proof. Cándida and Ramón suspect their son is dead, yet their attempts at sparing each other the tragic news suggest the depth of their love.

Following the generic conventions of the documentary, *Hamaca paraguaya* was shot on location with seemingly native actors who tell a significant story about that particular place.[2] Yet, instead of working nonprofessional actors or social actors who play roles similar to the ones of real life, Encina relies in her minimalist film on professional actors who impersonate an elderly peasant couple living in 1935. Further subverting the conventions of the observational documentary, the conflict is not contemporary but rather the Chaco War (1932–1935). This traumatic episode in the history of the nation arose because Bolivia became landlocked and claimed the land of modern Paraguay on the grounds that it had been granted to its colonial predecessor, the Audiencia de Charcas. The Chaco

Figure 16.3
Cándida refuses to accept her son's death.
Courtesy Wandavisión.

War followed the War of the Triple Alliance (against Argentina, Brazil, and Uruguay, 1864–1870), which devastated Paraguay. It lost half its national territory, and by 1870 the population was reduced to 116,000, about one-fourth of the 1864 figure; what remained of the country was a wasteland (Schofield Saeger, 193).

While Encina appears to follow certain conventions of the documentary such as long takes and shooting on location and in real time, *Hamaca paraguaya* resembles Pérez's work in a postmodern gesture that inscribes and subverts the conventions of the documentary's observational mode.[3] This mode offers a particularly apt framework to ground our analysis, as it shares similarities with neorealism and feature films and so offers a good venue to underscore the degree to which Encina's film subverts generic conventions of the documentary as well as of classic cinema. For instance, in observational documentaries, speech is overheard as the social actors engage with one another rather than speak to the camera. Accordingly, overheard speech follows some laws of folk narrative, such as the use of repetition and metaphoric language.[4]

Repetition is rampant because the couple's exchanges involve a limited set of themes—the barking dog, the heat, the drought and the impending storm, and the recollections about their son's farewell. Moreover, their respective conversations with the veterinarian and the messenger also focus on their son. At times silenced or metonymically transferred, the son is nonetheless the main theme. The dog barks because it misses him, the heat does not seem to have subsided since he left, Ramón hopes the rain will reach him in the Chaco, and the couple must come to terms with his absence and probable death. Finally, since their son was drafted, the war remains the unresolved trauma. The opening scene offers an instance of repetition:

Ramón: What's wrong with you?

Cándida: What's wrong with me? I can't go on like this, Ramón, changing the place of the hammock, waiting for that dog to stop barking.

Ramón: But why put the hammock closer to the dog, then?

Cándida: What else can I do? There is no other shade.

Ramón: Why didn't you leave it where it was, since it was far-
ther away from the dog? Answer me.

Cándida: Isn't it bigger here?

Ramón: Bigger, what do you mean bigger?

Cándida: The shade is bigger.

Ramón: But it's closer to the dog.

Cándida: Let's not talk about that again—and the dog stopped
barking.

Oral narratives are marked by temporal, spatial, and conceptual limitations. Despite the indeterminacy of the diegesis, the war lasts three years.
The peasants lead an isolated life in their farm and are acutely aware that
no one cares about them. The open-endedness typical of folk narratives
appears in the screenplay, as when Cándida refrains from giving Ramón
the messenger's news for fear he may suffer a heart attack. On the other
hand, she appears to be in denial:

Messenger: Do you know any relatives of the soldier Máximo
Caballero?

Cándida: My son's name is Máximo Ramón Caballero.

Messenger: The soldier Máximo Caballero died at the front.

Cándida: My son's name is Máximo Ramón Caballero.

Messenger: Is he your son, ma'am?

Cándida: All the men here have that name. No, he's not my son.
And take that piece of paper with you. And take that damn shirt
away as well. Who would want to have their son's shirt.

Metaphoric language is another trait of oral narratives. As she be-
seeches her son not to go to war, Cándida expresses her feelings through

metaphors: "If this heart were stone, it would have broken by now. If it were leather, if would have burst." Along these lines, the diegesis begins with the assumption of foreknowledge insofar as Cándida accepts her fate. She chides her husband for hoping against hope by asserting, "There's nothing we can do." Similarly, the dog is not personified but endowed with knowledge as Cándida wonders why it barks: "That old bitch howls and barks since he left. It seems as if she knows something." In addition to repetition, the dramatic impact of the script lies in the series of structural antitheses such as heat and cold, drought and storm, absence and waiting. Thus, Ramón complains, "That war has taken all our energy." When the son tells Ramón his mother doesn't want him to go to war, he spews a cliché: "Your mama is a woman. She doesn't understand." Oral narratives bear proverbs such as "Memories don't bring a dead person back" and "Nobody can escape death."

The distance between the stationary camera and the protagonists paradoxically creates and subverts the illusion of realism because it is too far away to ascertain whether the characters actually speak, so the audience attributes the Guaraní exchanges to the grain of the voice with which it endows the respective characters. By so doing, the audience follows age-old conventions of cinema based on the notion that it delivers real sounds, a legacy of the Western episteme. The voice is identified with the here and now, to the extent that speech is defined as the essence of presence and the construct of the voice as carrier of meaning undergirds the impression of reality. The subordination of the auditory to the visual track, nonhuman sounds to the human voice, and noise to speech, typical of classic cinema occurs throughout *Hamaca paraguaya*. Therefore, we attribute words to each character, and we locate the irritating barking of the dog in the background.

Yet, these effects hinge on synchronization, which is fundamental because it anchors sounds to an immediately visible source, and the emphasis upon diegetic speech acts to suture the viewer/listener into the story, as firmly as the sound analogue of the shot/reverse shot formation (Silverman, *Acoustic Mirror*, 45). Precisely by so doing we position ourselves as interlocutors. But, as we shall see, Encina's *Hamaca paraguaya* brackets synchronization thanks to the considerable distance between the camera and the actors: the lack of synchronization becomes clear as the camera zooms in to medium and close-up shots when the unseen messenger addresses Cándida. As the tracking shot captures her body we begin to notice that her lips remain shut despite the exchanges we hear

and attribute to her. Close-ups of Ramón's pursed lips in exchanges attributed to him underscore this asynchronicity. By bracketing lip synch Encina
subverts the auditory impression of reality in a strategic use of silence that
subverts the idea of a single rendition of events. For instance, rather than
assuming that the messenger talks to Cándida while her husband is at the
veterinarian's (his fear), she may be recalling an exchange that took place
on another occasion, which would certainly disrupt the apparent linearity
of the script.

Besides post-dubbing, another significant deviation from the rule of
synchronization is the voice-off, which occurs when its ostensible source
is not visible at the moment of emission (Silverman, *Acoustic Mirror*,
48). As we have mentioned, the only visible characters are Cándida and
Ramón. As the son remains outside the frame and his farewell purportedly
took place some time ago, we naturalize the scene as a recollection. The
messenger who gives Cándida the news and the veterinarian who saves
the dog also remain outside the frame. According to the diegesis, Ramón
takes the dog on that same day, and we presume the messenger arrives
while he's away. Nonetheless, the messenger may have come at another
point, since Cándida exists in the timelessness of "home," and the men
belong to the temporal realm of national history. Therefore, the episode
of the messenger could also be a recollection. When Ramón rebuts his
wife's comment regarding the worn hammock we notice that she is not to
be seen for another five minutes, which raises the question of whether he
is talking to himself, recalling their conversation, or thinking she can hear
him. Yet Encina's subversion goes even further. Silverman argues that the
voice-off exceeds the limits of the frame but not of the diegesis because
its "owner" occupies a potentially recoverable space and is almost always
brought within the field of vision at some point or other (*Acoustic Mirror*,
48). Encina adheres to Silverman's tenet in terms of the invisibility of the
voice-off, and it remains associated with significant figures in the story
such as the characters of the son, the veterinarian, and the postman, but
by keeping these interlocutors out of sight Encina subverts the conventional normalization of classic cinema, thus lending support to the idea
of trauma as an organizing principle of the film. Deleuze's definition of the
out-of-field supports this hypothesis because it may refer to that which
exists elsewhere or testify to a more disturbing presence, one that insists
or subsists outside of homogeneous space and time (*Cinema 1*, 17). Thus,
the presence of the voice given the absence of the son, the postman, and

the veterinarian as out-of-frame interlocutors underscores the traumatic nature of the couple's waiting for their son to return from war.

Following the conventions of observational documentaries, Encina places a stationary camera in front of the actors and alternates locale as she follows the couple through the day, that is, from the hammock to the cane field (Ramón) and the spring (Cándida), from the veterinarian (Ramón) to the tatakuá (Cándida), before returning to the hammock (Ramón and Cándida). Yet, while the photography in *Hamaca paraguaya* is spectacular, the camera work is minimalist, involving a series of wide-angle shots originating from a single camera.

The composition of the photography appears to follow the golden section in that the position of the protagonists maintains the relation-ship of two parts of a whole with each other and with the whole. This is particularly evident in the images of Cándida and Ramón sitting beside the tatakuá and at the veterinarian's porch, respectively, as their bodies take about one-third of the frame. The subdivision of the frame into thirds appears with Cándida set off toward the right in the scene at the spring and those of Ramón in the cane field.[5]

The fixed camera adds to the film's minimalism. According to Encina, the rationale was not financial but aimed instead to suggest the slow rhythms of nature that peasants endured in isolated environments almost eighty years ago. Also, Encina refuses the gaze by focusing on the profiles or backs of characters. The refused intimacy becomes timeless because the profile is like a coin. Turned back, the refusal of the gaze implies the refusal of history. From a cinematic point of view, the fixed camera is reminiscent of the inception of cinema. As Deleuze mentions, insofar as the frame is defined by a frontal point of view, that of the spectator on a fixed set, the shot is a slice of space at a given distance from the camera (*Cinema 1*, 25). Though Encina maintains the frontal point of view, she tends to set the establishing shot far away, making the audience aware of the distance. Then she generally zooms in, most often in two discernible steps (medium shots and close-ups), in a practice that underscores the variation in distance while maintaining the point of view. The variation in the distance of these shots creates a kind of montage.

The advantages of the wide-angle shot are not only that it allows for different options such as a long-duration fixed or mobile shot, a sequence shot, and depths of field but also that it includes all the slices of space at once, from close-up to long-distance shot, as it maintains a unity that

Figures 16.4 and 16.5
Montage through variations in distance.
Courtesy Wandavisión.

allows it to be defined as a shot (*Cinema 1*, 26). The unity in the different distances (planes) is underscored by having the clearing become a stage where the protagonists enter and exit from the back and set up and sit on the hammock, which they dismantle at dusk. The hammock's apparent immobility as an anchoring device is slightly disrupted when Cándida peels an orange in real time. A variation of the leitmotif of the hammock occurs when Ramón repeatedly and unsuccessfully stands up to see the birds he hears go by. As he picks up twigs, the variation in the planes con-tributes to the unity of the shot, which, as Deleuze has observed, involves the relationship of near and distant parts. This practice also reinscribes the golden mean, since Ramón is placed in the last third of the frame.

Encina's wide-angle camera allows for medium shots and close-ups of Cándida and Ramón as they remember their son's farewell. The tracking shot is most noticeable when it follows Cándida as she tries to make a butterfly leave. It zooms in on her as she burns it in the tatakuá. The shift between medium shot and close-up is apparent in the images of Ramón in the sugarcane plantation and Cándida at the stream. In each shot the close-up remains focused on the back of the head, showing part of the left side of the face. However, these close-ups are set against (as mon-tage) wide-angle shots of the protagonists surrounded by other people: Ramón's by four men sitting down in the clearing of the cane plantation and Cándida's by several women, one with a baby, by the river. Wide-angle shots that move into close-up develop the protagonists' growing suspicion of their son's death, following Ramón's dialogue with the veterinarian about the end of the war and the messenger's offer to give Cándida her son's torn and bloody shirt.

Exclusion of some interlocutors from the frame enables the audi-ence to naturalize the exchanges with the son, the messenger, and the veterinarian as if they were taking place chronologically. On the other hand, the initial chronological reading is disrupted once we realize that the sequences—especially the son's farewell and the arrival of the messen-ger—function independently and may change if in fact they represent the protagonists' recollections. Thus the audience can contest the realistic linearity of the diegesis, anchored as it is in the use of Guaraní and on-site locations. One way or the other, the diegesis maintains a certain char-acter development insofar as Ramón's hope diminishes as he becomes more despondent and needy. The apparent reality of no exit from trauma is emphasized by the claustrophobic location. Yet, the out-of-field may introduce the spiritual into the system (Deleuze, *Cinema 1*, 17), as the messenger and the veterinarian interrupt the stalemate of trauma and to that extent introduce the notion of historical time into the everyday, seasonal time of the diegesis. More importantly and perhaps more persuasively, Cándida appears to accept and suggest their son's death by mentioning the butterfly she had to dispose of in the tatakuá. Her recourse to the doxa is effective as metonymically Ramón feels the fleeting presence of death, an intimation of the reason their son has not returned, which supports Deleuze's reference to the spirit.

In observational documentaries, long takes anchor speech to images of observation that locate dialogue and sound in specific moments and historical places. Like Pérez, Encina subverts the actual anchoring of the voice along with other requirements for the dialogue and sound while reinscribing their verisimilitude for a rural couple in the rain forest of Paraguay. Turning the screw further, Encina offers a specific date, June 14, 1935, two days after the official end of hostilities.[6] Like *Suite Habana*, *Hamaca paraguaya* feels like a feature film. Despite the asynchronicity of the dialogue and the episodes of voice-off, the observer's location is readily determined in each scene, as in classic narrative fiction. As in observational documentary, the space gives every indication of belonging to the historical world rather than a fabricated mise-en-scène (Nichols, 39), which increases identification. Encina inscribes this notion by presenting verisimilar locations like the clearing in the woods where the hammock is set and more importantly the veterinarian's humble adobe home, the stream arising from the spring, and the cane fields. These locations become examples of any space whatever, that is, of a singular place that has lost its homogeneity, which therefore allows for linkages to be made in an infinite number of ways, ultimately underscoring their affective appeal (Deleuze, *Cinema 1*, 111).

Trauma may be defined as a response to an overwhelming event that is not fully grasped as it occurs but returns later in repeated flashbacks, nightmares, and other repetitive phenomena (Caruth, *Unclaimed Experience*, 91). Though it would seem that the recruitment of Ramón and Cándida's son is not a traumatic event equal to a violent natural catastrophe or a man-made disaster, the repeated recollections of his farewell underscore the unconscious enactment of trauma. The couple's suffering is worsened by the lack of news about the son, who changed his name to prevent his mother from being certain about his death. The film focuses on the suffering brought about by their recollections and the uncertainty of his fate. Since trauma symptoms include endless repetition, unheeded circularity, and lack of ordered sequences, the features of oral narratives identified in the peasants' speech replicate these markers.

Although Paraguay won the war and access to huge tracts of land, the human cost included the lives of 50,000 Bolivian and 40,000 Paraguayan soldiers (Farcau, 230). Given the series of dictatorships that plagued Paraguay from its inception (José Gaspar Rodríguez de Francia, Carlos Antonio López, and Francisco Solano López) and the War of the Triple Alliance that decimated Paraguay, the Chaco War reactivated a national trauma.

According to Kaja Silverman, historical trauma is based on the notion of dominant fiction, defined as the procedure by way of which a given society creates itself based on the triple axis of closure, fixation of meaning, and the (deconstructive) avoidance of the infinite play of differences (*Male Subjectivity*, 54). Despite and because of the traumatic losses of the War of the Triple Alliance, Paraguay ignored the very likely possibility of defeat, in the name of the dominant fiction of the nation. By fixating collective identity on the desire to win the war, Paraguay—and Bolivia—put an end to the infinite play of differences afforded by the diplomatic treaties drawn up in 1879, 1887, 1894, and 1907 that allowed for the option of mediation of territorial disputes for about thirty years (Farcau, 9). Although Paraguay did prevail in the ensuing conflict, the huge loss of life traumatized the Paraguayan people once again.

Evidence of trauma's foreclosing of possibilities occurs in Ramón's adherence to the necessity of national ideology: "You have to go to defend your country." But Cándida objects: "I don't care about this war. I don't care if they all die." Their son, by contrast, is honest about his misgivings: "I'm scared, Pa . . . What if I die?" Though Ramón does not go to the front, he is metaphorically emasculated by war neurosis, ultimately another synonym for the death drive (Silverman, *Male Subjectivity*, 60). Ramón is crushed by the absence of his son and the fear that he has died at the front. His repeated complaints about the war evidence his misgivings, which are transferred into chest pain and finally rearticulated as: "My son, that's what hurts." Though the fear that the son will not return is concealed by his apparent hope, Ramón finally accepts fate when he repeats Cándida's mantra "There's nothing we can do."

Paradoxically, even the strength placed in one another's love—"We

have each other . . . we're happy"—vanishes as suddenly as the falling
star: "Now we're sad." In Benedict Anderson's words, the construction of
national allegories characteristically requires the paradoxical need to
have forgotten the same tragedies about which one has to be constantly
reminded (200). In the case of Paraguay this translates as the need to
remember and to forget the devastating consequences of the War of the
Triple Alliance as well as the repeated dictatorships. In *Hamaca paraguaya* the seemingly endless cycle of remembrance in which Cándida and
Ramón appear immersed is a sign of trauma and a foundational process in
the construction of the nation.

By keeping the bad news to themselves to protect one another,
Cándida and Ramón unwittingly continue the cycle of trauma, which is
represented through the circular references to the heat and the impending rain, terms that hark back to their son and the war. Their sheer isolation, suggested by the silence intercut with the sounds of the barking dog,
conversations, birds, and thunder, highlights the claustrophobic environment. That claustrophobia is underscored as well by the repeated cycle
of activities of daily life that offer no escape from the circularity of trauma.
Waiting, their hell on earth is ultimately compounded with the cycle of
misery brought about by dictatorships and war.

Due to their isolation, the peasants' predicament underscores the
retraumatization of the nation, whose collectively suffered loss undercuts
the shared identifications and desires that neutralize the social formation's
contradictions (Silverman, *Male Subjectivity*, 54). By hurting for his son,
Ramón finally abandons the national ideology according to which men
defend the nation. Moreover, if we think of *Hamaca paraguaya* as an allegory, Cándida and Ramón's personal tragedy reinscribes the repeated
losses that lay the foundation for the fiction of the nation. To that extent,
the couple stands for all Paraguayans, whose losses fray the fabric of the
nation. However, since Encina's film focuses on the absence and possible
death of the couple's son, the drama arises from their uncertainty, which,
in the figure of the *desaparecido*, precludes both closure and mourning.
Precisely this in-between, this indeterminacy that generates the affective
pull of the interval, is so compelling because it is mirrored formally, for
Encina masterfully inscribes only to subvert the conventions of observational documentaries.

CONCLUSION

Possible Futures

The corpus of *Experimental Latin American Cinema: History and Aesthetics* consists of films that were, to a greater or lesser degree, influenced by the first and second European, American, and Latin American avant-gardes. The effect of the first avant-garde (late 1920s–early 1930s) may be summed up in terms of the experimental deployment of montage in a degree of experimentation that ranges tremendously. There is the inherent montage resulting from variations in the distance of the shots of a fixed camera (as in Encina's *Hamaca paraguaya*). Montage also appears in the typical editing mechanism evidenced in Salles's *Central do Brasil*, which either structures a series of close-ups thematically or suggests psychic phenomena such as fainting. Further variations on this traditional approach to montage appear to buttress characterization in Sorín's *El camino de San Diego* and to introduce the dream sections in Menis's *El cielito*. Despite the film's more industrial flair, the engaging montage of Bielinsky's *El aura* is buttressed by repetition that portrays psychic processes such as epilepsy, stream of consciousness, and recollections. Subverting the linear structure of the diegesis heightens awareness of the aura, ultimately creating uncertainty regarding the verisimilitude of events. Repetition with variation in Dhalia's *O cheiro do ralo* likewise results in a sense of impending danger due to multiple permutations of a pattern of exchange.

The range of montage spans traditional types identified by Eisenstein, such as dialectic, rhythmic, tonal, and associative montage, all of which are showcased in Pérez Valdéz's *Suite Habana*. Montage breaks the laws of causality in Reygadas's films when abrupt juxtaposition of scenes unhinges the linearity of the plot and reinforces the importance of the interval, resulting in a verfremdungs-effekt and eliciting the spectator's affective response to fill in the blanks. Oliveira Cézar's montage allows for a slippage of intertextual relations of similar narratives across temporal and spatial disjunctions. Although montage appears with more latitude as a paratactical structuring device in *Días de Santiago*, Méndez's experimental aesthetics may be defined as the alternation of shots in black and white with shots in color to contrast the past and the present. In *Madrigal*, Pérez Valdés resorts to a more unsettling slippage between mirroring circumstances in two plots, thus inscribing and subverting intratextual relations in offering alternate reversible plots.

The impact of the second avant-garde (1960s–1970s) may be traced to the influence of neorealism, which develops, in turn, into a characteristic synergy between features of the documentary and fiction in the New Latin American Cinema and Cinema Novo, its Brazilian manifestation. A combination of ideological and economic factors lead neorealist features to resurface in the early 1990s, well after the advent of democracy, in the New Argentine Cinema and in the Brazilian Cinema da Retomada. The combination of neorealism, documentary, and fictional film marks the work of a variety of relatively young filmmakers who graduated from film schools in countries with rich cinematic traditions, notably Brazil, Mexico, Argentina, and Cuba.

The classical approaches to neorealism are enhanced by Gilles Deleuze's framework, which defines it in terms of the time-image, emphasizing the importance of sight, together with the representation of time as possibility—a practice shared by most of the films in this corpus. The book purposefully begins with neonoir films, which adhere to the standards of the movement-image and the plot as the representation of a rationale, to show the impact of the transition by way of the attraction of the voyage as well as characters mesmerized by a vision and ultimately by the enigma of time.

Aesthetic tenets shared by all the films in this corpus and with neorealism generally include shooting on location and portraying life convincingly, with the harshness of documentaries, whether or not it is explicitly stated.

A salient difference between Italian neorealism and its Latin American manifestations is the avowed distance from Hollywood. With few exceptions (Salles, Bielinsky), the directors in this corpus should be considered independent filmmakers. In contradistinction to their predecessors, they tend to refrain from offering overt political messages. The deeply instilled doubt about the feasibility of metanarratives appears to preclude political manifestos; rather, the implied message is restricted to taking note of problems that perpetuate the state's malaise. In contrast to the 1960s avant-garde formal fireworks, most directors discussed herein tend to be mellower in their experimentation.

Since the corpus is ample enough to encompass a variety of genres, many other films share certain features with texts in this book. For instance, Colombian director Ciro Guerra's *Los viajes del viento* (*Journeys of the Wind*, 2009) inscribes and subverts the generic conventions of the road movie and its close relative, the male buddy movie. This journey centers on a professional accordion-player, Ignacio Carrillo (Marciano Martínez), who travels with Fermín (Yull Núñez), a teenage boy who insists on accompanying him despite the older man's continual silent rebuffs and occasional outright rejections. Their journey or quest—which involves riding donkeys, traveling by boat and ferry, and recovering from several near-death encounters—is slightly different for each character.

The pair experiences a series of misadventures, set against the quasi-ethnographic portrayal of the cultures they encounter as the accordion player has decided, in the wake of the death of his beloved wife, to return the musical instrument to the master who made it. While he became a great folk hero, triumphant in many musical competitions of poetry and song, the accordion is cursed by the devil. Yet his younger companion reveals that his own goal is precisely to follow in the footsteps of the master. Their lengthy and exhaustive travels offer the audience spectacular views of a vast and varied landscape. The pair generally avoids towns and all cities but cannot entirely skirt civilization. The protagonists' encounters with various other travelers bring the accordion player, against his will, to compete and triumph in a broad range of traditions of accordion playing as the open road becomes a metaphor not just for the life that the older man is hoping to leave behind but also for the new life that the boy wants so much to enter.

Tarkovksy's notion of sculpting time, evident in the films of Oliveira Cészar and Reygadas, reappears in the work of Argentine filmmaker Lisandro

Alonso. In *Los muertos* (2004) the camera seems to follow Vargas (Argentino Vargas) in real time as he is released from prison. As in Oliveira Cézar's films, the protagonist in *Los muertos* engages in actions that echo ancient rites, such as the cleansing ceremony alluded to by shaving and having a haircut. Re-entry into society involves proving his manhood, accomplished through engaging a prostitute. As Vargas purchases gifts to celebrate his freedom with his relatives, he commences to row upstream, toward his daughter's home, in a realist representation and symbol of life's struggles. While not for the faint-hearted, the slaughter of a goat recalls ancient rites of sacrifice and especially ritual feasts to celebrate the master's return.

The focus on social malaise is a final aspect of the representation of Latin America in the early twenty-first century. Much like Pérez Valdés's *Madrigal*, Brazilian filmmaker Lina Chamie's *A Via Lactea* (*The Milky Way*, 2007) presents a harrowing panorama of contemporary São Paulo. The alternating sequences juxtapose different spatial settings and time periods, naturalized as the mid-life crisis of Heitor (Marco Ricca), a literature professor who struggles with jealousy and unrequited love when Júlia (Alice Braga), his fiancée, admits that she no longer loves him. Crazed at the news, the protagonist crosses the street repeatedly until he decides to drive to her apartment. Caught in traffic, he slows down and grows irritable in searching out detours. Lost in a threatening and unfamiliar area of town, he witnesses child prostitution, runs over a dog, and tries to catch up with a young boy present at the time of the accident. The audience gradually realizes that the child is actually an image of the protagonist in the past. In addition to multiple time references, Chamie presents different points of view including that of Júlia's cat, intertextual references, and reversed-dialogue exchanges.

Through a series of Danteesque images of the suburbs, *A Via Lactea* suggests a descent into the unconscious with scenes that correspond sequentially to periods of the life of the protagonist, who is actually dying, rather than the dog that he believes he has hit. So does the movie play out the stream of consciousness of the dying protagonist, who was struck and run over in the film's opening scenes. Thus, Chamie has successfully taken Faulkner's experimental structure to portray the ills of Latin American megalopolises.

The topic of national trauma in Encina's *Hamaca paraguaya* emerges in other films, for example in the alternation between the past (slavery) and the present (*afavelados*, slum dwellers) that concerns Brazilian film director Sergio Bianchi in *Quanto vale ou é por quilo?* (What Is It Worth? 2005). The plot denounces the parasitical nature of nongovernmental organizations, NGOs, by noting that poverty could be eradicated if the funds allocated to them were distributed among the poor. The problem of profit as paramount likewise dominates the intertext of the past. In a script adapted from Machado de Assis's story "Pãe contra Mãe" and from Nireu Cavalcanti's eighteenth-century chronicles, bounty hunters and freed slaves have no qualms about profiting from the slavery system by keeping those of their own race in abject poverty and inhumane conditions. Bianchi brings the corruption of the past into the contemporary era through sequences that alternate present-day exploitation and greed with stylized theatrical performances of scenes of a traumatic past, illustrating, for example, punishments typically meted out to slaves who dared resist.

All of these experimental films develop a historical analysis in order to comment on the present. Their approach can be attentive to folk tradition, as in *Los viajes del viento*, or to a tradition of social critique that dates from the '60s, as when *Quanto vale ou é por quilo?* shows that the abject poverty of the underclass has only worsened with the implementation of neoliberal policies. *Quanto vale ou é por quilo?* refers to the national trauma of slavery, while *A Via Lactea* focuses on the relentless pace of urban life, with its continued stress and resulting violence. The restless protagonist of *A Via Lactea* finds solace in death, but former prisoner Vargas's predicament in *Los muertos* shows that there is no exit, no expectation other than mere subsistence.

This overview conveys something of the richness of the corpus of experimental movies being produced by Latin American directors. Their work shows how changes in filmic modes over the past hundred years offer multiple means for commenting on recent social tendencies, such as the failure of the left and the toxic impact of neoliberalism. A huge increase in the population living in substandard conditions has brought a resulting social malaise in crime, drugs, and prostitution. While these films engage in social critique by calling attention to the perpetuation of the cycle of poverty, their directors refrain from offering salvational panaceas.

From a theoretical viewpoint, in this book I offer multiple applications of Gilles Deleuze's philosophical musings about cinema to contemporary Latin American films. The text accordingly showcases certain aspects of the movement-image, such as the conventions of (neo)noir, and underscores the sea change brought about by the postwar or time- image (via neorealism and the nouvelle vague) in an understanding of cinema as being entranced by a vision, along with the exploration of time. As the cinematographic picture becomes a representation of time, the time-image puts thought into contact with the inexplicable and the incommensurable (*Cinema 2*, 214). Insofar as cinema offers images and a point of view, it introduces a type of language. By presenting a variety of films that underscore complex modes of aesthetic experimentation, I aspire to expand the cinematic imaginary through the analysis of a rich, novel, and promising corpus of independent films that offer an alternative to the hegemonic Hollywood model.

NOTES

Introduction

1. On Cavalcânti's contribution to the documentary in Britain see Aiken, 179–214. After leaving Vera Cruz Studios in São Paulo, an exiled Cavalcânti worked in France as well as in Germany and Israel.
2. Peixoto soon withdrew *Limite* from circulation, so few actually viewed the film in Brazil. See Avellar, 14–23, on the preservation of this film.
3. For the influence of documentary on the New Latin American Cinema see the works of Michael Chanan, Ana M. López, and Juliane Burton.
4. Trinh T. Minh-ha argues, "There is no such thing as documentary—whether the term designates a category of material, a genre, an approach, or a set of techniques" (29).
5. On the current emphasis on realism see Nagib, *World Cinema*.
6. On the other modes of the documentary—expository, interactive, and reflexive—see Burton, 4–5.
7. On *La hora de los hornos* see Tal, 111–120.
8. Burucúa, who lost a brother to Argentine state terrorism, objects to Stam's decision to accept Perón's populism as political avant-garde (62).
9. On the impact of Latin American revolutionary movements of the '60s on neorealist style and mode of production see Hess, 105, 111.
10. On the politics of neorealism see Brunetta, 111, 114.
11. For in-depth analysis of the New Latin American Cinema see Pick.

12.   For a more developed treatment of this period of Argentine cinema see
       works by Foster, Falicov, and España.

13.   Bentes argues that the 1960s "aesthetics of hunger" was superseded by the
       1990s "cosmetics of hunger" (124–125).

14.   On the effect of the withdrawal of Soviet support on Cuban GDP see
       Young, 33.

15.   For more about the inherent pressures of co-production on Méndez see
       Cobos and Vilches.

16.   On fictual faction see Rodríguez-Mangual. On recent Latin American films
       as direct and silent still-life portraits see León, 136.

17.   For a new reading of Hitchcock that finds Deleuze's description of the action
       image too narrow see Orr.

18.   On Italian neorealism's lengthy takes, a predominance of medium and long
       shots, respect for the continuity of time and space, unobtrusive editing,
       working-class protagonists, and active viewer involvement see Marcus, 22.

19.   Levy supports the autochthonous theory by noting that *Chinatown*, *The
       Conversation*, *Parallax View*, *Three Days of the Condor*, *All the President's
       Men*, and *Nashville* were produced in 1974–1976 (221).

20.   For a radically different theoretical approach to authorship that takes the
       entire production of a film as a unit see Daniel Frampton's *Filmosophy*.

21.   For a sobering account of co-productions in Cuba see Ambrosio Fornet's
       foreword to *Framing Latin American Cinema*. For Argentina see Getino's
       Cine argentino, and for Mexico see García Canclini, Rosas Mantecón, and
       Enrique Sánchez Ruiz.

22.   On intolerance in Ripstein's films see Schumann, 233.

23.   See Johnson, "TV Globo," 25.

Chapter One

1.   On Mamet and the con man see Levy, 238–242.

2.   Fellow neonoir directors include Marcelo Piñeyro, who directed *Cenizas en
      el paraíso* (*Ashes of Paradise*) and *Plata quemada* (*Burnt Money*), and Juan
      José Campanella, director of *El mismo amor la misma lluvia* (*Same Love
      Same Rain*) and *El hijo de la novia* (*Son of the Bride*). Bernardes, Lerer, and
      Wolf, 121.

3.   See Kaplan, *Women in Film Noir*.

4.   For a detailed examination of noir lighting, parody, pastiche, and fashion see
      Naremore's "Old Is New" in *More than Night*, 167–219.

5.   The corralito that began in 2001 under President Fernando de la Rúa's
      administration entailed freezing all bank deposits as major financial institu-
      tions, aware of an impending meltdown of the banking system, withdrew
      funds while still luring middle-class investors to make deposits. The mea-
      sure was taken by Domingo Cavallo, minister of finance. Upon the social
      unrest that led to de la Rúa's overthrow and Cavallo's resignation, Roberto

Lavagna, minister of finance in Duhalde's administration, converted deposits made in dollars into pesos and promptly liberalized the exchange rate from one dollar for one peso to one dollar for four pesos. See Stiglitz on the IMF origins of the bank run, the repayment of foreign financial institutions, and the assault on middle-class Argentines who bore the brunt of the collapse.

Chapter Two

1. Jorge Furtado (1959–), born in Porto Alegre, Rio Grande do Sul, Brazil, began his directorial career by working in television. His film production includes *Houve uma vez dois verões* (*Two Summers*, 2002), which tells the story of an adolescent who has a fling, only to become aware of the consequences the following summer. *Meu tio matou um cara* (My Uncle Murdered a Dude, 2004) centers on a teenager who tries to prove his uncle's innocence while attracting the attention of the girl he loves. By introducing video games that reflect the plot, Furtado incorporates intermediality. In *Saneamiento básico* (Basic Sanitation, 2007), a small community tries to dig a ditch to solve sanitation issues, but a lack of resources leads them to decide to generate funds by producing a film that, due to their inexperience, becomes self-reflexive.

2. Phillipe Barcinski's *Não por acaso* (2007) and Adrián Biniez's *Gigante* (2009) weave intermediality by means of security cameras.

3. See George Yúdice, 12–13, for a nuanced summary of Habermas's definition of instrumental rationality.

4. Despite its controversial depiction of indigenous peoples, the determined protagonist of Claudia Llosa's *Madeinusa* (2006) embarks on a quest for America, defined in terms of consumer society.

5. Consumers bask in the warmth of gratification. Baudrillard, *Consumer Society*, 159.

6. On the expansion of the sphere of exchange value see Jhally, 11.

7. Quoted English translations are from the films' subtitles.

8. On Brazilian conspicuous consumption see D'Angelo, 134, 138–143.

9. On pastiche see Jameson, 16.

10. On referential bracketing in the age of simulation see Baudrillard, *Simulations*, 4.

11. On the generation of new contexts by citation see Derrida, *Margins*, 320.

12. On a current femme fatale faithful to her role see Ricardo Darín's *La señal*. On the success of the neonoir femme fatale see Wager, 133.

Chapter Three

1. Heitor Dhalia (1970–) was born in Rio de Janeiro, grew up in Recife, and moved to São Paulo. Dhalia, a self-taught filmmaker and scriptwriter, transitioned into the United States riding on the success of his three movies. *Nina* (2004), his first feature film, is a dark psychological thriller inspired by Dostoyevsky's *Crime and Punishment* that mixes expressionist aesthetics with

mangalike animation. *À deriva* (*Adrift*, 2009) is a drama about a teenager undergoing her sexual awakening and torn about her allegiances toward her parents when she learns of her father's infidelities. Like Bielinsky, Dhalia admires American independent filmmakers such as the Cohen brothers, Paul Thomas Anderson, Todd Solondz, Miranda July, and Quentin Tarantino.

2. McElroy provides etymology and sources on the term *bunda*. For a summary on the Brazilian fixation with bundas see Kulick, 70–71. On female attractiveness resulting from the ratio of body mass see Singh. On the relationships of the body, sexuality, and gender see Goldenberg, 62, 68. On beauty and race in Brazil see Edmonds.

3. Portuguese quotes with page notations are from Lourenço Mutarelli's homonymous novel.

4. Lourenço Mutarelli (1964–), born in São Paulo and famous for his underground comics, starred in a 2009 adaptation of another text he penned, *O natimorto: Um musical silencioso* (2004).

5. On the gambler's behavior see Hallowell and Grace.

6. Intertextual references in Mutarelli's novel include Glauco Matoso's baroque poems *Geléia de rococó* (1999) (38), Anatole France's *Monsieur Bergeret* (1901) (60–61), Mario de Andrade's *Macunaíma* (1828) (61), Oscar Wilde's *Dorian Gray* (1890) (110), and *Manual prático do ódio* (2003) by Reginaldo Ferreira da Silva, aka Ferréz (18, 126). Authors mentioned include Camus and Machado de Assis (122) and Mauro dos Prazeres, an engineer who became a prized graphic artist (78).

7. There are very few black characters in the film. One sells silver cutlery, and another offers a music box.

8. On the ageless aura of Lourenço's classic clothes see the "Extras" section of the DVD.

9. See "The Making of *O cheiro do ralo*" in the "Extras" section of the DVD. See Mutarelli's interview in *IDE*, "A estranha arte de produzir efeito sem causa."

10. Regarding Lourenço's abuse of the drug addict, the movie elides his most humiliating order: "Pega um pouco de papel no banheiro. E vem me limpar" (Get some toilet paper from the bathroom and come clean me) (67).

11. For a psychoanalytical approach to the relationship between money and feces see Bornemann.

12. For a historical approach to the condemnation of usury see Vermeersch. The reference to the eye includes Bataille's *Story of an Eye*.

13. See Freud's "Beyond the Pleasure Principle" (1920) in *Essentials of Psycho-Analysis*.

Chapter Four

1. Walter Moreira Salles Jr. (1956—), born in Rio de Janeiro the son of an ambassador, is widely traveled. Salles graduated from the University of

Southern California's School of Cinematic Arts. His documentary on Socorro Nobre, a semiliterate female prisoner engaged in correspondence with a visual artist, led him to conceive of *Central do Brasil*. *Foreign Land* (*Terra estrangeira*, 1996) focuses on the story of a youth who decides to leave the country after the death of his mother. *O primeiro dia* (*Midnight*, 1998) tells the story of a fugitive prisoner and a middle-class teacher—suicidal after having broken up with her lover—who meet on New Year's Eve. *Behind the Sun* (*Abril despedaçado*, 2001) centers on the rebellion of a son who does not wish to obey his father's command to avenge his brother's death. *The Motorcycle Diaries* (*Diarios de motocicleta*, 2004) is based on Ernesto "Che" Guevara's notebooks. *Linha de passe* (Pass Line, 2008) follows the paths of a single mother's four sons as they attempt to escape the favela. At this writing, Salles, like Dhalia, has been directing a film in the United States.

2. Based on Martín-Barbero, Cisneros classifies the film as anachronistic melodrama (104).

3. On the impact of neoliberal economic measures in Brazil see Gutiérrez-Albilla, 143.

4. Shaw concludes, "Both for the audience and for Dora, these talking heads never acquire the status of individuals worth caring about" (166).

5. For changes in hegemonic ideology regarding religion see Oricchio, "Sertão," 156.

6. For a definition of "under erasure" see Spivak, xiv.

7. Bentes describes Glauber Rocha's sertão in *Deus e o diabo na terra do sol* (*Black God, White Devil*, 1964) as a land in crisis, typically scorched and barren (124).

8. On the supplement see Derrida, *Of Grammatology*, 144–145.

9. On the comparison between *Central do Brasil* and *Pixote* see Shaw, 158–160, and Xavier, 60.

10. On the similarity with Cinema Novo see Cowan. On the ideological shift between the sites shot by Salles and their representation in foundational Cinema Novo films see Nagib, *Brazil on Screen*, 33–41.

11. On the recuperation of images that remain frozen in time as they were some fifty years ago see Pellegrini, 225.

Chapter Five

1. Carlos Sorín (1944–), born in Buenos Aires, considers himself an independent director.

2. The smoke at the brick factory lends an eerie feel to the movie, and the sound of a *cumbia villera* is a clear reference to the lumpen.

3. See "That Dangerous Supplement" in *Of Grammatology*, 144–145.

4. On hierarchical relations among different types of masculinity see Connell, *Men and Boys*, 10, 30–31. The reference to sponsorships typical of sports

celebrities reinforces Bombón's effect on the construction of Villegas's masculinity.

5. Echoing the alienation of Osvaldo Dragún's "Historia del hombre que se convirtió en perro" (1956), Sorín both inscribes and subverts the Italian *grottesco* insofar as he maintains the traditional focus on sentimentality but displaces the motivation onto survival. Pelletieri, 55.

6. In the interview on the DVD, Sorín associates the tropical rainforest with mystery and magic.

7. Unemployment sheds light on the popular devotion to San Cayetano and the Virgen Desatanudos.

8. Though the inception of the piquetero movement has been traced back to 1996, roadblocks gained momentum with the economic meltdown of 2001. The lack of unemployment coverage contributes to these movements in Argentina.

9. According to Yoruba tradition, the orishás are the emissaries of Olodumaré, the highest deity in the pantheon. Like the Virgin of Guadalupe, the Virgin of Itatí represents religious syncretism, as the Guaraní found her in 1615. The fortune frog symbolizes richness and prosperity in feng shui. A mãe de santo is a priestess in Afro-Brazilian religions. On Gauchito Gil see Graziano, 119–140. On those left out by the myth of Argentina as a Catholic nation see Bianchi. For historical accounts of the Catholic Church in Argentina see Gustafson. On sects in Argentina see Silletta and Gorbato.

10. Director's introduction and Q&A on the movie, screened on March 5, 2010, during Mesa Community College's film festival in Phoenix. On the correlation between state religion and state regulation see Barro and McCleary, 763. On the association between the secular-rational dimension and the transition to an industrial society see Inglehart and Baker, 30.

11. On the influence of indigenous and African cultures on the Argentine imaginary see Frigerio, 227, 232. On Argentina as a screen on which Europe and the United States project an otherness that encompasses the same see Kaminsky, 12. On San La Muerte see Graziano, 77–111. On San Baltasar or Baltazar see Cirio.

12. Carlos Jiménez Rufino, aka La Mona Jiménez, born in Córdoba, Argentina, in 1951, has produced seventy-seven records over a forty-year period.

Chapter Six

1. María Victoria Menis graduated from the Centro Experimental del Instituto Nacional de Cinematografía Cortometrajista in Buenos Aires. Menis has garnered numerous awards for her shorts, television series, and work in theater. She has offered courses at the Universidad de Buenos Aires, the INCAA (Instituto Nacional de Cine y Artes Audiovisuales, the National Institute of Cinema and Audiovisual Arts), and the Escuela de Cine de

Avellaneda, Buenos Aires. Menis directed two comedies. In *Los espíritus patrióticos* (*Patriotic Spirits*, 1989), political satire and mystery center on a group of journalists who have uncovered a conspiracy. *Arregui, la noticia del día* (2001) revolves around an obscure employee who takes stock of his life when he learns that he has a terminal illness. Menis's feature film *La cámara oscura* (2008), based on the homonymous short story by Angélica Gorodischer, focuses on discriminatory practices and the intense imagination of an ugly duckling who becomes ostracized to the point of invisibility yet makes up for it in efficiency as a homemaker and in developing an intense inner world. The chance meeting with a surrealist French photographer changes her life, allowing for sensual self-discovery and liberation.

2. Despite Laura Mulvey's 1975 dictum that only women can be objectified (19), film critics Silverman (*Male Subjectivity*) and Lehman (21), among others, note that the gaze may be focused on the male as a desirable object.

3. According to Kristeva, the loss of an erotic object is experienced as castration insofar as it affects the body image and the entire psychic system. *Black Sun*, 81.

4. On the waves of immigrants see Costa, 45.

5. On the effects of neoliberal policies on different types of establishments see Nochteff and Abeles, 39. On trauma theory see Kaplan, *Trauma Culture*, 31–41.

6. On the increasing impoverishment of the Argentine middle class since the 1976 military coup see Grimson and Kessler, 87.

7. On bonding through boxing see Connell, "El imperialismo," 86. On the construction of masculinity as an extended adolescence see Connell, *Men and Boys*, 85.

8. On the constellation of factors affecting the construction of motherhood see Hardy and Wiedmer, 2. On the reproduction of mothering see Chodorow.

9. The description comes from the personal account of Norma López, a Bolivian anthropologist who lived in a Guaraní community in the Bolivian Amazon. I am grateful to Norma López also for the references to the lullaby "La cantuta" and firewood as symbol of the hearth. Félix's actions may be attributed to remnants of the matriarchal nature of Guaraní ideology. On Guaraní family structure, child rearing, and the transmission of language and culture see Rocca and Rossi, 27.

10. On what has become known as the Washington Consensus on Latin America see Wiarda and Skelley's chapter "Neoliberalism and Its Problems," 164–187. On the origin and development of neoliberalism and its relation to the diminishing returns of production see Dierckxsens, 90–91.

11. Adrián Caetano's film *Bolivia* (2001) illustrates Argentine racism against Bolivian immigrants. On battered women and post-traumatic stress disorder see Morewitz, 173.

12. On machismo as performance designed to disguise insecurity see Meler, 83. On feelings of worthlessness unleashing domestic violence see Liendro Zingoni, 135.

13. *Echolalia* is an almost bodily rhythm reminiscent of Kristeva's notion of *chora*, defined as the preverbal state that connects the body (in the process of constituting itself as an independent being), objects, and family members. *Revolution*, 26–27.

Chapter Seven

1. Inés de Oliveira Cézar (1964–), born in Buenos Aires, has blended her interest in theater direction and acting with an interest in psychology.

2. For the symbolic connotation of homes see Bachelard.

3. For the anamorphic shots see http://www.fdk-berlin.de/en/forum/forum-archive/2005/main-program/como-pasan-las-horas.html.

Chapter Eight

1. Josué Méndez Bisbal (1976–), born in Lima, graduated in 1998 from Yale University with degrees in film and Latin American studies. Méndez has also worked in advertising, documentaries, theater, and television for Peruvian and foreign producers. *Dioses* (*Gods*, 2008), his second feature film, dwells on the lives of the rich in Peru, perhaps as a counterpoint to the social class depicted in *Días de Santiago*.

2. On Shining Path see Gorriti. On the 70,000 victims of the twenty-year war between guerrilla and government forces (1980–2000) see the *Report of the Peruvian Truth and Reconciliation Commission* at http://www.cverdad .org.pe/ingles/ifinal/index.php and the documentary *State of Fear* (2005).

3. PTSD can result from man-made, deliberate, malicious stressors, unintentional human accidents, or technological or natural disasters. PTSD tables list symptoms in four main categories, labeled A through D. Within each category are more specific manifestations of the disorder; a certain number of these discrete symptoms is required for clinical diagnosis. For descriptions of these terms see Schiraldi, 1–6. Category A involves exposure to a stressor, defined as a life threat or violation or witnessing such an event and experiencing intense fear, helplessness, or horror as a result. Category B involves persistent re-experience in at least one of the following five ways: 1) recurrent, intrusive recollections of the event; 2) recurrent, distressing dreams of the event; 3) acting or feeling as if the trauma were recurring; 4) intense psychological distress upon exposure to internal or external cues that resemble an aspect of the trauma; 5) psychological reactivity upon exposure to such cues. Category C involves persistent avoidance of stimuli, of which diagnosis requires three of seven factors: 1) efforts to avoid thoughts, feelings, or conversations that remind one of the trauma; 2) efforts

to avoid activities, people, or places that arouse recollections; 3) inability to recall an important aspect of the trauma; 4) markedly diminished interest or participation in significant activities that used to be pleasurable; 5) feeling of detachment or estrangement from others; 6) restricted range of affect; 7) sense of foreshortened future. Santiago evidences three, C1, C6, and C7. Category D involves persistent symptoms of increased arousal. Two of five manifestations of D are required for diagnosis: 1) difficulty falling or staying asleep; 2) irritability or outbursts of anger; 3) difficulty concentrating; 4) hypervigilance; 5) exaggerated startle response. Three are discernible in the film, D1, D2, and D4. Considering that Santiago lived and witnessed these traumatic events because he perpetrated them (category A), the plot line would allow us to identify PTSD due to the appearance of the listed after-effects.

4. Like Freud, in developing a theory of psychological trauma to explain hysteria, Pierre Janet discovered the fundamental tenets of PTSD (Flora, 4). For Freud's views on "traumatic neurosis" see section 2 of *Beyond the Pleasure Principle* (1920). In 1941 Abram Kardiner identified five constant features: "1) Fixation on the trauma; 2) Typical dream life; 3) Irritability and startle pattern [sudden unexpected noises take the victim back to trauma]; 4) Tendency to explosive aggressive actions; 5) Contraction of the general level of functioning" (in Flora, 6).

5. The English subtitles of *Días de Santiago* are problematic. There are typos such as "psychollogy." Perhaps the worst one is the translation of the section on the DVD titled "Fan Club," literally rendered "Club del ventilador," with "fan" translated as a machine that blows air.

6. The veteran returns to normal functioning as long as she or he can dissociate and deny the traumatic war memories (Flora, 7).

Chapter Nine

1. Carlos Reygadas Castillo (1971–) was born in Mexico City, studied law in Mexico, specialized in armed conflicts in London, and worked for the United Nations. Reygadas discovered his filmic passion after watching Andrei Tarkovsky's films in 1987. Auteurs whom Reygadas admires are Abel Ferrara, Iranian directors, and Dreyer (in Romero, 180). Reygadas, in Wood, *Talking Movies*, 191, cites three more: "The first films of Carlos Saura are also very dear to me as are, for different reasons, Ozu and Kurosawa."

2. Mariana Carreño King argues that "the title comes from the rising-sun symbol associated with Japan."

3. The beheading of the shot pigeon by the unnamed protagonist is reminiscent of Buñuel's *Un chien andalou* (1929).

4. See Rowlandson, 1028–1031, on *Japón* as an allegory of the act of reading, which allows for the fusion of actor, filmmaker, and viewer.

5. On abjection resulting from the pollution of the representation of decaying bodies see Kristeva, *Powers of Horror*, 109. The man's request of Ascen reinserts him into the hegemonic construction of masculinity. Although from a hegemonic stance impotence is a flaw, freedom from instincts is an advantage.

6. In setting up the Reygadas interview, Fraser defines the Kuleshov effect as the construction of meaning through the juxtaposition of images (montage) to create ideas not present in either image by itself.

Chapter Ten

1. Regarding the couple's motive Reygadas states in the interview by Higgins, "It's just a fact. I don't want to talk about the kidnapping, I want to talk about the internal struggle of a man."

2. According to Reygadas in the Higgins interview, this scene suggests that "we long for things and we long for love. Hope is the most important feeling we can have."

3. On the funeral march and the death pact see the interview with Reygadas on the *Batalla en el cielo* DVD. On the effect of music in the film and as a structural device see Reygadas's interview with Badt, "No Slave to Realism."

4. On Reygadas and this scene in terms of Titian and Tintoretto see his interview by Higgins.

5. On iterability see Derrida's *Margins*, 320.

6. Sociologist Aleksandra Jablonska has asserted that Mexican hegemonic ideology does not rely on phenotypes to define ethnicity. Instead, indigenous peoples are recognized as such only if they choose to embrace their ancestral cultures. Comments at the Universidade Federal de São Carlos, Brazil, May 17–18, 2011.

Chapter Eleven

1. On Mennonite migration and adaptation in Mexico see Bennion.

2. Miriam Toews is a Canadian novelist. Romney, 42.

3. On Munk's wavering between a miracle and the coroner's mistake see Drum and Drum, 224. Dreyer refers to Einstein's theory of relativity in discussing the fourth dimension, time, and a fifth dimension, the psychical, in arguing for a deeper understanding of the divine and a natural explanation for supernatural things. Skoller, 164.

4. Adaptation theory entails "translation, reading, dialogization, cannibalization, transmutation, transfiguration, and signifying transmutation." Stam, "Beyond Fidelity," 62.

5. In a 2006 interview by Le Cain in *Senses of Cinema*, Reygadas argues that while Bresson expects his actors to be neutral models for his ideas, Reygadas tries to respect their individual energy.

6. Reygadas set a camera on a cart and cross-faded a series of takes shot over the course of an hour and a half to create the initial and last shots without having to depend on computer-generated images. Romney, 43.

7. On Dreyer's work toward the generation of a new dimension of cinematic consciousness see Skoller, 163.

Chapter Twelve

1. Oliveira Cézar's film draws from the material of the Trojan wars—Euripides's *Iphigenia at Aulis* (408–406 BCE) and *Iphigenia at Tauris* (414–412 BCE) and Aeschylus's "Oresteia," that is, *Agamemnon, The Libation Bearers*, and *The Eumenides* (458 BCE)—to represent the cultural passage from a matriarchal to a patriarchal order.

2. As in the Greek play, the "unspeakable and unspoken" is elided: "What came next?" is answered by "I neither saw, nor do I tell." Gurd, 16.

3. During this period, infanticide of sickly, crippled, "wrong gender" (girls), or illegitimate babies seems to have been common, as was their exposure to harm; these practices were "legally prescribed" in Sparta; Kamen, 89. Exposure to starvation, dehydration, hypothermia, and dangers from nature amounted to infanticide for most such babies albeit tempered by the possibility of their being rescued.

4. Some of the competing theories regarding the disappearance of the palace states are the migration of great masses of warlike people, warfare, climate changes, volcanic eruptions, plagues, earthquakes, and overpopulation. Thompson, 17.

5. Dates on the Comechingones vary from Pedro González's *Probanza* (1548) to Diego Fernández's account (1571). Aparicio, 675.

6. The Cordobés accent, considered a remnant of the Comechingones, consists in the prolongation of vowels. A Spaniard says "tráe-me-lo," a Cordobés, "tra-ée-me-lo."

7. Lefebvre, 317, notes that social relations retain a relative stability, while the members of a society are constantly changing.

8. In defining "habitus" Bourdieu avoids objectivism or mechanical reaction as well as subjectivism or conscious intent. In Bourdieu and Wacquant, 120.

9. Although there are many texts on the Trojan Cycle, Oliveira Cézar follows Euripides's version, which emphasizes the importance of family, as it depicts women as speaking historical agents.

Chapter Thirteen

1. On Elena Holmberg in Paris see Lewis, 168.

2. Jorge Luis Borges stakes the claim of universal culture for Argentines.

3. See Rudnytsky, 253–274, for ambivalence in Freud's articulation of the Oedipus complex.

4.   On the disappeared see CONADEP and Penchaszadeh, 291–292. On the
      400 missing grandchildren and the 100-plus who recovered their identities
      see http://www.abuelas.org.ar.

Chapter Fourteen

1.   For a biographical snapshot see Santos Moray.
2.   On the different co-production agreements offered by Ibermedia, a film fund
      sponsored by Spain, Portugal, and thirteen countries in Latin America, see
      Falicov, "Programa Ibermedia."
3.   The unbridled and sad sexuality of the sci-fi story may be an allusion to the
      current boom in sex tourism, suggested by Elvira's reference to Eva's small
      role as a "jinetera."
4.   I borrow Ann E. Kaplan's thesis of the projection of trauma into the future, a
      feature shared by various Latin American directors of transnational projects
      like Fernando Meirelles's *Blindness* (2008).

Chapter Fifteen

1.   On the influence of Godfrey Reggio's *Koyaanisqatsi* (1982) see Young, 35. On
      digital media in *Suite Habana* see Stock, 70.
2.   On Castro's changing attitute toward Lennon see Young, 40.
3.   On the Aristotelic-Hegelian aporia of time see Derrida, *Aporias*, 15.
4.   Patterson notes (188) that the teacher's commands denote her influence
      over her charges as well as state hegemony.
5.   Marcelo Fajardo Cárdenas, in email, notes that "suite" in the title also means
      a luxurious hotel room, all the more ironic given the dilapidated state of most
      of the dwellings.
6.   In the Cuban context a *transformista* cross-dresses only to perform in drag.
      Young, 42.
7.   Though sexist, these shots register plausible male reactions. Additionally,
      the women's narratives speak to their dependence on masculine figures.
      Redruello, 192.
8.   See Tierney, 51, on the distancing effect of the religious choir's "amen"
      set against a baseball game, just prior to a shot of partners dancing at
      the Benny Moré, and as an allusion to Gutiérrez Alea's *Memorias del
      subdesarrollo*.
9.   Conversely, Young (36) contrasts the gritty realism of the scenes with the
      poetic imagery and the haunting sound track.
10.   On associative montage in *Berlin* see Macrae.
11.   Even ordinary actions like bathing allow for comparisons, since only Francis-
      quito enjoys running water.
12.   See Rodríguez-Mangual, 311, on the composition of the frame and the light-
      ing, even when the sequences were shot in the characters' homes.

13.   On the cathartic expression of lack and the artistic expression of the failed project of the nation see Goldman, 880.

Chapter Sixteen

1.   Paz Encina (1971–) was born in Asunción, Paraguay, where she studied law and communications prior to taking courses at the Escuela de Cine y Televisión de San Antonio de los Baños, Cuba, in 1993. In 2001 she graduated from the Universidad del Cine in Buenos Aires, Argentina. In 2005 she produced a seventy-two-minute documentary titled *Río Arriba* and set in the northern province of Salta, Argentina. Encina shot in 35mm because Holland, Argentina, and France co-produced *Hamaca paraguaya*.

2.   Although Encina reads and writes Guaraní, she wrote the screenplay in Spanish and had it translated.

3.   Hutcheon argues that simultaneous inscription and subversion is characteristic of postmodern intertextuality (118).

4.   Partyka also identifies temporal, spatial, and conceptual limitations, open-endedness, assumption of forehand knowledge, and extensive usage of metaphors, personification, antitheses, clichés, and proverbs (93).

5.   Yorgos's blog post concentrates on the shots that structure the film. Distance occludes Encina's stress on real time, as evidenced by Cándida fanning herself and peeling and eating an orange.

6.   The date of the end of the Chaco War varies between June 12 and June 14, 1935, because some at the front were unaware of the official ending of the conflict. Thus, Ríos (334) mentions June 12, 1935, and Farcau (229) June 14, 1935.

BIBLIOGRAPHY

Films

8½. Dir. Federico Fellini. Perf. Marcelo Mastroiani, Anouk Aimée, Claudia Cardinale. Italy, 1963.

21 Grams. Dir. Alejandro González Iñárritu. Perf. Sean Penn, Benicio del Toro, Naomi Watts. USA, 2003.

Las aguas bajan turbias. Dir. Hugo del Carril. Perf. Hugo del Carril, Adriana Benetti, Raúl del Valle. Argentina, 1952.

Amores perros. Dir. Alejandro González Iñárritu. Perf. Emilio Echeverría, Gael García Bernal, Gaya Toledo. Mexico, 2000.

Arregui, la noticia del día. Dir. María Victoria Menis. Perf. Enrique Pinti, Carmen Maura, Damián Dreyzik. Argentina, 2001.

Asesinato en el Senado de la Nación. Dir. Juan José Jusid. Perf. José Soriano, Miguel Solá, Oscar Martínez. Argentina, 1984.

El aura. Dir. Fabián Bielinsky. Perf. Ricardo Darín, Dolores Fonzi, Pablo Cedrón. Argentina, 2005.

Azyllo muito louco. Dir. Nelson Pereira dos Santos. Perf. Nildo Parente, Isabel Ribeiro, Arduíno Colassanti. Brazil, 1970.

Babel. Dir. Alejandro González Iñárritu. Perf. Brad Pitt, Cate Blanchett, Gael García Bernal. USA, 2006.

El baño del papa. Dir. César Charlone, Enrique Fernández. Perf. César Troncoso, Virginia Méndez, Virginia Ruiz. Uruguay, 2007.

Batalla en el cielo. Dir. Carlos Reygadas. Perf. Marcos Hernández, Anapola Mushkadiz. Mexico, 2005.

Battleship Potemkin. Dir. Sergei Eisenstein. Perf. Aleksandr Antonov, Vladimir Barsky, Grigori Aleksandrov. USSR, 1924.

Berlin: Die symphonie der Großstadt. Dir. Walter Ruttmann, 1927.

Biutiful. Dir. Alejandro González Iñárritu. Perf. Javier Bardem, Maricel Álvarez, Hannaa Bouchaib. Mexico, 2010.

Blindness. Dir. Fernando Meirelles. Perf. Julianne Moore, Mark Ruffalo, Gael García Bernal. USA, 2008.

Bolivia. Dir. Adrián Caetano. Perf. Freddy Flores, Rosa Sánchez, Oscar Bertea. Argentina, 2001.

Bombón: El perro. Dir. Carlos Sorín. Perf. Juan Villegas, Walter Donado. Argentina, 2004.

Buenos Aires viceversa. Dir. Alejandro Agresti. Perf. Vera Fogwill, Nicolás Pauls, Fernán Mirás. Argentina, 1996.

La caída. Dir. Leopoldo Torre Nilsson. Perf. Elsa Daniel, Duilio Marzio, Lautaro Murúa. Argentina, 1959.

Call of the Oboe. Dir. Claudio MacDowell. Perf. Paule Betti, Mario Lozano, Arturo Fleitas. Paraguay, 1998.

La cámara oscura. Dir. María Victoria Menis. Perf. Mirta Bogdasarian, Fernando Armani, Patrick Dell'Isola. Argentina, 2008.

Camila. Dir. María Luisa Bemberg. Perf. Susú Pecoraro, Imanol Arias, Héctor Alterio. Argentina, 1984.

O caminho das nuvens. Dir. Vicente Amorím. Perf. Wagner Moura, Claudia Abreu, Ravi Ramos Lacerda. Brazil, 2003.

El camino de San Diego. Dir. Carlos Sorín. Perf. Ignacio Benítez, Carlos Wagner La Bella. Argentina, 2006.

O cangaceiro. Dir. Lima Barreto. Perf. Alberto Ruschel, Marisa Prado, Milton Ribeiro. Brazil, 1953.

La casa del ángel. Dir. Leopoldo Torre Nilsson. Perf. Elsa Daniel, Lautaro Murúa. Argentina, 1957.

Cenizas en el paraíso. Dir. Marcelo Piñeyro. Perf. Héctor Alterio, Cecilia Roth, Leonardo Sbaraglia. Argentina, 1997.

Central do Brasil. Dir. Walter Salles. Perf. Fernanda Montenegro. Brazil. 1998.

Cerro Corá. Dir. Guillermo Vera. Perf. Roberto De Felice, Rosa Ros, Pedro Ignacio Aceval. Paraguay, 1977.

O cheiro do ralo. Dir. Heitor Dhalia. Perf. Selton Mello, Paula Braun. Brazil, 2007.

Chelovek s kino-apparatom. Dir. Dziga Vertov. Perf. Mikhail Kaufman. USSR, 1929.

Un chien andalou. Dir. Luis Buñuel. Perf. Pierre Batcheff, Simone Mareuil. France, 1929.

Children of Men. Dir. Alfonso Cuarón. Perf. Julianne Moore, Clive Owen, Chiwetel Ejiofor. USA, 2006.

Cidade de Deus. Dir. Fernando Meirelles. Perf. Alexandre Rodrigues, Matheus Nachtergaele, Leandro Firmino. Brazil, 2002.

El cielito. Dir. María Victoria Menis. Perf. Leonardo Ramírez, Darío Levy, Mónica
    Lairana. Argentina, 2004.

La ciénaga. Dir. Lucrecia Martel. Perf. Mercedes Morán, Graciela Borges, Martín
    Adjemián. Argentina, 2001.

Cinema, aspirinas, e urubus. Dir. Marcelo Gomes. Perf. João Miguel, Peter Ketnath.
    Brazil, 2005.

Citizen Kane. Dir. Orson Welles. Perf. Orson Welles, Joseph Cotten, Dorothy Co-
    mingore. USA, 1941.

Clandestinos. Dir. Fernando Pérez Valdés. Perf. Luis Alberto García, Isabel Santos,
    Oscar Alvarez. Cuba, 1987.

Como agua para chocolate. Dir. Alfonso Arau. Perf. Marco Leonardi, Lumi Cavazos,
    Regina Torné. Mexico, 1991.

Como pasan las horas. Dir. Inés de Oliveira Cézar. Perf. Susana Campos, Susana
    Berco, Guillermo Arengo, Agustín Alcoba. Argentina, 2005.

Criminal. Dir. Gregory Jacobs. Perf. John C. Reilly, Diego Luna, Maggie Gyllenhaal.
    USA, 2004.

Cronos. Dir. Guillermo del Toro. Perf. Federico Luppi, Ron Perlman, Claudio Brook.
    Mexico, 1993.

De cierta manera. Dir. Sara Gómez. Perf. Mario Balmaceda, Yolanda Cuéllar. Cuba,
    1974.

Demasiado miedo a la vida o plaff! Dir. Juan Carlos Tabío. Perf. Daisy Granados,
    Thais Valdés, Raúl Pomares. Cuba, 1988.

A deriva. Dir. Heitor Dhalia. Perf. Laura Neiva, Vincent Cassel, Camilla Belle. Brazil,
    2009.

Deus e o diabo na terra do sol. Dir. Glauber Rocha. Perf. Geraldo del Rey, Yoná Mag-
    alhães, Othon Bastos. Brazil, 1964.

Días de Santiago. Dir. Josué Méndez. Perf. Pietro Sibile, Milagros Román. Peru 2004.

Diarios de motocicleta. Dir. Walter Salles. Perf. Gael García Bernal, Rodrigo de la
    Serna, USA, 2004.

Dioses. Dir. Josué Méndez. Perf. Maricielo Effio, Sergio Gjurinovic, and Edgar Saba.
    Peru, 2008.

Entre'acte. Dir. René Clair. Perf. Jean Börlin, Inge Frïs, Francis Picabia, Marcel Du-
    champ, Man Ray. France, 1924.

El espinazo del diablo. Dir. Guillermo del Toro. Perf. Marisa Paredes, Federico Luppi,
    Fernando Tielve. Spain, 1993.

Los espíritus patrióticos. Dir. María Victoria Menis. Perf. Ana María Caso, Jorge
    D'Elía, Mauricio Dayub. Argentina, 1989.

Extranjera. Dir. Inés de Oliveira Cézar. Perf. Angelina Muñoz, Carlos Portaluppi, Eva
    Bianco. Argentina, 2007.

La familia rodante. Dir. Pablo Trapero. Perf. Graciana Chironi, Nicolás López, Liliana
    Capurro. Argentina, 2004.

Favela dos meus amores. Dir. Humberto Mauro. Perf. Sílvio Caldas, Jaime Costa,
    Belmira de Almeida. Brazil, 1935.

Fome de amor. Dir. Nelson Pereira dos Santos. Perf. Arduíno Colassanti, Manfredo Colassanti, Olga Danitch. Brazil, 1968.

Ganga bruta. Dir. Humberto Mauro. Perf. Durval Bellini, Dea Selva, Lu Marival. Brazil, 1933.

El gato desaparece. Dir. Carlos Sorín. Perf. Maria Abadi, Norma Argentina, Gisela Aringoli. Argentina, 2011.

Gigante. Dir. Adrián Biniez. Perf. Horacio Camandule, Leonor Svarcas. Uruguay, 2009.

Guantanamera. Dir. Tomás Gutiérrez Alea. Perf. Carlos Cruz, Mirta Ibarra. Cuba 1995.

Hamaca paraguaya. Dir. Paz Encina. Perf. Ramón del Río, Georgina Genes. Paraguay, 2008.

Hasta cierto punto. Dir. Tomás Guitérrez Alea. Perf. Oscar Álvarez, Mirta Ibarra, Omar Valdés. Cuba, 1983.

Harry Potter and the Prisoner of Azkaban. Dir. Alfonso Cuarón. Perf. Daniel Radcliffe, Emma Watson, Rupert Grint. USA, 2004.

Hello Hemingway. Dir. Fernando Pérez Valdés. Perf. Laura de la Uz, Raúl Paz, Herminia Sánchez. Cuba, 1990.

El hijo de la novia. Dir. Juan José Campanella. Perf. Ricardo Darín, Héctor Alterio, Norma Aleandro. Argentina, 2001.

La historia oficial. Dir. Luis Puenzo. Perf. Héctor Alterio, Norma Aleandro. Argentina, 1986.

Historias mínimas. Dir. Carlos Sorín. Perf. Javier Lombardo, Antonio Benedicti. Argentina, 2002.

O homem que copiava. Dir. Jorge Furtado. Perf. Lázaro Ramos. Brazil, 2003.

La hora de los hornos. Dir. Oscar Getino and Fernando E. Solanas. Perf. María de la Paz, Fernando Solanas, narrators. Argentina, 1968.

Iluminados por el fuego. Dir. Tristán Bauer. Perf. Gastón Pauls, Pablo Riva, César Albarracín. Argentina, 2005.

Japón. Dir. Carlos Reygadas. Perf. Alejandro Ferretis. Mexico, 2002.

Kukuli. Dir. Luis Figueroa, Eulogio Nishiyama, and César Villanueva. Perf. Victor Chambi, Martina Mamani, Lizardo Pérez. Peru, 1961.

El laberinto del Fauno. Dir. Guillermo del Toro. Perf. Ivana Baquero, Adrianda Gil, Sergi López, Maribel Verdú. Spain, Mexico, 2006.

Lady from Shanghai. Dir. Orson Welles. Perf. Orson Welles, Rita Hayworth, Everett Sloane. USA, 1947.

Limite. Dir. Mario Peixoto. Perf. Olga Breno, Tatiana Rey, Raul Schnoor, Brutus Pedreira. Brazil, 1931.

Lucía. Dir. Humberto Solás. Perf. Raquel Revuelta, Eslinda Núñez, Adela Legrá. Cuba, 1969.

Macunaíma. Dir. Joaquim Pedro de Andrade. Perf. Grande Otelo, Paulo José, Jardel Filho. Brazil, 1969.

Madagascar. Dir. Fernando Pérez Valdés. Perf. Elena Bolaños, Zaida Castellanos, Laura de la Uz. Cuba, 1994.

Madeinusa. Dir. Claudia Llosa. Perf. Magaly Solier, Yliana Chong, Carlos J. de la Torre. Peru, 2006.

Madrigal. Dir. Fernando Pérez Valdés. Perf. Liety Chaviano, Carlos Enrique Almirante, Luis Alberto García, Carla Sánchez. Cuba, 2006.

María Escobar. Dir. Galia Giménez. Perf. Ruth Ferreira, José Carlos Aguayo, Miguel María Aguayo. Paraguay, 2001.

El mégano. Dir. Tomás Gutiérrez Alea and Julio García Espinosa. Perf. Ciénaga del Zapata workers. Cuba, 1955.

Memorias del subdesarrollo. Dir. Tomás Gutiérrez Alea. Perf. Sergio Corrieri, Daisy Granados, Eslinda Núñez. Cuba, 1968.

Meu tio matou um cara. Dir. Jorge Furtado. Perf. Darlan Cunha, Sophia Reis, Lázaro Ramos. Brazil, 2004.

El mismo amor la misma lluvia. Dir. Juan José Campanella. Perf. Ricardo Darín, Soledad Villamil, Ulises Dumont. Argentina, 1999.

Muerte al amanecer. Dir. Francisco Lombardi. Perf. Gustavo Rodríguez, William Moreno, Jorge Rodríguez. Peru, 1977.

Los muertos. Dir. Lisandro Alonso. Perf. Argentino Vargas, Francisco Dornez, Yolanda Galarza. Argentina, 2004.

Mundo grúa. Dir. Pablo Trapero. Perf. Luis Margani, Adriana Aizemberg, Daniel Valenzuela. Argentina, 1999.

Un muro de silencio. Dir. Lita Stantic. Perf. Vanessa Redgrave, Ofelia Medina, Lautaro Murúa, Julio Chávez. Argentina, 1993.

Não por acaso. Dir. Phillipe Barcinski. Perf. Rodrigo Santoro, Leonardo Medeiros, Leticia Sabatella. Brazil, 2007.

Nina. Dir. Heitor Dhalia. Perf. Guta Stresser, Milhem Cortaz, Anderson Faganello. Brazil, 2004.

La nueva Francia. Dir. Juan Fresán. Perf. Rodolfo Dallorso, Bertha Dreschler, Rubén Falbo. Argentina, 1972.

Nueve reinas. Dir. Fabián Bielinsky. Perf. Ricardo Darín, Gastón Pauls, Leticia Bredice, Eduardo Fonzi. Argentina, 2000.

Ojos que no ven. Dir. Francisco Lombardi. Perf. Gianfranco Brero, Gustavo Bueno, Patricia Pereya. Peru, 2003.

Los olvidados. Dir. Luis Buñuel. Perf. Estela Inda, Miguel Inclán, Alfonso Mejía. Mexico, 1950.

Ordet. Dir. Carl Theodor Dreyer. Perf. Birgitte Federspiel, Emil Hass Christensen, Cay Kristiansen. Denmark, 1954.

Papeles secundarios. Dir. Orlando Rojas. Perf. Paula Ali, Leonor Arocha, Ferndando Bermúdez. Cuba, 1989.

The Pawnbroker. Dir. Sydney Lumet. Perf. Rod Steiger, Geraldine Fitzgerald, Brock Peters. USA, 1964.

La película del rey. Dir. Carlos Sorín. Perf. Ulises Dumont, Julio Chávez, David Llewelyn. Argentina, 1986.

Picado fino. Dir. Eduardo Sapir. Perf. Belén Blanco, Marcela Guerty, Facundo Luengo. Argentina, 1998.

Piedra libre. Dir. Leopoldo Torres Nilsson. Perf. Marilina Ross, Juan José Camero, Mecha Ortiz. Argentina, 1976.

Pixote: A lei do mais fraco. Dir. Héctor Babenco. Fernando Ramos da Silva, Jorge Julião, Gilberto Moura. Brazil, 1981.

Pizza, birra, fasso. Dir. Adrián Caetano and Bruno Stagnaro. Perf. Héctor Anglada, Jorge Sesán, Pamela Jordán. Argentina, 1998.

Plata quemada. Dir. Marcelo Piñeyro. Perf. Eduardo Noriega, Leonardo Sbaraglia. Argentina, 2000.

El poder de las tinieblas. Dir. Mario Sábato. Perf. Carlos Cantón, Christina Banegas, Aldo Barbero. Argentina, 1979.

El portón de los sueños. Dir. Hugo Gamarra Echeverry. Perf. Justina Aguero, Rosa Elena Blanco, Juanita Espinola. Paraguay, 1998.

Primera noche. Dir. Luis Alberto Restrepo. Perf. Carolina Lizarazo, John Alex Toro. Colombia, 2003.

Quanto vale ou é por quilo?. Dir. Sergio Bianchi. Perf. Antonio Abujamra, Caio Blat, Herson Capri. Brazil, 2007.

El rapado. Dir. Martín Rejtman. Perf. Ezequiel Cavia, Damián Dreyzik, Mirta Busnelli. Argentina, 1996.

Rear Window. Dir. Alfred Hitchcock. Perf. James Stewart, Grace Kelly, Wendell Corey. USA, 1954.

Recuento de los daños. Dir. Inés de Oliveira Cézar. Perf. Eva Bianco, Santiago Gobernori, Marcelo D'Andrea. Argentina, 2010.

Rien que les heures. Dir. Alberto Cavalcânti. Perf. Blanche Bernis, Nina Chousvalowa, Phillippe Hériat. France, 1926.

Rio 40 graus. Dir. Nelson Pereira dos Santos. Perf. Modesto de Souza, Roberto Bataglin, Jece Valadão. Brazil, 1955.

Rodrigo D no futuro. Dir. Víctor Gaviria. Perf. Rodrigo Meneses, Carlos Mario Restrepo, Jackson Idrian Gallego. Colombia, 1991.

São Paulo, sinfonia da metrópole. Dir. Adalberto Kemeny and Rudolf Rex Lustig. Brazil, 1929.

El secreto de sus ojos. Dir. Juan José Campanella. Perf. Ricardo Darín, Soledad Villamil, Pablo Rago. Argentina, 2010.

La señal. Dir. Ricardo Darín and Martín Hodara. Perf. Ricardo Darín, Diego Peretti, Julieta Díaz. 2007.

Sin dejar huella. Dir. María Novaro. Perf. Aitana Sánchez-Guijón, Tiaré Scanda, Jesús Ochoa. Mexico, 2000.

Sólo con tu pareja. Dir. Afonso Cuarón. Perf. Daniel Giménez Cacho, Claudia Ramírez, Luis de Icaza. Mexico, 1991.

State of Fear. Dir. Pamela Yates. Archival. 2005.

Stellet licht. Dir. Carlos Reygadas. Perf. Cornelius Wall, Miriam Toews. Mexico, 2008.

The Strike. Dir. Sergei M. Eisenstein. Perf. Grigori Aleksandrov, Maksim Shtraukh, Mikhail Gomorov. USSR, 1925.

Suite Habana. Dir. Fernando Pérez Valdés. Perf. Iván Carbonell, Francisco Cardet. Cuba, 2003.

La teta asustada. Dir. Claudia Llosa. Perf. Magaly Solier, Susi Sánchez, Efraín Solís. Peru, 2009.

Terra em transe. Dir. Glauber Rocha. Perf. Jardel Filho, Paula Autran, José Lewgoy. Brazil, 1967.

Tiempo de revancha. Dir. Adolfo Aristarain. Perf. Federico Luppi, Haydée Padilla, Julio de Grazia. Argentina, 1981.

Tire dié. Dir. Fernando Birri. Perf. Guillermo Cervantes Luro, María Rosa Gallo, Francisco Petrone. Argentina, 1960.

Touch of Evil. Dir. Orson Welles. Perf. Charlton Heston, Orson Welles, Janet Leigh. USA, 1958.

Vendedora de rosas. Dir. Víctor Gaviria. Perf. Lady Tabares, Marta Correa, Mileider Gil. Colombia, 1998.

La ventana. Dir. Carlos Sorín. Perf. Antonio Larreta, María del Carmen Jiménez, Emilse Roldán. Argentina, 2008.

A Via Lactea. Dir. Lina Chamie. Perf. Marco Ricca, Alice Braga. Brazil, 2007.

El viaje. Dir. Fernando E. Solanas. Perf. Walter Quiroz, Soledad Alfaro, Ricardo Bartis. Argentina, 1992.

Los viajes del viento. Dir. Ciro Guerra. Perf. Marciano Martínez, Yull Núñez. Colombia, 2009.

La vida es silbar. Dir. Fernando Pérez Valdés. Perf. Luis Alberto García, Coralia Veloz, Bebé Perez. Cuba, 1998.

Vidas secas. Dir. Pereira dos Santos. Perf. Atila Iório, Maria Ribeiro, Orlando Macedo. Brazil, 1963.

La virgen de los sicarios. Dir. Barbet Schroeder. Perf. Germán Jaramillo, Anderson Ballesteros, Juan David Restrepo. Colombia, 2000.

Yo, la peor de todas. Dir. María Luisa Bemberg. Perf. Assumpta Serna, Dominique Sanda, Héctor Alterio. Argentina, 1990.

Y tu mamá también. Dir. Alfonso Cuarón. Perf. Maribel Verdú, Gael García Bernal, Diego Luna. Mexico, 2001.

Secondary Sources

Abrams, Jerold J. "Space, Time, and Subjectivity in Neo-Noir Cinema." In *The Philosophy of Neo-Noir*, ed. Mark T. Conard, 7–20. Lexington: UP of Kentucky, 2007.

Aguilar, Gonzalo Moisés. *Other Worlds: New Argentine Film*. Trans. Sarah Ann Wells. New York: Palgrave Macmillan, 2008.

Aitken, Ian. *The Documentary Film Movement*. Edinburgh, Scotland: Edinburgh UP, 1998.

Amiot, Julie. "Carlos Reygadas, el cine mexicano y la crítica, una bonita historia?" *Cinémas d'Amerique Latine* 14 (2006): 154–165.

Anderson, Benedict Richard O'Gorman. *Imagined Communities: Reflections on the Origin and Spread of Nationalism.* London: Verso, 2006.

Aparicio, Francisco de. "Comechingón and Their Neighbors of the Sierras de Córdoba." *Handbook of South American Indians: The Andean Civilizations* 143.2 (1946): 673–685.

Aubert, Jean-Paul. "*Suite Habana.* Les rêveries mélancoliques de Fernando Pérez." In *Cuba: Cinema et revolution,* ed. Julie Amiot-Guillouet, Nancy Berthier, and Ignacio Ramonet, 255–266. Lyon, France: Grimh, 2006.

Avellar, José Carlos. "*Limite*: Mário Peixoto, Brazil, 1931." *The Cinema of Latin America,* ed. Alberto Elena and Marina Díaz López, 14–23. London: Wallflower, 2003.

Bachelard, Gaston. *La poétique de l'espace.* Paris: Presses Universitaires de France, 1957.

Badt, Karin Luisa. "No Slave to Realism: An Interview with Carlos Reygadas." *Cineaste* (Summer 2006): 21–23.

———. "*Silent Light* or Absolute Miracle: An Interview with Carlos Reygadas at Cannes 2007." *Bright Lights Film Journal* 57 (Aug. 2007): n.p.

Barro, Robert J., and Rachel M. McCleary. "Religion and Economic Growth across Countries." *American Sociological Review* 68.5 (Oct. 2003): 760–781.

Bassi, Raúl, and Federico Fuentes. "Argentina: Who's Afraid of the *Piqueteros?*" http://www.greenleft.org.au/node/31535.

Bataille, Georges. *Story of an Eye.* Trans. Joachim Neugroschel. San Francisco: City Lights Books, 1987.

Baudrillard, Jean. *The Consumer Society: Myths and Structures.* London: Sage, 1998.

———. *Simulations.* New York City: Semiotext(e), 1983.

Bauman, Zygmunt. *Consuming Life.* Cambridge, England: Polity, 2007.

———. *Liquid Life.* Cambridge, England: Polity, 2005.

———. *Work, Consumerism, and the New Poor.* Buckingham, England: Open UP, 1998.

Beattie, Keith. *Documentary Screens: Non-Fiction Film and Television.* New York: Palgrave Houndmills, 2004.

Beceyro, Raúl. *Ensayos sobre cine argentino.* Santa Fe, Argentina: Universidad Nacional del Litoral, 1986.

Bennion, Janet. *Desert Patriarchy: Mormon and Mennonite Communities in the Chihuahua Valley.* Tucson: U of Arizona P, 2004.

Bentes, Ivana. "The *Sertão* and the *Favela* in Contemporary Brazilian Film." In *The New Brazilian Cinema,* ed. Lúcia Nagib, 121–137. London: I. B. Tauris, 2003.

Bernardes, Horacio, Diego Lerer, and Sergio Wolf. "From Industry to Independent Cinema: Are There 'Industry Auteurs'?" In *New Argentine Cinema,* ed. Bernardes, Lerer, and Wolf, 119–131.

———. "Introduction: A Brief History." In *New Argentine Cinema*, ed. Bernardes, Lerer, and Wolf, 9–14.

———, eds. *New Argentine Cinema: Themes, Auteurs, and Trends of Innovation.* Buenos Aires: Ediciones Tatanka, Fibresci, 2002.

Bianchi, Susana. *Historia de las religiones en la Argentina: Las minorías religiosas.* Buenos Aires: Editorial Sudamericana, 2004.

Birri, Fernando. *La escuela documental de Santa Fe.* Rosario, Argentina: Prohistoria Ediciones, Instituto Superior de Cine y Artes Audiovisuales de Santa Fe, 2008.

Borde, Raymonde, and Etienne Chaumeton. "Toward the Definition of Film Noir." In *Perspectives on Film Noir*, ed. and trans. R. Barton Palmer, 59–65. New York: G. K. Hall, 1996.

Borges, Jorge Luis. *Obras completas.* Buenos Aires: Editorial Emecé, 1974.

Bornemann, Ernest. *The Psychoanalysis of Money.* New York: Urizen Books, 1976.

Boulter, Jonathan. "The Negative Way of Trauma: Georges Bataille's 'Story of the Eye.'" *Cultural Critique* 46 (Autumn 2000): 153–178.

Bourdieu, Pierre, and Loïc J.D. Wacquant. *An Invitation to Reflexive Sociology.* Chicago: U of Chicago P, 1992.

Burucúa, Costanza. *Confronting the "Dirty War" in Argentine Cinema 1983–1993: Memory and Gender in Historical Representations.* Suffolk, England: Tamesis, 2009.

Burin, Mabel, and Irene Meler. *Varones: Género y subjetividad masculina.* Buenos Aires: Paidós, 2004.

Burton, Juliane. *The Social Documentary in Latin America.* Pittsburgh, PA: U of Pittsburgh P: 1990.

Brunetta, Gian Piero. *The History of Italian Cinema.* Trans. Jeremy Parzen. Princeton, NJ: Princeton UP, 2009.

Calderón de la Barca, Pedro. *La vida es sueño.* Madrid: Alhambra, 1987.

Canals Frau, Salvador. "El grupo huarpe-comechingón." *Anales del Instituto de Etnografía Americana* 5 (1944): 9–47.

Carney, Raymond. *Speaking the Language of Desire: The Films of Carl Dreyer.* Cambridge, England: Cambridge UP, 1989.

Carrard Araujo, Marcelo. "Walter Salles." In *O Cinema da Retomada: Depoimentos de 90 cineastas dos anos 90*, Lúcia Nagib, 416–422. São Paulo: Editora 34, 2002.

Carreño King, Mariana. "Journey to the End of the World." *Offoffoff Film*, March 19, 2003. http://www.offoffoff.com/film/2003/japon.php.

Caruth, Cathy. Introduction. *Trauma: Explorations in Memory*, ed. Cathy Caruth, 3–12. Baltimore: Johns Hopkins UP, 1995.

———. *Unclaimed Experience: Trauma, Narrative, and History.* Baltimore: Johns Hopkins UP, 1996.

Chadwick, John. *The Mycenaean World.* Cambridge, England: Cambridge UP, 1976.

Chanan, Michael. *Cuban Cinema.* Minneapolis: U of Minnesota P, 2004.

Chodorow, Nancy. *The Reproduction of Mothering: Psychoanalysis and the Sociology of Gender*. Berkeley: U of California P, 1978.

Chopra-Gant, Mike. *Hollywood Genres and Postwar America: Masculinity, Family, and Nation in Popular Movies and Film Noir*. London: Tauris, 2006.

Cirio, Norberto Pablo. "Antecedentes históricos del culto a San Baltazar en la Argentina: 'La Cofradía de San Baltazar y Animas' (1772–1856)." *Latin American Music Review/Revista de Música Latinoamericana* 21.2 (Autumn–Winter 2000): 190–214.

Cirlot, Juan Eduardo. *Diccionario de símbolos*. Barcelona: Editorial Labor, 1979.

Cisneros, James. "The Neoliberal City in the Brazilian Retomada: *Central Station* and *City of God*." *Cine, historia y sociedad: Cine argentino y brasileño desde los años 80*, ed. Gastón Lillo and Walter Moser, 101–120. Ottawa: Legas, 2007.

Clarke, Paul. Film review, *Japón*. *Kamera.co.uk*, n.d. http://www.kamera.co.uk/article.php/15.

Cobos, Mario Castro, and Fernando Vilches. "*Dioses*, la segunda película de Josué Méndez." *La Cinefilia No Es Patriota* blog, Feb. 20, 2007. http://lacinefilianoespatriota.blogspot.com/2007/02/dioses-la-segunda-pelcula-de-josu-mndez.html.

CONADEP, Comisión Nacional sobre la Desaparición de Personas. *Nunca más: Informe de la Comisión Nacional sobre la Desaparición de Personas*. Buenos Aires: Eudeba, 1984.

Conard, Mark T. "*Reservoir Dogs*: Redemption in a Postmodern World." In *The Philosophy of Neo-Noir*, ed. Mark T. Conard, 101–116. Lexington: UP of Kentucky, 2007.

Conley, Tom. "Noir in the Red and the Nineties in the Black." In *Film Genre 2000: New Critical Essays*, ed. Wheeler Winston Dixon, 193–210. Albany: SUNY P, 2000.

Connell, Robert W. "El imperialismo y el cuerpo de los hombres." In *Masculinidades y equidad de género en América Latina*, ed. Teresa Valdés and José Olavarría, 76–89. Santiago: FLACSO-Chile, 1998.

———. *The Men and the Boys*. Berkeley: U of California P, 2000.

Costa, Marta. *Los inmigrantes*. Buenos Aires: Centro Editor de América Latina, 1972.

Cottle, Thomas J. *Perceiving Time: A Psychological Investigation with Men and Women*. New York: John Wiley and Sons, 1976.

Cowan, Noah. "Special Delivery." *Filmmaker* 6.2 (Jan. 1998): 72.

D'Angelo, André Cauduro. *Precisar, não precisa*. São Paulo: Editorial Lazuli, 2006.

Debord, Guy. *The Society of the Spectacle*. New York: Zone Books, 1994.

Deleuze, Gilles. *Cinema 1: The Movement-Image*. Trans. Hugh Tomlinson and Barbara Habberjam. Minneapolis: U of Minnesota P, 2003.

———. *Cinema 2: The Time-Image*. Trans. Hugh Tomlinson and Robert Galeta. Minneapolis: U of Minnesota P, 2003.

———. *Difference and Repetition*. Trans. Paul Patton. New York: Columbia UP, 1994.

Derrida, Jacques. *Aporias*. Trans. Thomas Dutoit. Stanford, CA: Stanford UP, 1993.

———. *Margins of Philosophy*. Trans. Alan Bass. Chicago: U of Chicago P, 1982.

———. *Of Grammatology*. Trans. Gayatri Chakravorty Spivak. Baltimore: Johns Hopkins UP, 1974.

Dierckxsens, Wim. *Del neoliberalismo al poscapitalismo*. San José, Costa Rica: Editorial Departamento Ecuménico de Investigaciones, 2000.

Dimendberg, Edward. *Film Noir and the Spaces of Modernity*. Cambridge, MA: Harvard UP, 2004.

Dimock, E. George. Introduction. *Euripides's Iphigenia at Aulis*, trans. W. S. Mervin and George E. Dimock, 3–21. New York: Oxford UP, 1978.

Dixon, Paul. *Reversible Readings: Ambiguity in Four Modern Latin American Novels*. Tuscaloosa: U of Alabama P, 1985.

Dragún, Osvaldo. *Historias para ser contadas*. Buenos Aires: Editorial Astral, 1967.

Drum, Jean, and Dale D. Drum. *My Only Great Passion: The Life and Films of Carl Th. Dreyer*. Lanham, MD: Scarecrow, 2000.

Dueck, Al. "Psychology and Mennonite Self-Understanding." In *Mennonite Identity: Historical and Contemporary Perspectives*, ed. Calvin Wall Redekop, 203–224. Lanham, MD: UP of America, 1988.

Eco, Umberto. *De los espejos y otros ensayos*. Barcelona: Lumen, 2000.

Etcheverry, Hugo. "Existe el cine paraguayo?" *Cinémas d'Amérique Latine* 11 (2003): 156–162.

Edmonds, Alexander. "Triumphant Miscegenation: Reflections on Beauty and Race in Brazil." *Journal of Intercultural Studies* 28.1 (Feb. 2007): 83–97.

Eisenstein, Sergei. *The Film Sense*. Trans. Jay Leyda. New York: Harcourt, Brace, and World, 1947.

———. *Selected Works*. Vol. 1, *Writings, 1922–34*. Trans. Richard Taylor. London: British Film Institute, 1988.

Elena, Alberto, and Marina Díaz López. Introduction. *The Cinema of Latin America*, ed. Alberto Elena and Marina Díaz López, 1–12. London: Wallflower, 2003.

Elsaesser, Thomas. "Tales of Sound and Fury: Observations on the Family Melodrama." In *Movies and Methods*, ed. Bill Nichols, 165–189. Berkeley: U of California P, 1994.

Encina, Paz. Interview. "Paz Encina habla sobre 'Hamaca Paraguaya' en Cannes." Associated Press, published in *Terra*, May 26, 2006. http://www.terra.com/ocio/entretenimiento/noticias/paz_encina_habla_sobre_hamaca_paraguaya_en_cannes/oci87756.htm.

———. Interview by Diego Jemio. "Entrevista a la cineasta Paz Encina: 'Quería narrar la tristeza.'" *Clarín*, Oct. 31, 2006. http://www.clarin.com/diario/2006/10/31/espectaculos/c-00403.htm.

España, Claudio, ed. *Cine argentino: Modernidad y vanguardias 1957–1983*. 2 vols. Buenos Aires: Fondo Nacional de las Artes, 2004, 2005.

Falicov, Tamara L. *The Cinematic Tango: Contemporary Argentine Film*. London: Wallflower, 2007.

————. "Programa Ibermedia: Co-Production and the Cultural Politics of Constructing an Ibero-American Audiovisual Space." *Spectator* 27.2 (Fall 2007): 21–30.

Farcau, Bruce W. *The Chaco War: Bolivia and Paraguay, 1932–1935*. Westport, CT:
Praeger, 1996.

Fillmore, Charles J. "Scenes and Frames Semantics." In *Linguistic Structures Pro-
cessing*, ed. Antonio Zampolli, 55–81. Amsterdam: North-Holland, 1977.

Flora, Charles M. "Short History of PTSD from the Military Perspective." In *Simple
and Complex Post-Traumatic Stress Disorder: Strategies for Comprehensive
Treatment in Clinical Practice*, ed. Mary Beth Williams and John F. Sommer Jr.,
3–8. New York: Haworth, 2002.

Fornet, Ambrosio. Foreword. *Framing Latin American Cinema*, ed. Ann Marie Stock,
xi-xviii. Minneapolis: U of Minnesota P, 1993.

Foster, David William. *Contemporary Argentine Cinema*. Columbia: U of Missouri P,
1992.

Frampton, Daniel. *Filmosophy*. London: Wallflower, 2006.

Frank, Nino. "The Crime Adventure Story: A New Kind of Detective Film." In *Perspectives on Film Noir*, ed. R. Barton Palmer, 21–24. New York: G. K. Hall, 1996.

Freud, Sigmund. *The Essentials of Psycho-Analysis*. Trans. James Strachey. London:
Hogarth, 1986.

————. *Introductory Lectures on Psycho-Analysis*. Trans. James Strachey. New
York: Liveright, 1989.

Frigerio, Alejandro. "Identidades porosas, estructuras sincréticas y narrativas domi-
nantes: Miradas cruzadas entre Pierre Sanchis y la Argentina." *Ciencias Sociales
y Religión/Ciências Sociais e Religião* 7.7 (Sept. 2005): 223–237.

García Canclini, Néstor, Ana Rosas Mantecón, and Enrique Sánchez Ruiz, eds. *Situación actual y perspectivas de la industria cinematográfica en México y en el
extranjero*. Guadalajara: Universidad de Guadalajara and Instituto Mexicano de
Cinematografía, 2006.

García Espinosa, Julio. *Una imagen recorre el mundo*. Havana: Editorial Letras
Cubanas, 1979.

Getino, Octavio. *Cine argentino: Entre lo possible y lo deseable*. Buenos Aires: Ediciones Ciccus, 1998.

————. *Cine iberoamericano: Los desafíos del nuevo siglo*. Buenos Aires: INCAA and
Ediciones Ciccus, 2007.

Glissant, Edouard. *Poetics of Relation*. Trans. Betsy Wing. Ann Arbor: U of Michigan
P, 1997.

Goldenberg, Mirian. *De perto ninguém é normal: Estudos sobre corpo, sexualidade,
gênero e desvio na cultura brasileira*. Rio de Janeiro: Editora Record, 2004.

Goldman, Dara E. "Urban Desires: Melancholia and Fernando Pérez's Portrayal of
Havana." *Bulletin of Hispanic Studies* 85.6 (Dec. 2008): 867–882.

Gorbato, Viviana. *La Argentina embrujada*. Buenos Aires: Editorial Atlántida, 1996.

Gorriti, Gustavo. *The Shining Path: A History of the Millenarian War in Peru*. Trans.
Robin Kirk. Chapel Hill: U of North Carolina P, 1999.

Graziano, Frank. *Cultures of Devotion: Folk Saints of Spanish America*. New York: Oxford UP, 2006.

Grierson, John. "First Principles of the Documentary." In *The Documentary Film Movement*, ed. Ian Aitken, 81–93. Edinburgh, Scotland: Edinburgh UP, 1998.

Grimson, Alejandro, and Gabriel Kessler. *On Argentina and the Southern Cone: Neoliberalism and National Imaginations*. New York: Routledge, 2005.

Grosz, Elizabeth. *Space, Time, and Perversion: Essays on the Politics of Bodies*. New York: Routledge, 1995.

Gurd, Sean Alexander. *Iphigenias at Aulis: Textual Multiplicity, Radical Philology*. Ithaca, NY: Cornell UP, 2005.

Gustafson, Lowell S. "Church and State in Argentina." In *The Religious Challenge to the State*, ed. Matthew C. Moen and Lowell S. Gustafson, 19–50. Philadelphia: Temple UP, 1992.

Gutiérrez-Albilla, Julián Daniel. "The Gender Ethics and Politics of Affection: The 'Feminine' Melodramatic Mode in Walter Salles' *Central do Brasil* (1998)." *Bulletin of Latin American Research* 29.2 (2010): 141–154.

Gutiérrez Alea, Tomás. *Dialéctica del espectador*. Havana: Unión de Escritores y Artistas de Cuba, 1982.

Hallowell, Edward M., and William Grace. "Money Styles." In *Money and Mind*, ed. Sheila Klebanow and Eugene L. Lowenkopf, 15–26. New York: Plenum, 1991.

Hardy, Sarah, and Caroline Wiedmer. Introduction. *Motherhood and Space: Configurations of the Maternal through Politics, Home, and the Body*, ed. Sarah Hardy and Caroline Wiedmer, 1–11. New York: Palgrave Macmillan, 2005.

Hershfield, Joanne, and David R. Maciel, eds. *Mexico's Cinema: A Century of Film and Filmmakers*. Wilmington, DE: Scholarly Resources Book, 1999.

Hess, John. "Neorealism and New Latin American Cinema: *Bicycle Thieves* and *Blood of the Condor*." In *Mediating Two Worlds: Cinematic Encounters in the Americas*, ed. John King, Ana M. López, and Manuel Alvarado, 104–118. London: British Film Institute, 1993.

Hirsch, Foster. *The Dark Side of the Screen: Film Noir*. San Diego, CA: Barnes, 1981.

———. *Detours and Lost Highways: A Map of Neo-Noir*. New York: Limelight, 1999.

Holt, Jason. "A Darker Side: Realism in Neo-Noir." In *The Philosophy of Noir*, ed. Mark T. Conard, 23–40. Lexington: UP of Kentucky, 2006.

Hutcheon, Linda. *A Poetics of Postmodernism: History, Theory, Fiction*. New York: Routledge, 1988.

Huyssen, Andreas. "Trauma and Memory: A New Imaginary Temporality." In *World Memory: Personal Trajectories in Global Time*, ed. Jill Bennett and Roseanne Kennedy, 16–29. Houndmills, England: Palgrave Macmillan, 2003.

Inglehart, Ronald, and Wayne E. Baker. "Modernization, Cultural Change, and the Persistence of Traditional Values." *American Sociological Review* 65 (Feb. 2000): 19–51.

James, Nick. "Angels and Demons." *Sight and Sound* 15.11 (Nov. 2005): 30–33.

———. "Heartbreak and Miracles." *Sight and Sound* 9.3 (March 1999): 12–15.

Jameson, Fredric. *Postmodernism, or The Cultural Logic of Late Capitalism*. Durham, NC: Duke UP, 1991.

Jhally, Sut. *The Codes of Advertising: Fetishism and the Political Economy of Meaning in the Consumer Society*. London: Frances Pinter, 1987.

Johnson, Randal. *Cinema Novo × 5*. Austin: U of Texas P, 1984.

———. "TV Globo, the MPA, and Contemporary Brazilian Cinema." In *Latin American Cinema: Essays on Modernity, Gender, and National Identity*, ed. Lisa Shaw and Stephanie Dennison, 11–38. Jefferson, NC: McFarland, 2005.

Johnson, Randal, and Robert Stam. "The Shape of Brazilian Film History." In *Brazilian Cinema*, ed. Randal Johnson and Robert Stam, 17–51. East Brunswick, NJ: Associated University Presses, 1982.

Kaiser-Lenoir, Claudia. *El grotesco criollo: Estilo teatral de una época*. Havana: Casa de las Américas, 1977.

Kamen, Deborah. "The Life Cycle in Archaic Greece." In *The Cambridge Companion to Archaic Greece*, ed. H. A. Shapiro, 85–110. Cambridge, England: Cambridge UP, 2007.

Kaminsky, Amy K. *Argentina: Stories for a Nation*. Minneapolis: U of Minnesota P, 2008.

Kaplan, E. Ann. *Trauma Culture: The Politics of Terror and Loss in Media and Literature*. New Brunswick, NJ: Rutgers UP, 2005.

———, ed. *Women in Film Noir*. London: British Film Institute, 2001.

King, John. "Cinema." In *A Cultural History of Latin America*, ed. Leslie Bethell, 455–518. Cambridge, England: Cambridge UP, 1998.

———. *Magical Reels: A History of Cinema in Latin America*. London: Verso, 1990.

King, John, Ana M. López, and Manuel Alvarado, eds. *Mediating Two Worlds: Cinematic Encounters in the Americas*. London: British Film Institute, 1993.

Kolker, Robert Phillip. *The Altering Eye: Contemporary International Cinema*. Oxford, England: Oxford UP, 1983.

Korstanje, Maximiliano. "Formas urbanas de religiosidad popular. El caso Cromañón en Buenos Aires." *Rev Mad* 16 (May 2007): 79–92.

Kristeva, Julia. *Black Sun: Depression and Melancholia*. Trans. Leon S. Roudiez. New York: Columbia UP, 1989.

———. *Powers of Horror: An Essay on Abjection*. Trans. Leon S. Roudiez. New York: Columbia UP, 1982.

———. *Revolution in Poetic Language*. Trans. Leon S. Roudiez. New York: Columbia UP, 1984.

Kulick, Don. *Travesti: Sex, Gender, and Culture among Brazilian Transgendered Prostitutes*. Chicago: U of Chicago P, 1998.

LaCapra, Dominick. *Writing History, Writing Trauma*. Baltimore: Johns Hopkins UP, 2001.

Laderman, David. *Driving Visions*. Austin: U of Texas P, 2002.

Lefebvre, Henri. *Critique of Everyday Life: Foundations for a Sociology of the Everyday*. Vol. 2. Trans. John Moore. London: Verso, 1991.

Lehman, Peter. *Running Scared: Masculinity and the Representation of the Male Body*. Philadelphia: Temple UP, 1993.

Leitch, Thomas. *Film Adaptation and Its Discontents*. Baltimore: Johns Hopkins UP, 2007.

León, Christian. *El cine de la marginalidad: Realismo sucio y violencia urbana.* Quito: Universidad Andina Simón Bolívar, Abya Yala, Corporación Editora Nacional, 2005.

Levinas, Emmanuel. *Otherwise than Being or Beyond Essence*. Trans. Alphonso Lingis. The Hague: Martinus Nijhoff, 1981.

Levy, Emmanuel. *Cinema of Outsiders: The Rise of American Independent Film*. New York: New York UP, 1999.

Leys, Ruth. *Trauma*. Chicago: U of Chicago P, 2000.

Lewis, Paul H. *Guerrillas and Generals: The Dirty War in Argentina*. Westport, CT: Praeger, 2002.

Liendro Zingoni, Eduardo. "Masculinidades y violencia en un programa de acción en México." *Masculinidades y equidad de género en América Latina*, ed. Teresa Valdés and José Olavarría, 130–136. Santiago: FLACSO-Chile, 1998.

Lipovetsky, Gilles. *Hypermodern Times*. Trans. Andrew Brown. Cambridge, England: Polity, 2005.

López, Ana M. "An 'Other' History: The New Latin American Cinema." In *New Latin American Cinema*, ed. Michael Martin, 1:135–156. Detroit: Wayne State UP, 1997.

Macrae, David. "On Berlin. The Symphony of a Great City." In *Expressionist Film: New Perspectives*, comp. Dietrich Scheunemann, 251–270. Rochester, NY: Camden House, 2003.

Maranghello, César. *Breve historia del cine argentino*. Buenos Aires: Laertes, 2005.

Marcel, Mary. *Freud's Traumatic Memory: Reclaiming Seduction Theory and Revisiting Oedipus*. Pittsburgh: Duquesne UP, 2005.

Marcus, Millicent Joy. *Italian Film in the Light of Neorealism*. Princeton: Princeton UP, 1986.

McElroy, Isis Costa. "AxéNgolo Poetics: A Cultural and Cosmological Conceptualization of AfroBrazil in Space and Process." PhD diss., New York University, 2004.

Meler, Irene. "La masculinidad. Diversidad y similitudes entre los grupos humanos." In *Varones: Género y subjetividad masculina*, ed. Mabel Burin and Irene Meler, 71–121. Buenos Aires: Paidós, 2004.

Méndez, Josué. "Dias de Santiago. Nota del director." *Cinencuentro*. Feb. 2006. http://www.cinencuentro.com/dias-de-santiago.

Michieli, Catalina Teresa. *Los comechingones según la crónica de Gerónimo de Bibar y su confrontación con otras fuentes*. San Juan, Argentina: Universidad Nacional de San Juan, 1985.

Middents, Jeffrey. *Writing National Cinema: Film Journals and Film Culture in Peru*. Hanover, NH: UP of New England, 2009.

Mignona, Eduardo. *La señal*. Buenos Aires: Planeta, 2002.

Milne, Tom. *The Cinema of Carl Dreyer*. New York: Barnes, 1998.

Minh-ha, Trinh T. *When the Moon Waxes Red: Representation, Gender, and Cultural Politics.* New York: Routledge, 1991.

Morewitz, Stephen J. *Domestic Violence and Maternal and Child Health: New Patterns of Trauma, Treatment, and Criminal Justice Responses.* New York: Kluwer Academic, Plenum, 2004.

Mulvey, Laura. *Visual and Other Pleasures.* Bloomington: Indiana UP, 1989.

Mutarelli, Lourenço. *O cheiro do ralo.* São Paulo: Devir Livraria, 2002.

————. "A estranha arte de produzir efeito sem causa." *IDE: Psicanálise e Cultura* 31.47 (2008): 170–179.

————. *O natimorto: Um musical silencioso.* São Paulo: Companhia das Letras, 2004.

Nagib, Lúcia. *Brazil on Screen: Cinema Novo, New Cinema, Utopia.* New York: I. B. Tauris, 2007.

————. Introduction. *O Cinema da Retomada: Depoimentos de 90 cineastas dos anos 90.* São Paulo: Editora 34, 2002.

————. *World Cinema and the Ethics of Realism.* New York: Continuum, 2011.

Naremore, James. "Authorship." In *A Companion to Film Theory,* ed. Toby Miller and Robert Stam, 19–24. Malden, MA: Blackwell, 1999.

————. *More than Night: Film Noir in Its Contexts.* Berkeley, Los Angeles, London: U of California P, 1998.

Nichols, Bill. *Representing Reality: Issues and Concepts in Documentary.* Bloomington: Indiana UP, 1991.

Nochteff, Hugo, and Martin Abeles. *Economic Shocks without Vision: Neoliberalism in the Transition of Socio-Economic Systems. Lessons from the Argentine Case.* Frankfurt: Vervuert, 2000.

Oliveira, Sandro de. "Jorge Furtado." In *O Cinema da Retomada: Depoimentos de 90 cineastas dos anos 90,* Lúcia Nagib, 209–212. São Paulo: Editora 34, 2002.

Oricchio, Luis Zanin. *Cinemadenovo: Um balanço crítico da Retomada.* São Paulo: Editora Estação Liberdade, 2003.

————. "The *Sertão* in the Brazilian Imaginary at the End of the Millennium." In *The New Brazilian Cinema,* ed. Lúcia Nagib, 139–156. London: I. B. Tauris, 2003.

Orr, John. *Hitchcock and the 20th-Century Cinema.* London: Wallflower, 2005.

Partyka, Betsy. "Traditional Oral Techniques in the Fiction of Augusto Roa Bastos (1953–1974)." *Chasqui* 26.1 (1997): 93–101.

Patterson, Enrique. "Tres testimonios cinematográficos." *Encuentro de la Cultura Cubana* 36 (Spring 2005): 181–189.

Pellegrini, Tânia. *Despropósitos: Estudos de ficção brasileira contemporânea.* São Paulo: Annablume Editora, 2008.

Pelletieri, Osvaldo. "Armando Discépolo: Entre el grotesco italiano y el grotesco criollo." *Latin American Theater Review* 22.1 (Fall 1988): 55–71.

Penchaszadeh, Victor B. "Abduction of Children of Political Dissidents in Argentina and the Role of Human Genetics in Their Restitution." *Journal of Public Health Policy* 13.3 (Autumn 1992): 291–305.

Pfeufer Khan, Robbie, "Women and Time in Childbirth and during Lactation." In *Taking Our Time: Feminist Perspectives on Temporality*, ed. Frieda Johles Forman and Caoran Sowton, 20–36. Oxford: Pergamon, 1989.

Pick, Zuzana M. *The New Latin American Cinema: A Continental Project*. Austin: U of Texas P, 1993.

Rafter, Nicole. *Shots in the Mirror: Crime Films and Society*. 2nd edition. New York: Oxford UP, 2006.

Rangil, Viviana. *Otro punto de vista: Mujer y cine en Argentina*. Rosario, Argentina: Beatriz Viterbo Editora, 2005.

Redruello, Laura. "El caso de Suite Habana: Diferencias genéricas." *Encuentro de la cultura cubana* 36 (Spring 2005): 190–196.

Reygadas, Carlos. Interview by Peter Fraser. "An Interview with Carlos Reygadas, Director of *Battle in Heaven*." *Close-Up Film*, Oct. 2005. http://www.close-upfilm .com/2005/10/an-interview-with-carlos-reygadas-director-of-battle-in-heaven.

———. Interview by Charlotte Higgins. "I Am the Only Normal Director." *The Guardian*, Aug. 22, 2005. http://film.guardian.co.uk/interview/interviewpages /0,,1554105,00.html.

———. Interview by Maximilian Le Cain. "*Battle in Heaven*: An Interview with Carlos Reygadas." *Senses of Cinema* 38 (Feb. 7, 2006). http://www.sensesofcinema .com/2006/feature-articles/reygadas.

Ríos, Ángel F. *Defensa del Chaco: Verdades y mentiras de una victoria*. Asunción: Archivo del Liberalismo, 1989.

Rocca, Manuel, and Juan José Rossi. *Los chané-chiriguano: Arawak y guaraní*. Buenos Aires: Editorial Galerna, 2004.

Rocco, Debora. "'Colagem de linguagens': Re-midiação em *O homen que copiava* e *Meu tio matou um cara* de Jorge Furtado." *Analecta* 9.1 (Jan.–June 2008): 25–34.

Rocha, Glauber. *Revolução do Cinema Novo*. São Paulo: Cosac Naify, 2004.

Rodowick, D. N. *Gilles Deleuze's Time Machine*. Durham, NC: Duke UP, 1997.

Rodríguez-Mangual, Edna M. "Fictual Factions: On the Emergence of a Documentary Style in Recent Cuban Films." *Screen* 49.3 (Autumn 2008): 298–315.

Romero, Miranda. "La nueva historia del cine mexicano: Dos visiones." *Cinémas d'Amerique Latine* 14 (2006): 176–185.

Romney, Jonathan. "The Sheltering Sky." *Sight and Sound* 18.1 (Jan. 2008): 42–44.

Roston, Tom. "Art with Heart." *Premiere* 11.4 (Dec. 1998): 68.

Rowlandson, William. "The Journey into the Text: Reading Rulfo in Carlos Reygadas's 2002 Feature Film 'Japón.' *Modern Language Review* 101.4 (Oct. 2006): 1025–1034.

Ruberto, Laura, and Kristi Wilson. Introduction. *Italian Neorealism and Global Cinema*, ed. Laura Ruberto and Kristi Wilson, 1–24. Detroit: Wayne State UP, 2007.

Rudnytsky, Peter L. *Freud and Oedipus*. New York: Columbia UP, 1987.

Salles, Walter. Interview by Geoff Andrew. The Guardian Interviews at the BFI series. *The Guardian*, Aug. 26, 2004. http://www.guardian.co.uk/film/2004/aug/26 /features.

Salazar Navarro, Salvador. "Suite Habana, la ciudad de Fernando Pérez." *Caribbean Studies* 36.2 (July-Dec. 2008): 281–285.

Sanjinés, Jorge, and Grupo Ukamau. *Teoría y práctica de un cine junto al pueblo.* Mexico City: Siglo XXI, 1979.

Santos Moray, Mercedes. "The Creative Work of Two Cuban Filmmakers: Tomás Gutiérrez Alea and Fernando Pérez." *Le Mouvement Social* 219–220.2 (2007): 57–64.

Schiraldi, Glenn R. *The Post-Traumatic Stress Disorder Sourcebook.* Los Angeles: Lowell House, 2000.

Schofield Saeger, James. *Francisco Solano Lópes and the Ruination of Paraguay.* Lanham, MD: Rowman and Littlefield, 2007.

Schrader, Paul. "Notes on Film Noir." In *Film Genre Reader II*, ed. Barry Keith Grant, 213–226. Austin: U of Texas P, 1995.

Schumann, Peter. *Historia del cine latinoamericano.* Trans. Oscar Zambrano. Buenos Aires: Editorial Legasa, 1987.

Seger, Linda. *The Art of Adaptation: Turning Fact and Fiction into Film.* New York: Henry Holt, 1992.

Semali, Ladislaus M., and Ann Watts Pailliotet. "Introduction. What Is Intermediality and Why Study It in U.S. Classrooms?" In *Intermediality: The Teacher's Handbook of Critical Media Literacy*, ed. Ladislaus M. Semali and Ann Watts Pailliotet, 1–29. Boulder, CO: Westview, 1999.

Shaw, Deborah. *Contemporary Cinema of Latin America: 10 Key Films.* New York: Continuum, 2003.

Shelton, Martin S. *Communicating Ideas with Film, Video, and Multimedia: A Practical Guide to Information Motion-Media.* Carbondale: Southern Illinois UP, 2004.

Shiel, Mark. *Italian Neorealism: Rebuilding the Cinematic City.* London: Wallflower, 2006.

Skoller, Donald. *Dreyer in Double Reflection. Translation of Carl Th. Dreyer's Writings about the Film (Om Filmen).* New York: Dutton, 1973.

Silverman, Kaja. *The Acoustic Mirror.* Bloomington: Indiana UP, 1988.

———. *Male Subjectivity at the Margins.* New York: Routledge, 1992.

Silletta, Alfredo. *Las sectas invaden Argentina.* Buenos Aires: Puntosur, 1991.

Singh, Devendra. "Body Weight, Waist-to-Hip Ratio, Breasts, and Hips: Role in Judgments of Female Attractiveness and Desirability for Relationships." *Ethnology and Sociobiology* 16.6 (Nov. 1995): 483–507.

Solanas, Fernando Ezequiel, and Octavio Getino. *Cine, cultura, y descolonización.* Buenos Aires: Siglo XXI, 1973.

Sommer, Roy. "Initial Framings in Film." In *Framing Borders in Literature and Other Media*, ed. Werner Wolf and Walter Bernhart, 383–406. Amsterdam: Rodopi, 2006.

Sophocles. *Oedipus the King.* Trans. Robert Bagg. Amherst: U of Massachusetts P, 2004.

Spain, Daphne. *Gendered Spaces*. Chapel Hill: U of North Carolina P, 1992.

Spivak, Gayatri Chakravorty. Translator's preface. *Of Grammatology*, by Jacques Derrida, ix-lxxxvii. Baltimore: Johns Hopkins UP, 1974.

Stam, Robert. "Beyond Fidelity: The Dialogics of Adaptation." In *Film Adaptation*, ed. James Naremore, 54–76. New Brunswick, NJ: Rutgers UP, 2000.

———. "The Hour of the Furnaces and the Two Avant-Gardes." In *The Social Documentary in Latin America*, ed. Julianne Burton, 250–266. Pittsburgh: U of Pittsburgh P, 1990.

———. "On the Margins: Brazilian Avant-Garde Cinema." In *Brazilian Cinema*, ed. Randal Johnson and Robert Stam, 306–327. East Brunswick, NJ: Associated University Presses, 1982.

Stephens, Michael L. *Film Noir: A Comprehensive Illustrated Reference to Movies, Terms, and Persons*. Jefferson, NC: McFarland, 1995.

Stiglitz, Joseph E. *Globalization and Its Discontents*. New York: W. W. Norton, 2002.

Stock, Anne Marie. "Imagining the Future in Revolutionary Cuba: An Interview with Fernando Pérez." *Film Quarterly* 60.3 (Spring 2007): 68–75.

Tal, Tzvi. *Pantallas y revolución: Una visión comparativa del Cine de Liberación y el Cinema Novo*. Buenos Aires: Ediciones Lumiere, 2005.

Tarkovsky, Andrey. *Sculpting in Time: Reflections on Cinema*. Trans. Kitty Hunter-Blair: London: Bodley Head, 1998.

Thompson, Diane P. *The Trojan War: Literature and Legends from the Bronze Age to the Present*. Jefferson, NC: McFarland, 2004.

Tierney, Dolores. "La imagen digital en Cuba y en Colombia." *Cuadernos Hispano-americanos* 679 (Jan. 2007): 45–54.

Tompkins, Cynthia. "A Deleuzian Approach to Carlos Reygadas' *Japón* and *Battle of Heaven*." *Hispanic Journal* 29.1 (Spring 2008): 155–169.

———. "A Deleuzian Approach to Carlos Reygadas's *Stellet Licht* [*Silent Light*] (2008)." U of New Mexico Latin American and Iberian Institute Research Paper Series, no. 51 (Nov. 15, 2010).

———. "A Deleuzian Approach to Jorge Furtado's *O Homem que Copiava* (2003) and Heitor Dhalia's *O Cheiro do Ralo* (2006)." *Dissidences* 6–7 (May 2010): 1–31.

———. "Fabián Bielinsky's *El aura* [*The Aura*]: Neo-noir Inscription and Subversion of the Action Image." *Confluencia* 24.1 (Fall 2008): 17–27.

———. "Montage in Fernando Pérez' *Suite Habana* (2003)." *Confluencia* 26.2 (Spring 2011): 31–45.

———. "Paradoxical Inscription and Subversion of the Gendered Construction of Time, Space, and Roles in María Victoria Menis' *El cielito* (2004) and Inés de Oliveira Cézar's *Como pasan las horas* (2005) and *Extranjera* (2007)." *Chasqui* 38.1 (May 2009): 38–56.

———. "Walter Salles's *Central do Brasil*: The Paradoxical Effect of the Conventions of the Documentary." *Studies in Twentieth- and Twenty-First-Century Literature* 33.1 (Winter 2009): 9–27.

Torrents, Nissa. "Mexican Cinema Becomes Alive." In *Mediating Two Worlds: Cinematic Encounters in the Americas*, ed. John King, Ana M. López, and Manuel Alvarado, 222–229. London: British Film Institute, 1993.

Torres, Carlos Alberto. *The Church, Society, and Hegemony: A Critical Sociology of Religion in Latin America*. Trans. Richard A. Young. Westport, CT: Praeger, 1992.

Torres, Félix. "Las armas de los comechingones." *Todo Es Historia* 23.266 (Aug. 1989): 18–27.

Traverso, Antonio. "Migrations of Cinema: Italian Neorealism and Brazilian Cinema." In *Italian Neorealism and Global Cinema*, ed. Laura E. Ruberto and Kristi M. Wilson, 165–186. Detroit: Wayne State UP, 2007.

Van der Kolk, Bessel A., and Otto van der Hart. "The Intrusive Past: The Flexibility of Memory and The Engraving of Trauma." In *Trauma: Explorations in Memory*, ed. Cathy Caruth, 158–182. Baltimore: Johns Hopkins UP, 1995.

Vermeersch, Arthur. "Usury." *New Advent*. http://www.newadvent.org/cathen/15235c.htm. Originally published in *The Catholic Encyclopedia*, vol. 15; New York: Robert Appleton, 1912.

Wager, Jans. *Dangerous Dames: Women and Representation in the Weimar Street Film and Film Noir*. Athens: Ohio UP, 1999.

Warren, Harris Gaylord, and Katherine F. Warren. *Paraguay and the Triple Alliance: The Postwar Decade, 1869–1878*. Austin: Institute of Latin American Studies, 1978.

West, Dennis. *Contemporary Brazilian Cinema*. Albuquerque: U of New Mexico Latin American and Iberian Institute, 1993.

Wiarda, Howard J., with Esther M. Skelley. "Neoliberalism and Its Problems." *Dilemmas of Democracy in Latin America: Crises and Opportunity*. Lanham, MD: Rowman and Littlefield, 2005.

Wolf, Sergio. "The Aesthetics of the New Argentine Cinema: The Map Is the Territory." In *New Argentine Cinema: Themes, Auteurs, and Trends of Innovation*, ed. Horacio Bernardes, Diego Lerer, and Sergio Wolf, 29–39. Buenos Aires: Ediciones Tatanka, 2002.

Wolf, Werner. "Introduction: Frames, Framings and Framing Borders in Literature and Other Media." *Framing Borders in Literature and Other Media*, ed. Werner Wolf and Walter Bernhart, 1–40. Amsterdam: Rodopi, 2006.

Wood, Jason. *100 Road Movies*. London: British Film Institute, 2007.

———. *Talking Movies: Contemporary World Filmmakers in Interview*. London: Wallflower, 2006.

Xavier, Ismail. "Brazilian Cinema in the 1990s: The Unexpected Encounter and the Resentful Character." In *The New Brazilian Cinema*, ed. Lúcia Nagib, 39–63. London: I. B. Tauris, 2003.

Yorgos. "*Hamaca paraguaya* (2006), Paz Encina." *La Linterna Mágica* blog, July 5, 2008. http://seteart.blogspot.com/2008_07_01_archive.html.

Young, Elliott. "Between the Market and a Hard Place: Fernando Pérez's *Suite Habana* in a Post-Utopian Cuba." *Cuban Studies* 38.1 (2007): 26–49.

Yúdice, George. "Postmodernity and Transnational Capitalism in Latin America." In *On Edge: The Crisis of Contemporary Latin American Culture*, ed. George Yúdice, Jean Franco, and Juan Flores, 1–28. Minneapolis: U of Minnesota P, 1992.

Žižek, Slavoj. *The Metastases of Enjoyment*. London: Verso, 1994.

INDEX

DH

791.
430
98
TOM